Deborah Gewertz and Frederick Errington have worked as anthropologists in Papua New Guinea for nearly two decades. In their second joint study of the Chambri, they consider the way those in a small-scale society, peripheral to the major centers of influence, struggle to sustain some degree of autonomy. They describe the Chambri caught up in world processes of social and cultural change, and attempt to create a "collective biography" which conveys the intelligibility and significance of the twentieth-century experience of these Papua New Guineans whom they have come to know well. This biography consists of interlocking stories, twisted histories, commentaries and contexts about Chambri who are negotiating their objectives while entangled in systemic change and confronting Western representations of modernization and development.

Twisted histories, altered contexts

Twisted histories, altered contexts
Representing the Chambri in a world system

Deborah Gewertz
Amherst College

Frederick Errington
Mount Holyoke College

CAMBRIDGE
UNIVERSITY PRESS

PUBLISHED BY THE PRESS SYNDICATE OF THE UNIVERSITY OF CAMBRIDGE
The Pitt Building, Trumpington Street, Cambridge, United Kingdom

CAMBRIDGE UNIVERSITY PRESS
The Edinburgh Building, Cambrige CB2 2RU, UK
40 West 20th Street, New York, NY 10011–4211, USA
477 Williamstown Road Port Melbourne, VIC 3207, Australia
Ruiz de Alarcón 13, 28014 Madrid, Spain
Dock House, The Waterfront, Cape Town 8001, South Africa

http://www.cambridge.org

First published 1991
Reprinted 1994 (twice), 1997, 2000, 2001, 2002

Printed in the United Kingdom at the University Press, Cambridge

British Library Cataloguing in Publication data
Gewertz, Deborah B. *1948–*
Twisted histories, altered contexts in Papua New Guinea:
on ethnography and Chambri lives in a world system.
1. Papua New Guinea. Chambri, history
I. Title II. Errington, Frederick Karl
995.3

Library of Congress Cataloguing in Publication data
Twisted histories, altered contexts in Papua New Guinea
on ethnography and Chambri lives in a world system/Deborah Gewertz,
Frederick Errington.
  p.   cm.
Includes bibliographical references and index.
ISBN 0-521-40012-0. – ISBN 0-521-39587-9 (pbk.)
1. Chambri (Papua New Guinea people) – Social conditions.
2. Chambri (Papua New Guinea) – Ethnic identity. 3. Acculturation –
Papua New Guinea.   I. Errington, Frederick Karl.   II. Title.
DU740.42.G47   1991
305.89'912–dc20   90-43063 CIP

ISBN 0 521 39587 9   paperback

GO

To Andrew Tambwi Kwolikumbwi Yorondu   1922–1988

Contents

Illustrations

Acknowledgements

We are grateful to the three granting agencies that supported our field trip to the Chambri during 1987. We were joint recipients of Interpretive Research Grant No. RO-21584–87 from the National Endowment for the Humanities; Frederick, in addition, was awarded a Grant-in-Aid from the American Council of Learned Societies; and Deborah, a Faculty Research Grant from Amherst College. We also wish to thank the Department of Anthropology of the Research School of Pacific Studies at the Australian National University for sponsoring our research among the Chambri during 1983. Deborah had, prior to 1983, made two trips. On the first, from 1974 through 1975, she was supported by the Population Institute of the East–West Centre, the National Geographic Society and the Graduate School of the City University of New York. The second, during the summer of 1979, was paid for by the National Endowment for the Humanities and the Miner D. Crary Fellowship from Amherst College. She expresses gratitude to each of these institutions, as well as to the Wenner-Gren Foundation for Anthropological Research which enabled her to investigate archival material during 1981.

We also wish to thank the many individuals who helped us complete this project. We particularly appreciate the willingness of our colleagues to read and comment on portions of this manuscript. Among those who deserve special mention are: Debbora Battaglia, Jan Dizard, Jerome Himmelstein, Brad Klein, Andrew Parker and Marilyn Strathern. We are extremely grateful, as always, to Carolyn Errington for her invaluable editorial advice.

Our greatest debt is to the Chambri people with whom we have by now become connected by a kinship constructed through a history of reciprocity. In particular, we thank Seby Asawi, Michael and Jacoba Fox, Francis and Scola Imbang, Michael Kamban, Teresia Kambukwat, Rex Kamilus, Godfried Kolly, Cosimos Kompar, Kosemp, Maliwan, Mepi, Theo Pekur, Anna Sapui, Cherobim Subur, Conny Tangi, Aron Tom, Margarita Wani, Leo Wasi, Patrick Yarapat. And, of course, our old and valued friend, the late Andrew Yorondu.

Finally, in listing our names as authors, we wish to note that one of us will no longer accept the tyranny of alphabetical order. Both of us contributed equally to the project and each wishes to thank the other for making this possible.

Introduction
On writing the Chambri

"When there is development there is always changes. We must choose the best way to cause the development." We found this unelaborated statement in 1987, under the heading of "Social Studies," on one of the last pages of Angela Imbang's school notebook still remaining in the outhouse. When Angela copied it the previous year from the blackboard of the Chambri Community School, she was in her sixth and for her, as for most Chambri and other Papua New Guinea children, the final year of formal education in a nationally determined curriculum.[1]

Angela was not a strong student. Certainly she felt scant motivation to preserve her notebooks, and she in fact understood little of the English she had written down. Because she had not done well enough to be admitted to high school, she doubted she would ever have a regular job. Yet, the expectations about development contained in the statement she copied had become pervasive in Papua New Guinea and were fully endorsed by Angela and other Chambri (and, in our experience, by many other Papua New Guineans).[2] While recognizing that their lives were constrained by, for instance, the educational requirements of even low-level clerical jobs they had come to believe, nonetheless, that their lives were, and should be, significantly different from the lives of those who came before and those who would come after them. Furthermore, they believed that they would, through their choices, be able to lead better lives.

This book is primarily about the changes, choices and constraints in the lives of the twentieth-century Chambri we have come to know either directly, through our own continuing field work which first began some fifteen years ago, or indirectly, through (in large measure) the research during 1933 of Margaret

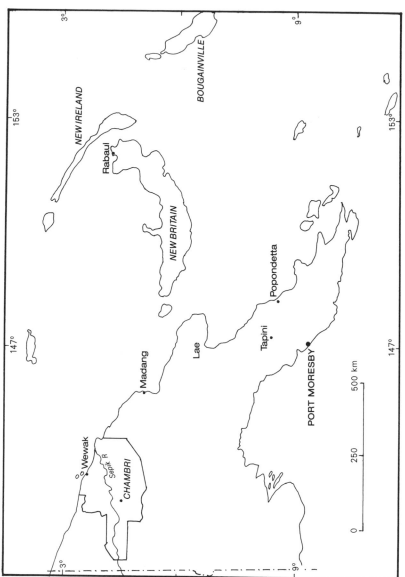

Map 1   Chambri within the East Sepik Province, Papua New Guinea.

Mead and Reo Fortune. This book is also about how small-scale societies like Chambri, peripheral to the major centers of influence, must struggle to fashion lives of relative autonomy within a world system premised on assumptions concerning social relationships, about power and control different from their own. Throughout, our effort has been to pursue an anthropology in which ethnographic representations convey the encounter between such peripheral societies and the larger system in a manner that might foster rather than subvert their attempts to maintain autonomy.

Well before European contact in the twentieth century, the Chambri lived in three densely settled, largely endogamous villages of Indingai, Wombun and Kilimbit on an island-mountain in Chambri Lake, south of the Sepik River (see Map 1). Their sociocultural system had developed in complex interaction with those of their neighbors of the Middle Sepik: the Iatmul, Sawos and the Sepik Hill peoples.[3] All were sedentary; they had different environmental resources; and they exchanged their surpluses in a regional system. None was economically autonomous. Principally, the Chambri supplied fish to the Sepik Hills peoples and the Iatmul supplied fish to the Sawos. Each received sago in return. (See Maps 2 and 3 for the location of peoples and places mentioned throughout this book.) This was a system of regional dependency in which the development of particular villages within each group was shaped and constrained by that of the others. However, within this context of dependency and mutual influence, the Iatmul became militarily and culturally dominant. Although never able to act with full autonomy or authority, and often at war among themselves, they were able through a masterly blend of warfare, intimidation and flattery to shape and maintain the regional pattern for their own benefit.[4]

From their position on the fish-rich Sepik waters the Iatmul were able to develop larger and more powerful villages than their sago-supplying neighbors of the bush and swamps.[5] However, these large villages faced nutritional problems. They had need of regular deliveries of sago to be exchanged for fish. As long as the Iatmul remained powerful they could require the Sawos to make the necessary deliveries. Their strategy was to keep the Sawos in their niche and that niche was away from the water. The Sawos were to produce sago and remain dependent on Iatmul for fish.[6]

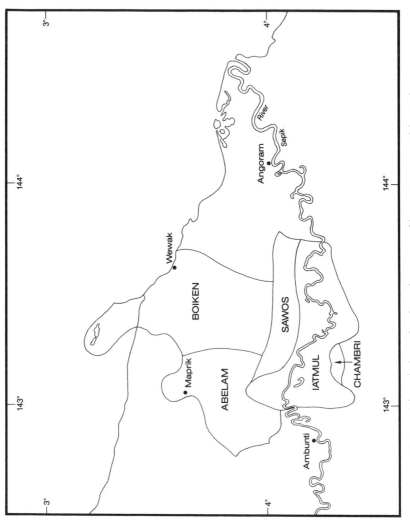

Map 2   Linguistic and cultural groups of importance to this study.

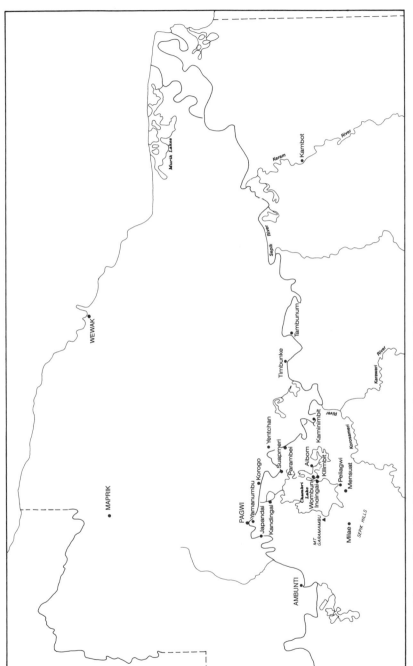

Map 3   Some Sepik villages within the East Sepik Province.

These large Iatmul villages also faced organizational problems. The internal cohesion which gave them their military power rested in large part on a complex system of exchanges, focused on ties created by marriage. These ties required shell valuables.[7] The importance of these valuables to the Iatmul and, eventually, to the Chambri, determined in major part the relationship between these two groups. The Chambri resources of principal interest to the Iatmul were their specialized trade goods of stone tools (made by men from Chambri quarries) and woven mosquito bags (made by women from reeds found in Chambri Lake). The Iatmul acquired these Chambri commodities with shell valuables previously obtained from the Sawos. Then, reserving a portion of these commodities for their own use, they traded the rest to the Sawos for yet further valuables. These they used in their own internal transactions and in trading for additional Chambri goods.

The Iatmul strategy to ensure Chambri cooperation in providing these items was to treat them as valued allies. Under these conditions of Iatmul hegemony but relative peace,[8] the Chambri could closely observe and emulate their formidable and impressive neighbors.[9] Indeed, the Iatmul encouraged the Chambri to elaborate a ritual and social system based largely on a Iatmul model. This stimulated Chambri demand for shell valuables and, in turn, increased their incentive to trade their specialized goods to the Iatmul. In fact, through imitation and interaction, and through occupying a comparable ecological position as fish producers, the Chambri came to duplicate many features of the Iatmul pattern. Their villages did become relatively large; they sought to control their Sepik Hills neighbors as the Iatmul did the Sawos. They never, however, developed a comparable military capacity.[10]

The Chambri lived largely safe from Iatmul attack until Europeans arrived on the coast of New Guinea at the turn of the century. The system then changed: in particular, the introduction and diffusion of European steel tools and cloth mosquito nets destroyed the market for Chambri products and transformed the relationship between the Chambri and the Iatmul. Fighting between the two became increasingly frequent until about 1905, when the Chambri fled their island rather than risk further military encounters with Iatmul, whose ferocity had been augmented by the acquisition of a German shotgun.[11]

In 1986, when Angela copied the passage on development, change and choice into her notebook, some eighty years had passed since the Iatmul drove the Chambri from their island.

Sixty-two years had passed since the Australian Administration had sufficiently pacified the Iatmul to allow the Chambri to return home. Fifty-three years had passed since Margaret Mead and Reo Fortune visited them and then made them famous as the "Tchambuli." (In Mead's view, Tchambuli women dominated over men.)[12] Some thirty-five years had passed since the beginning of extensive labor migration to distant plantations. Twenty-seven years had passed since the completion on Chambri of an impressive Catholic church, constructed of Western materials including colored glass panes. Thirteen years had passed since Deborah Gewertz first began her research among the Chambri. Some ten years had passed since *Salvinia molesta*, a South American fern, had been accidentally introduced, probably by a Catholic priest. It had so choked the lakes and rivers that the fishing and trading economy of the entire region was devastated.[13] And some two years had passed since a weevil, *Cyrtobagus singularis*, introduced by a research scientist and paid for largely by the Food and Agricultural Organization of the United Nations, brought the *Salvinia* under control. And, of course, much more happened in those intervening years, including a world war, the achievement of Independence for Papua New Guinea and the inauguration of education, Western style. In this new educational system Papua New Guinea teachers required their students, Angela among them, to copy statements in partially understood English about development . . .

But, to understand the nature and significance of this history, a portion of individual and community experiences and actions during the period must be brought into better focus. These experiences and actions, after all, both registered and to some extent shaped events.

Angela was the daughter of Deborah's best Chambri female friend and one of her most helpful informants. Angela was also, through her mother, the granddaughter of Walinakwan, a man described by Margaret Mead as one of the best dancers in the three Chambri villages.[14] Walinakwan, we were to discover during this most recent field-trip, had been much more than a dancer of renown. He had been entrusted with the care of two beautifully carved and powerful water drums, Posump and Ponor, named after the two ancestral crocodiles whose spirits animated them. Anyone participating at an initiation when these drums were used knew by the resonance of their thumping bark that these spirit crocodiles were fully present. (The resonance was produced when

1   Posump and Ponor displayed in the National Museum.

their open ends were thrust up and down in the water.) So knowledgeable of the secret names that invoked ancestral power were those who carved and bespelled these powerful drums that Walinakwan, according to Angela's mother and many others, had slept next to them inside his woven mosquito bag. His purpose was to absorb their power and to protect them from enemy raids. As both sources and repositories of his power, his viability and that of his clan depended on their safety.

We had seen these drums, but not at Chambri. We saw them in Port Moresby, at the National Museum. During Deborah's first period of field-work in 1974, they had been sold by Walinakwan's successor and clan brother, Wapiyeri, for several hundred dollars to an Australian artifact buyer. He, in turn, sold them to the museum for considerably more.

Wapiyeri had been desperate for money; although his sons were away at work, they were not remitting and he alone had to fulfill the obligations incurred through his own three marriages and those of his sons. (Money had by this time replaced shell valuables for ceremonial payments.[15]) He had hoped the sale of the drums would enable him to maintain his prestige. Instead, the sale provoked widespread condemnation and ill feeling. Even before the actual sale, when news of the impending sale leaked, many objected. They argued that because these drums were essential to the initiatory complex, they should be inalienable. Others claimed that, if the drums were to be sold, they were entitled to a major portion of the payment: after all, their ancestors had provided the trees from which the drums had been made or the tools with which they had been carved.

After several weeks of uproar, Wapiyeri nevertheless accomplished the sale with Deborah's unwilling and unwitting help. Wapiyeri instructed his youngest son to smuggle them out to the waiting buyer when next, as Deborah's research assistant, he accompanied her to the coastal town of Wewak where she went to resupply. Thus, unbeknown to Deborah, Posump and Ponor, concealed by her assistant in copra bags as though they were smoked fish destined for urban kin, left Chambri in her canoe, powered by her motor, operated by her boatman.

The trouble was not over. Suangin, the eldest member of Walinakwan's line still living on Chambri in 1987, made this clear to us when he came to enlist our help near the time of our departure. He explained that ever since Posump and Ponor had left Chambri sickness and misfortune had beset members of his

2   Suangin asked us to take exact measurements and
photographs of the water drums.

family. Not only had Wapiyeri and many others died – he named them – but many had gone to live in the towns and were not sending money back to Chambri. He and one younger man were the only adult males of his line remaining on Chambri. To add to his troubles, he had just lost a local court case and had been fined (the substantial sum of) K35.[16] Furthermore, the drums carved to replace Posump and Ponor had little power: they resonated only weakly. Clearly, the ancestral crocodiles who should have been embodied in these drums had themselves departed. In fact, the actual path of their departure was evident in a deep fissure which had opened in the ancestral land near his house. The crocodiles, angry that these drums were sold, and dissatisfied with the replacements that had been carved for them, had gone. This left Suangin and his family bereft of important support.

He wanted us to visit the museum when we passed through Port Moresby on our way home and arrange for the return of Posump and Ponor. Or, if unable to effect their return, we should take exact measurements and photographs of them, front and back. Suangin might then be able to have drums made that the spirit crocodiles could again be induced to inhabit (provided they were invoked by recitation of their secret names). If so, the fortunes of his clan would be restored and the replaced Posump and Ponor would again boom with the authoritative force of those sold.

Regardless of whether Suangin, with the measurements and pictures we did, in fact, send him,[17] could satisfactorily recreate the drums, we doubt that anyone in this Chambri universe of ramifying consequences – of "twisted histories," as one of our informants put it – could fully put to rest the repercussions of Wapiyeri's choice. Indeed, we ourselves were still involved: the boatman who transported the drums to Wewak was again in our employ in 1987, and thus thought to have access to our resources. He was being sued for damages in the Chambri village court by a woman who sought K25 from him because in 1974 he was implicated in the disposal of the drums in which she claimed an interest.

That Angela was the granddaughter of Walinakwan – a man whom we knew about from Mead's writings before we came to Chambri; that Walinakwan's drums were in the National Museum of an independent Papua New Guinea; and that we were indirectly held responsible by one for their loss and charged by another, Suangin, with their recovery, were not just components of a twisted history.[18] They provided more than an illustration of what was to the Chambri the evident truth that one thing led to another and that choices always had a profusion of consequences. They were, as well, an indication that the nature of the context in which choices were made and consequences appraised had altered: the world of Walinakwan and Mead and the present world, that of Angela, Suangin and us, while part of the same twisted history, were different worlds. Because a whole process of "development" had intervened, Walinakwan had become a curiosity to the Chambri. He was, nevertheless, a curiosity they could still readily understand and somewhat admire.

The fact that Posump and Ponor were so impressive[19] that Walinakwan slept with them influenced the sequence of choices and consequences which led Suangin to enlist our aid in getting them back. However, the fact that Walinakwan slept with his drums also marked his world in the eyes of contemporary Chambri as very different from their own. Although Suangin might desperately wish to regain Posump and Ponor, neither he nor any contemporary would seriously consider sleeping with them or with any ritually powerful object at his side under his cotton mosquito net. Walinakwan's behavior was described with a mixture of respect and amusement: his behavior was that of a powerful man but it was old-fashioned and unsophisticated. Such behavior, while probably still prudent and effective, would be decidedly anachronistic in the independent nation of Papua New Guinea where his grand-daughter went to a local school and was taught about development.

Indeed, the very idea of anachronism existed because development, whether conveyed through formal education or not, had become part of the consciousness of Chambri and other Papua New Guineans. With the idea of development had come the Chambri *perception* that their lives were, and would continue to be, different from the lives of those before and after them. What was appropriate for Walinakwan in the early days of European contact would no longer be so for Suangin more than fifty years later. For the Chambri, the linked ideas of development and anachronism followed from their recognition that they had made a transition from one kind of political economy into another: Walinakwan had acted in the context of a regional political economy, regulated primarily, although by no means exclusively, by the interests of Iatmul; Suangin and Angela acted in the wider context of a world economy, regulated by the interests of industrialized countries such as Australia, Japan and the United States. Moreover, contemporary Chambri understood not only that their system had changed but that it was, with its emphasis on development, premised on continuing change.

It must be emphasized that the Chambri did not expect their choices would be made free either from the constraint `that stemmed from prior choices, or from the regional or world system that constructed the range of present choices. And they probably never had expected that. However, the present circumstances of development were, we think, new to the Chambri in two important regards: the Chambri were more aware than formerly that the system of constraints in which they pursued interests and made and appraised choices had changed. They realized also that they did not yet fully understand the constraints of this present system. Significantly, those urban Chambri most subject to the exigencies and vicissitudes of a cash economy were fortunate since they knew they could still choose to return home to the (as yet) intact subsistence base provided by their fish-rich lake. Indeed, for these and many other Chambri, the perception that they were operating in an expanded system had evoked a sense of opportunity.

Thus, introduction of an artifact market provided Wapiyeri with the welcome opportunity to meet obligations through selling Posump and Ponor; our arrival as anthropologists provided Suangin with a means to recover the drums from the National Museum. To be sure, as these twisted histories became played out in the expanded system, one person's opportunity might become another person's problem, as with Wapiyeri and Suangin, and individuals might make decisions they would regret. But this had been true in the past and recognition that such was still the case did little to diminish a sense that life, in part because of its increased possibilities, had become enhanced. After all, much as Suangin wanted to recover the lost Posump and Ponor, he would not have wished to change places with Walinakwan in whose possession they had been indubitably secure.

As we will see in many of the cases that comprise this book, Chambri were attempting to determine the conditions and con- straints of development: they were trying to take advantage of the altered and expanded context by exploring, in ways that made cultural sense to them, the parameters of the new system. And, apparently discounting intimations or experiences of uncertainty or vulnerability, most exhibited a substantial degree of optimism about the future.

But, as before indicated, there was much the Chambri did not yet understand about the world system. They did not fully recognize, for example, that this system was premised on such institutionalized inequalities as class and on the perpetuation of underdevelopment.[20] Although they did recognize that choice and the system in which choice was made both affected and reflected relations of power, they did not fully realize that, whereas they had some influence on their regional system, they would have virtually none on the world system.[21] Yet, they were not entirely hapless. While the survival of their village economy might, indeed, serve to underwrite national and international capitalism (by absorbing many of the costs involved in reproducing the labor force), nonetheless, as the Chambri themselves knew, so long as the home environment was in working order, they would not be completely at the mercy of a precarious cash economy in a "developing" country.[22] Stated in another way, they would not be hapless so long as they were successful in their efforts to maintain their subsistence economy, that most essential basis of autonomy.

The autonomy the Chambri wished for themselves was not the autonomy of the pristine, the untouched, the remote, that we first traveled to Papua New Guinea to find. (Late 1960s for Frederick and early 1970s for Deborah.) Papua New Guinea at that time was for anthropologists, as for others in the West, still the "last unknown." Before going into the field, we read books such as *Patrol into Yesterday* (McCarthy, 1963) and *New Guinea: The Last Unknown* (Souter, 1963). And if we were not to be the first "Europeans" to "discover" a people, we would, we thought, be at least the first actually to live among one group. We would document thoroughly and sensitively the culture of what would become "our" society. Indeed, both our personal and professional aspirations seemed well served by work in a place such as Papua New Guinea, characterized, as it was, by remoteness. (As Salzman wrote in a recent edition of the *Anthropology Newsletter*: "The image of an anthropologist, in the general public and in academe, is that of a lone adventurer who strikes out to parts unknown, finds exotic and unknown peoples, engages sympathetically with them, and discovers unusual social lives and astonishing customs" [1989: 33].)

It would be through a combined process of self-discovery and transformation in such an isolated and unfamiliar setting that we as fledgling anthropologists could be validated. That validation, however, would be according to our own cultural standards that defined personal worth in terms of autonomy and individuality.[23] It would be, as well, in such a setting that we could collect data of signal importance. There, supposedly shielded from external and Western pressures for change, cultures would have best preserved their original discrete and varied forms.[24] Arriving before the main transforming thrust of Western influence, we could document distinctive social and cultural arrangements that, in turn, could be used in controlled comparisons to examine hypotheses about, for instance, the relationship of cultural and biological determinants. In fact, because of its remoteness and cultural diversity (a diversity suggested by the existence of over 700 distinct languages), Papua New Guinea appeared an almost ideal "natural laboratory." It had been in Papua New Guinea, after all, that Mead had found the three cultures which, through their contrast with each other and with the American instance, supported her argument that gender roles and dispositions were culturally rather than biologically produced. (See *Sex and Temperament*, 1935.)

However, ventures into the remoteness of the third world have by now come to seem less romantic. They have come to require more careful scrutiny than they did when we first began our anthropological careers. Perhaps the most forceful scrutiny of the assumptions that have defined personal and professional efficacy in terms of encountering the remote "other" has been initiated by those anthropologists loosely characterized as "post-modern." Their criticism takes the form of a challenge to "ethnographic authority." They ask: With what understanding and by what right do anthropologists speak for those among whom they have worked? They contend that ethnographic convention permitting anthropologists *because they alone were there* to speak with substantial authority about particular groups, no matter how different from their own, describing them as if presenting fixed and incontestable facts, can no longer be taken as epistemologically acceptable (Clifford and Marcus, 1986; Clifford 1988a). Nor can this convention be regarded as politically justifiable: to assume that one has the authority to speak for another is ultimately an act of hegemony. The difficulties in understanding and representing the "other" do indeed appear substantial.

Some of these critics question the degree to which anthropologists gain a mastery of cultures very different from their own. They remind their colleagues that "participant observation" may be actually quite limited and ineffective: anthropologists may spend considerable periods in the field incapacitated by illness or depression or engaged in escapist reading; when they do venture out they may largely limit their conversations to the few informants among whom they feel relatively comfortable; and despite their efforts, they may acquire only minimal linguistic and social competence. Consequently, according to this charge, anthropologists often return from the field with seriously incomplete knowledge of "their" particular people. As the logical extension of this position, it has been argued that anthropologists are little different from tourists.[25] Yet, we think it fair to say that despite the genuine difficulties of engaging in fieldwork, anthropologists do generally come to know a great deal about the peoples among whom they have lived. (For comparison between anthropologists and tourists, see Chapters 1 and 2.)

In any case, the major problems in doing ethnography, particularly for Western anthropologists working in non-Western contexts, are recognized to reside elsewhere. Others, and not only "post-modernists," have argued with more telling effect that the fundamental problem in reaching an adequate though much less authoritative ethnographic understanding lies in the virtual inevitability that the data anthropologists collect will be strongly affected, if not determined, by their own cultural and disciplinary assumptions. These include assumptions concerning the way knowledge is recognized and analyzed. Western anthropologists may, therefore, misunderstand systems of classification by viewing them according to concepts that distinguish between, for example, nature and culture (MacCormack and Strathern, 1982); they may misunderstand social forms by viewing them according to concepts that distinguish between the individual and the society (Strathern, 1988); they may misunderstand social processes by viewing them according to the concepts that distinguish between past, present and future (Fabian, 1983); they may misunderstand systems of perception by viewing them according to the concepts that give relative importance to the visual over the aural (Feld, 1982). Because such forms of ethnocentrism are elusive and pervasive, anthropologists are likely to comprehend the "other" in important measure through their own terms.

A related criticism points to operation of the assumptions that are tied to the definition and experience of professional competence. In the concern to have entities that can be analyzed, represented and otherwise used to sustain professional identities, anthropologists are likely to misconstrue the nature of process. To be sure, relatively few would still, as Mead did in the 1930s, subscribe to a scientism that found it unproblematic to regard places like Papua New Guinea as a "laboratory" composed of discrete societies which, like distinct and relatively fixed variables, could be neatly compared and contrasted. Nonetheless, to the extent that anthropologists do think and speak in terms that approximate "in 'my' society they do such and such," they are likely to discount the degree to which societies (if one should use that term at all) are caught up in complex histories of change generated by internal and external political processes. Nor should these processes be regarded as only the recent effect of Western intrusion. As has already been noted with respect to the Sepik, the Chambri and their neighbors had a relationship of mutual dependence, influence, negotiation and contention long before their regional system was encompassed by a world system.

For such reasons as these personal, professional and more broadly cultural preoccupations, anthropologists will wittingly, unwittingly and to some extent unavoidably distort, simplify and reify. In addition, it is argued that the representations of anthropologists, based as they may be on misunderstandings, give these epistemological problems important political dimensions (Clifford and Marcus, 1986; Clifford, 1988a). Particularly in contexts where there are vast disparities of power, representations have significant consequences. The view anthropologists (and others) convey to the first world about the Chambri and others in Papua New Guinea affects, for instance, the definition of the "primitive." And the definition of the "primitive," in turn, affects tourism, investment and other matters pertaining to "development."[26]

Moreover, simply for a Western anthropologist to describe a non-Western "other" to a largely first-world audience in authoritatively delineated form as, for example, "these are the Chambri," presents them as known, encompassed and unproblematic. They become drained of the capacity to confront or otherwise engage that audience. Representations of this sort, especially, concern autonomy: who speaks for whom and to whom. The autonomy that Chambri and, we think, other Papua New Guineans wanted was indeed not one based on some idea of remoteness. Rather than escape or be sheltered from historical process, they wished to engage fully and be paid attention to as prime negotiators in that process.

This critique of ethnography thus outlined can, we think, be accepted as largely correct. It can also be accepted in its fully elaborated form as numbingly daunting and as engendering virtual ethnographic paralysis. Indeed, many of those most active in the development of the critique are no longer engaged in non-Western ethnography. Yet, it seems to us that it would be an act of hegemony, for those whom the system of hegemony favors, not to act at all. To be other than passive agents of Western hegemony, we must, as Western anthropologists, consider what we can do to foster Chambri efforts to control, to some extent at least, their own future. At the very least, we must consider what we can do so that the Chambri, and those still relatively fortunate third-world others, will be able to preserve their subsistence base, the most essential source of their autonomy. (We believe this is so whether or not the preservation of that base may also subsidize the capitalist sector.)

The vulnerability of groups like the Chambri in the world system more than justifies accepting the epistemological and political risks inherent in ethnographic research and writing. And indeed there are risks in creating ethnographic texts. We must emphasize, though, that in expressing our concern for the Chambri we are not simply posing a modern variant of the "whiteman's burden." Our advocacy of their interests stems not from some perception that the Chambri were benighted, left behind, or lacked adult status either individually or collectively in the world at large. It comes from the realization that in this world, power is unequally distributed. We concur, therefore, with di Leonardo's observation in a review of two recent books which argue that anthropological "texts" are potentially hegemonous in their representation of non-Western "others": "Texts are political, but they do not constitute the whole of politics." She further warns that when evaluating the sources of the power ethnography has, we must be aware not only of "rhetorical force [but also of] . . . First World economic and political privileges" (1989: 352).

Thus, although Chambri lives may be viewed as texts, we must not be so preoccupied with textual concerns focusing on representation as to forget that they were also lives, lives affected in important ways by our Western power and interests. In this regard we would insist that while a text-based position, which views informants "as parables, as foci of textuality, as things spoken rather than speaking" (Dorst, 1989: 209), might be appropriate when applied, for instance, to the residents of a wealthy American suburb such as Chadds Ford, Pennsylvania, this position, if applied to the Chambri, would deny the very real effects on them of that suburb (and other sources of Western power and interest).

In writing this book about the Chambri as they were caught up in world processes of social and cultural change, we have not ignored issues concerning understanding and representation. We have struggled to get important aspects of the epistemology (relatively) right. By focusing on *Chambri* concepts of person, power, politics, gender, and worth, we have provided some basis for a non-ethnocentric understanding of their experience. We have also been concerned that Chambri political objectives be heard. Although we do on many occasions present Chambri voices, we have not cast this book as a "dialogue," a form some have advocated as a means of resolving both the epistemological and political difficulties of writing ethnography. Those favoring the "dialogue" form argue that local people should speak for themselves rather than have anthropologists put inaccurate and politically inauthentic words in their mouths: local people should at least be co-creators of the ethnographic text.[27] We believe, however, that such a text of self-representation would not be either feasible or effective in the Chambri instance.

Simply put, we cannot imagine Chambri reaching agreement on what such a text should contain. As will be evident, particularly in our discussion of literacy in Chapter 5, Chambri regarded their anthropologists as resources to be employed in local competition. Whose voice and hence whose partisan perspective became inscribed in written form was a matter of serious contention among Chambri. (It followed that contention among the Chambri became a potential source of resentment against us, the inscribers.) Nor can we imagine that such accounts, filled as they were with ancestral names and precedents, would in themselves have much intelligibility or significance for a Western audience, that audience that has the greatest power to affect Chambri lives. (These unexplicated accounts would, at best, be accommodated within a post-modern view that the world often displays a "funda-mental weirdness" [Polan, as cited by Dorst, 1989: 210] in which different perspectives, none more authoritative, more compelling, more valid than any other, are juxtaposed. Thus Chambri would be another item for personal consumption or rejection.)

It is to convey the intelligibility and significance of Chambri experience and lives to a relatively broad Western audience that we have chosen, through presentation of interlocking stories, twisted histories, commentaries and contexts, to create a collective (although partial and unfinished) biography. In particular, rather than delivering Chambri as some fixed and determinant entity, we have sought to convey them caught up in systemic change, insistent that they retain their autonomy as they negotiate in pursuit of their objectives, including those of "development."

To the extent that Chambri have been able in fact to retain autonomy, their views of change, and especially their experiences of it, should be seen as a component of the processes of change.[28] Indeed, as we have already seen in our discussion of the process of "development" linking Walinakwan and his descendants, the Chambri pursuit of their objectives in steadily changing circumstances has altered and may further alter both those objectives and those circumstances. It is in this regard that the specifics of the Chambri experience may contribute to what has recently been called for as a focus of anthropological research: that is, to reach a more complete "understanding of experience and of the *precise ways by which experience enters historical-cultural processes*" (Rebel, 1989: 123, emphasis ours). In an effort to provide a fine-grained understanding of the way in which this happens, we have written what is essentially a case study. In it, we wish to convey specifically and clearly, and to as wide an audience as we can reach, how Chambri view and negotiate their linkages with the first world system.[29]

Because we have ourselves been working with the Chambri for a considerable time and have available the earlier published and unpublished research of Mead and Fortune, we know a great deal about the actions, responses, experiences and interpretations of many Chambri lives during the period of transition between a regional and a world system. Through use of these data that are both first-hand and relatively long-term we seek in this case study to understand more completely the intersection between the processes of cultural elaboration, transformation and practice, within systems in which power was not only negotiated but also imposed. From the perspective of anthropological theory, our most general concerns in the relationship of experience and process are ones that encompass, link and, we think importantly, *ethnographically embody* those of Bourdieu (1977) on the ways that political systems are maintained through the actions of individuals; those of Barth (1988) on the ways that cosmological systems become modified and embellished through the speculations of individuals; those of Sahlins (1985) on the ways that sociocultural systems are altered through efforts of individuals to maintain them in changing circumstances; and those of Gramsci (1977) on the ways that systems of constraint are embodied in consciousness.

Finally, during times of substantial elaboration and transformation, an understanding of Chambri experience is essential in any *political* effort to properly appraise and appropriately respond to the Chambri circumstances in the world at large. We have thus chosen, in writing an ethnography of Chambri experience, to do more than understand a significant component of social change within a world system. In recognition that interests of some within a world system readily determined the destinies of others, we have *as well* sought to provide the basis for a politically compelling acknowledgement of common humanity.

In affirming this latter objective we do realize that, in a world filled with the politics of oppression, terror and counter-terror, such recognition of common humanity and political responsibility may not go very far.[30] But what else is there to serve those who have significant power neither to withhold nor to threaten? (We again insist that our advocacy on behalf of the Chambri stems from a conviction that we should take responsibility for the effects of our actions, not that we should shoulder a "whiteman's burden.")

We have intentionally separated most of our academic discourse from the main text and have placed it in footnotes in order to preserve the integrity and continuity of the Chambri stories. Our decision to write an ethnography that is unconventional in these (and other) regards may, we recognize, at least initially trouble some of our anthropological colleagues. Nonetheless, we have taken advantage of the present ethnographic times to be somewhat experimental as we try to make Chambri lives *as accessible as possible to as many as possible*.[31]

Correspondingly, the interpretive discussions we have included in the text are designed to enhance engagement with Chambri lives rather than to distract from that engagement. In these discussions we have sought to employ the insights of those writing for a more exclusively professional audience than are we (in this particular work) without creating complexities so dense as to make Chambri life inaccessible. (We have tried to avoid the opposite problem of rendering Chambri life as unduly transparent.) And, although on occasion, as in Chapter 6, we do compare the Chambri circumstances with those of other Papua New Guinea groups, our concerns in this ethnography are not primarily comparative. This is so, in part, because comparable material is often lacking in the literature and, in part, because we wish the Chambri to remain our principal focus. Throughout, our primary effort has been to harness and direct whatever anthropological sophistication we and others can provide so as to represent the *Chambri* with an intelligible immediacy.

Although we readily admit our book is a construct, it is a story of real lives, written to facilitate both understanding and empathy, and not just a self-interested fiction.[32] It is a story in which we have personally played a direct part. Therefore, we have intentionally written ourselves into this ethnography to a degree that might strike some as obtrusive. We wished to avoid the ethnographic conventions suggesting authorial omniscience. In addition, as fieldworkers we were for the Chambri both representative of, and mediators with, the West; and we were, consequently, a significant political component in their circumstances.

It follows that this ethnography is not primarily to provide a distance that will grant those of us in the West a fresh look at our own lives.[33] Nor have we written it to document Chambri lives apart from our own. Rather, we have sought to bring Chambri lives into conjunction with our own Western ones so that we can understand, and begin to take responsibility for, the effects our collective lives have had and will continue to have on theirs within the world system.

In Chapter 1 we discuss the consequences of tourism to Chambri: tourism had become for them the principal source of income and thus the primary road to development. It affected their internal politics, their artistic production and their sense of place in the world. Unlike the earlier interaction between the Chambri and their neighbors in a regional system of similar – commensurate – differences, Chambri and tourists met in a world system of incommensurate differences. It was a world system in which the

Chambri were of value primarily because they lacked development.

In Chapter 2 we describe a Chambri initiation to which the tourists were invited. The money they provided in admission fees enabled the sponsor of the ceremony to stage a more lavishly traditional performance than he could otherwise have afforded. The presence, though, of tourists as an audience to be entertained also meant that the initiators were partially deflected from the objective of conveying Chambri custom to the initiates as weighty, comprehensive and binding. Although offering important ceremonies for sale as tourist attractions provided enhanced opportunities for some Chambri, this increasing commoditization of social relations and even of culture itself, carried the important but largely unrecognized possibility that both Chambri and their ceremonies might be transformed.

In Chapter 3 we focus on the lives of Chambri living in town where relationships were already substantially commoditized. Virtually cut off from traditional forms of subsistence, and fully immersed in a cash economy, Chambri found urban life hard and sometimes dangerous. But for many, life in town was preferable to that in their home villages: it allowed them to redefine obligations and to evade sorcery and other forms of traditional coercion. Nonetheless, Chambri did not use the relative freedom of town to repudiate their identity as Chambri. Despite the fact that their relationships with other Chambri were often irksome, other Chambri remained their primary reference point.

In Chapter 4 we examine the influence on Chambri youth of Western representations pertaining to freedom and choice. Our principal concentration in this chapter is on the life, death and subsequent funeral of a young popular musician who, many Chambri believed, was ensorcelled by his father for marrying against his father's wishes. Particularly affected by his death and committed to altering those social arrangements they believed had led to it were members of an emergent social category, that of "youth." The questions of what changes were acceptable and what sorts of persons Chambri youths and others should be in a changing and developing Papua New Guinea were largely unanswered, even after the mortuary ceremonies for the young musician were concluded. The question of how, if at all, to redefine persons, social relationships and social and cultural practices was unsettled and unsettling.

In Chapter 5 we appraise the uses by, and effects on, the Chambri of literacy. As anthropologists we were often asked to produce written accounts that were valued in this highly competitive system because they enhanced the authority of clan-based claims and perspectives. Significantly, the Chambri were to produce their own transcriber of ancestral stories, their own indigenous ethnographer. He combined a very large number of fragmentary, inconsistent and often esoteric clan-based accounts into a single, comprehensive and authoritative history called a "Chambri Bible." This was to preserve and display ancestral precedent and be a source of continuing strength and a guide to proper conduct in the changing and developing world. We then consider some of the Chambri responses to this project, conceivable only with literacy. We especially focus on the potential such a project of inclusive representation had to transform the system of competition between relative equals into a system based on hierarchical control.

In Chapter 6 we analyze the Chambri relationship to the national state, an institution that at least in its design was comprehensive and authoritative. In particular, we examine the Chambri resistance to representation and control by the state and their concurrent insistence that their relationships with other Papua New Guinea groups as well as with the government itself be based not on rights in the abstract but on the social entailments they themselves had negotiated.

In our Conclusion, we consider a letter we received after leaving the field announcing the death of Yorondu, an old friend, one of Walinakwan's last contemporaries. It provides a context for our reflections on the processes of social change we have discussed. The letter, as well, reminded us of our kinship with the Chambri, constructed through a history of reciprocity in which we had each negotiated for the resources of the other. The letter implied that by helping us to do anthropology among them, the Chambri had extended to us a generosity for which we should reciprocate.

In a world where the Chambri were unlikely to achieve the development they would choose, we offer this book in the hope that it may in some useful measure assist them in averting a development they might regret.

1

The new traditionalism: tourism and its transformations

Maliwan had been telling us of his plans for the forthcoming initiation of five of his eight sons, a ceremony we very much wanted to witness. The initiation, during which young men received hundreds of incisions on their arms, backs and sometimes on their buttocks and legs, was intended to transform them into productive adults. Although Deborah had seen two such initiations before – in 1974–75, during her first fieldwork among the Chambri[1] – Frederick had never seen one. We wanted to know how maturity was defined and effected in 1987[2] and to what extent, if any, the ceremony would reflect the changes that the Chambri had been experiencing since the time of Deborah's first research among them.

Our first intimation of change in the initiation came when Maliwan said that we would each be charged an admission fee of K10, the amount decreed by custom, to enter the Walindimi men's house and attend the ceremony: this was the fee he was going to charge the tourists. "But," we said in shocked surprise, "we have been living at Chambri a long time." In response to our objection that we be grouped with the tourists for this occasion, he replied that any person not himself initiated who entered the men's house during the ceremony of initiation would either have to undergo initiation at that time or pay K10. Or, he added somewhat ominously, pay K20 or contribute a pig. Indeed, such a person would have to pay whatever amount the sponsor of the ceremony, in this case Maliwan, decided was enough to show appropriate respect for custom. Moreover, K10 was the amount tourists were being charged to witness initiations in the Iatmul villages along the Sepik River.

Given our concern with social change we were intrigued to

25

discover that it was now regarded as both a matter of tradition and as indicating respect for tradition that tourists be charged admission to what had theretofore been a carefully guarded ceremony.[3] Interested as we were in this turn of events, we nonetheless continued to object to his classification of us with those who were to be paying customers. We pointed out to Maliwan how in other ways we differed from tourists, mentioning, for instance, that because we had lived in Chambri a long time we had come to know well and to respect Chambri customs.[4] In addition, throughout this long period we had always helped Chambri in a variety of ways including giving them medicine and first aid. We also reminded Maliwan that the immediate reason we were having this conversation with him at all was that he had come to our house to pick up an application to the national government for funds which we had typed at his request: Maliwan was asking the government to give him K4,600, primarily for the renovation of the major Chambri tourist attraction, Maliwan's own Walindimi men's house.

More than our match in the rhetoric of obligations, Maliwan expressed his great pleasure that we had all lived so well together: the Chambri had given us help in teaching us their customs and we had reciprocated with our help. Similarly, the Chambri had helped the government and now the government must help the Chambri. In fact, the Chambri had built the Walindimi men's house to celebrate the inauguration of the government in 1975, when Papua New Guinea had achieved independence. Moreover, the Chambri had been following the government's exhortation that they (and other Papua New Guinea societies) must keep their traditional culture strong. It was to be an important resource that would both guide them and, as an attraction for tourists, provide the basis of prosperity in their future course of development in the new Papua New Guinea. Now that the men's house needed repairs, the national government should reciprocate for all of the hard work the Chambri had done on its behalf. The Chambri needed this help if development was to proceed: that is, if tourists were to continue to visit Chambri to see the Walindimi men's house.

Finally, Maliwan said that the initiation was going to be very expensive to sponsor. As far as he knew, his sons alone would be initiated. That meant that he and his family would have to bear the full expense.[5] He would need all the money he could get from visitors. If he were to allow us free entry, he would not only lose our fees, but perhaps those of the tourists. They might balk at paying if we revealed to them that we had been admitted without charge. And the likelihood was that we would reveal that to them: after all, they were our countrymen.

Maliwan was both amiable and adamant and so we paid up. Finally, to mollify us, he said that he would explain anything we wanted to know about the ceremony. Indeed, he seemed anxious to have us record and photograph the ceremony in detail.

The circumstances Milawan described appeared to us as filled with irony, as pregnant with expectations that would be confounded by unpredicted consequences.

Our own expectations, as we have mentioned, in first coming to Papua New Guinea had been to validate ourselves through sur-mounting the challenge of fitting into an entirely unfamiliar cultural context. According to these criteria of defining worth, to be admitted into the secret phases of an initiation that featured such an exotic practice as extensive scarification would provide clear confirmation of our hard-won status as anthropological insiders and as accredited ethnographers. Flawed as we eventually saw these criteria to be, it struck us, nonetheless, as a most curious and unsatisfactory turn of events that tourists, although outsiders, were to be given the insiders' seats at the initiation, while we, who had struggled to become insiders, were to be classified with the tourists as those who had to pay admission. Paying admission was not the same as paying one's dues, we thought resentfully.

During our stay at Chambri we did come to like most of the tourists, at least as individuals. We often enjoyed our conversa-tions with them when they arrived at Chambri and when, as guest lecturers of the tour company, we once joined them on a circuit of Sepik villages. Well educated and, in most cases, persons of good will, they were usually disposed to appear respectful of the customs of those they were visiting.[6] And, we thought, it was probably to their credit that they had sufficient curiosity to come to Papua New Guinea at all. However, ironies less personal and more enduring than those concerning our relationship to the tourists remained.

Our conversation with Maliwan had evoked, as well, a far more significant irony: it was that tourism was likely to have conse-quences quite different from those the Chambri sought, in part, because the tourists and the Chambri had largely contradictory objectives. Simply put, the tourists were drawn to Chambri primarily to see those less developed whereas the Chambri sought to attract tourists so that they could become more developed. Correspondingly, to the extent that the Chambri were successful in developing, they would endanger the basis of their development: the Chambri would remain of special interest to tourists only as long as they remained "primitive" and "unchanged." In fact, as we shall see, many of the tourists thought that they had come to the Sepik just in time, before too much change had taken place. Although few Chambri clearly realized that the tourists found them primarily of value, that is, of interest, for characteristics that the Chambri did not value in themselves, many Chambri were coming to recognize the moral component of this irony. Tourism, the source of their future strength and autonomy in the world, was premised on continuing inequality.

In another important regard, tourism was likely to have consequences very different from those the Chambri recognized or intended. The "traditional" culture that was to attract tourists would almost inevitably in the course of tourist performances become much less traditional: Chambri culture was subject to change simply by being performed for an outside audience.

Chambri certainly recognized and accepted a number of the consequences of tourism. They realized, for instance, that in their concern to carve artifacts for sale to tourists, they no longer carved ritually efficacious figures and images. But in this and other situations, they were eager for change. Yet, in certain contexts, they had every intention of precisely following past practices. Indeed, Maliwan wished to invite tourists to the initiation of his sons so that he could fulfill his traditional obligations in an exemplary fashion. (Consistent with this objective, he argued that it was in accord with tradition that they be invited and charged admission.) It was in such cases as these, in which precise replication of ancestral pattern was particularly important to the Chambri, that we think the presence of the tourists would have quite unintended and to a great extent, unperceived, effects.

Given their reliance on tourism with its only partially recognized ironies, negotiating a future that the Chambri would find satisfactory was not going to be easy, even for a tactician as skilled as Maliwan. In this chapter and the next, we discuss in more detail the significance to the Chambri of their individual and collective decisions to offer aspects of their culture, particularly those concerning ritual, for display or sale to tourists in order that they might "develop." We will examine in special detail the initiation Maliwan staged as a tourist attraction. Specifically, we will explore the meaning for Chambri youth of coming of age in 1987 in a men's house built to attract tourists, filled with artifacts made to sell to tourists and in front of an audience of tourists who paid, as we will see, to photograph esoteric ritual procedures and paraphernalia as well as the freshly cut backs of the initiates. And, in understanding the transformations, both intended and unintended, that both created the context for coming of age and were likely to follow from it, we will be concerned, as we are throughout this book, in examining the relationship, both recognized and unrecognized, of the Chambri to the more powerful others within a world system.

Maliwan's men's house

The Walindimi men's house in Wombun Village where Maliwan planned to initiate his five sons was the only full-sized, two-story men's house then standing in the three Chambri villages. It was built between 1974 and 1976 as a major collective undertaking. According to Maliwan, men from all three of the Chambri villages contributed their labor and resources. The work was often dangerous as large trees had to be felled on Chambri mountain. Maliwan told us of the alarm men working in the forest felt when the tree destined to become a main house post toppled unexpectedly: men called out to each other for assurance that no one had been killed. In addition, the work was frequently arduous as the trees had to be dragged across and down the slopes to the construction site in Wombun.

Maliwan had himself supported and enlisted the cooperation of others in this project. In this effort he was acting on the advice and encouragement of Peter Barter, owner of a tour company bringing wealthy sightseers up the Sepik on the Melanesian Explorer, a luxury cruise ship. Barter had convinced the Chambri that if they had a traditional men's house, they would be able to attract tourists who would buy their artifacts. Indeed, he would have the Melanesian Explorer make Chambri one of its regular stops.

And, as Maliwan had also explained to us, the Walindimi men's house was built as well to commemorate the emergence of Papua

New Guinea as an independent nation-state. Michael Somare, the first Prime Minister, had been invited to attend the grand opening. Although Somare could not come, the Chambri had a big party to celebrate and publicize the project that would inaugurate their post-Independence era of prosperity.[7]

Significantly, then, the only full-sized, "traditional" men's house on Chambri Island was built largely as a tourist attraction. Moreover, this "traditional" men's house could only be built in a non-traditional way. Whereas men's houses were customarily constructed by men of two or three residentially adjacent clans within a single community, this one was constructed by men drawn from all of the three communities. In fact, by the mid 1970s, with many Chambri away at work or at school in the towns,[8] only by defining the Walindimi men's house as representing all Chambri was it possible to mobilize enough men to complete such a project. Such a definition of the men's house as representing all of Chambri was, in turn, possible only in a context in which they became, however temporarily, doubly unified. They were unified as a sociopolitical entity among the many groups competing for governmental resources in a newly independent Papua New Guinea and also as a particular attraction among the many Sepik villages competing to sell artifacts to tourists.

Maliwan's strategy

Even though the building of Walindimi was an all-Chambri project, Walindimi was still Maliwan's own men's house: it was still the men's house where he and the men of a localized cluster of clans would store their ritual accouterments, recite their totemic names and perform their ceremonies and their cosmological observances. It was where they would participate in debates, make marriage arrangements and hold shamanistic seances. In the present instance, it was where they would initiate their sons. (Of the five men's houses existing at Wombun at this time, Walindimi was the most elaborate and the most architecturally complete. Some of the fifteen existing at Chambri were simply rudimentary shelters and, in a few instances, little more than house sites.[9])

Maliwan sought both to achieve leadership in his own men's house and to make that men's house, not simply one among many, but pre-eminent. Indeed, he wished to make Walindimi all encompassing. In his attempts to do so, he would show himself to be a particularly skilled player in a system of ceaseless male competition where accumulations of power and authority were possible only through the most shrewd and assiduous efforts. In this system, each senior Chambri man was likely to challenge the accomplishments of others and in so doing maintain himself as at least a potential equal of all others. In such circumstances, the achievements of those such as Maliwan could only be temporary, never becoming institutionalized into such patterned and enduring forms of inequality as social class. Yet, transitory as his accomplishments might prove to be, Maliwan could insist on taking full credit for effecting them. In this respect his accomplishments were unlike inherited privileges.

(As we have discussed at length in *Cultural Alternatives and a Feminist Anthropology* [1987a], Chambri women were also preoccupied with achieving worth, but in a manner different from that of Chambri men. A woman's strategy focused on the payment of what we have called "ontological debts" to those predecessors who gave up power on her behalf. By bearing children and by acting in the life-cycle rituals of those children and others related to her so as to facilitate their generational succession, a woman was able to replace those who had provided her with her own existence. Achieving worth in this fashion did not involve women in competition with each other, or with men. Chambri women were, thus, far more relaxed about their competencies than were Chambri men. As we will see throughout this book, ritual events were occasions for women to worry, grieve, celebrate but not, as for men, to compete.)

Maliwan's specific strategy in the present situation was to use traditional arguments in terms of clan ancestrality both to justify his dominant position in his men's house and to assert that Walindimi appropriately represented all Chambri in the Chambri relationship to the outside world. The benefits of this arrangement to Maliwan were evident: he could gain access to more than traditional resources to support Walindimi; he could supervise the labor of all three Chambri villages to construct and maintain his men's house; he could collect tourist income to defray his initiation expenses; and he could solicit and use government funds. However, access to these resources sometimes required the cooperation of other Chambri and Maliwan's principal task was to convince an often skeptical audience that support of him and his plans for his men's house would also channel resources to them. In short, he needed to convince them that the best way of dealing with the outside was through him and his enterprise. Specifically, Maliwan had to show that he could attract money not just to himself or to those in his men's house group but to other Chambri more generally. In other words, he had to show that he could continue to attract tourists and induce them to buy Chambri artifacts. That was a novel and risky undertaking for a big man.

As part of his effort to demonstrate that Walindimi belonged to him yet represented all Chambri and that he could continue to attract tourists, he asked us to record an account of how the Walindimi men's house was founded. This we present below. It would be posted in typed form, in both Pidgin English and English, in the men's house for everyone to read, Chambri and tourists alike.

Certainly a Chambri audience would have no difficulty understanding the significance Maliwan intended his story to have: it was his assertion that he had power and, thus, eminence because his ancestors had performed crucially important primordial acts. Moreover, Chambri would regard Maliwan's account as formidable rhetoric. In recounting his story, Maliwan undoubtedly had anticipated the kind of challenge he might encounter. He knew that his rivals would attempt to demonstrate, perhaps through recounting their own clan myths, that Maliwan had only an incomplete understanding of his ancestors and their activities and that, in addition, Maliwan's ancestors were, in their own time, men of little real consequence. To counter such a challenge, Maliwan had included in his story a wealth of strategic detail and a careful specification of the relationships his apical ancestor established with other ancestral figures. In so doing, he had constructed a story that other Chambri would immediately recognise as not readily to be discounted.

Maliwan was also seeking to address a larger and mostly Western audience, that of the tourists and those to whom the tourists would speak on their return home. However, he did not apparently recognize the extent to which this audience differed from a Chambri audience in political understanding. Whereas Chambri and other Sepiks could respond to his account with (often grudging) admiration, acknowledging it to be a virtual paradigm of a politically effective claim, those not themselves of the regional system could only find his story confusing. Nor did he fully realize that this larger, first-world audience held the decisive power to affect Chambri lives. It is, therefore, to make Maliwan's (and, by extension, Chambri) claims for significance intelligible to this first-world audience that we are here presenting both his story as he asked us to write it in English and our explication, in which we attempt to reveal its logic and rhetorical force.

The story of the Walindimi men's house

Yerenowi, Maliwan's ancestor, originated with the ground. He lived in the area [of Wombun Village] called Pampanchankwi. He married the daughter of Emosuie [the first Chambri, a half-pig, half-man who lived in a stone on the top of Chambri Mountain]. His wife's name was Klaboro. Yerenowi was not actually a man; he was an *uncheban* [a non-human spirit]. No one sired him; he came up with the ground.

Yerenowi's men's house was called Pluwelilman. It was not the kind of men's house we have today. It was a grove of pandanus trees. The grove was called Pluwel. The stone house in which Yerenowi lived was called Kanasuimeri. He lived in a hole in this stone and would leave it to walk to his men's house which was near the shore of Chambri Lake; here, Luke Kolly [Maliwan's brother] now resides. That is how he lived.

Meanwhile, Walindimi and his older brother, Yambukay, lived at Indingai Village. One day, Walindimi carried some dry sago to his men's house, Wiarmanagwi. As he tried to eat it, his mouth became very parched and he wished he had some moister food to eat with it. He decided to check the slitgong, in which men sometimes hid food they did not want others to find. Sure enough, he found a bunch of bananas, broke off several, and ate them.

Shortly after this, Yambukay left his house with his net bag and his basket of sago and walked to the Wiarmanagwi men's house. He put his net bag and his basket of sago on the bench of his men's house, got a broom, swept the floor of the men's house and built a fire. His tasks completed, he checked the slitgong where he had put his ripe bananas. When he retrieved them he found a cluster had been broken off and asked: "Who took some of my bananas?"

His brother, Walindimi, answered him: "I took some because I had only dry sago to eat and I wanted some other food with which to moisten my mouth."

Yambukay became very angry and said: "Why did you take them? I did not bring them here for you. They belong to me. I have come here to cook bananas and eat them with the sago I brought in my basket." Then Yambukay pulled out the stick for striking the slitgong, ran over to his brother and hit him repeatedly on the head with it.

Walindimi's face became covered with blood but he did not fight back. He just stood there and let his older brother beat him.

After venting his anger, Yambukay picked up his net bag and basket of sago and went to this house. He left the bananas on the bench in the men's house; he did not want to eat them anymore.

Walindimi decided to leave Indingai for good. He took his bundle of native tobacco and made three little cigars. One he kept in his hand; another, he put behind his ear; the third, he lit and put in his mouth. He walked away from the Wiarmanagwi men's house, taking the road that Yerenowi used to go to this men's house. He followed this and came upon Yerenowi's men's house of pandanus trees. Yerenowi was not there as he had gone to get *pliplimank* [a wild water plant supposedly once used instead of tobacco] at his house. Walindimi took a dry leaf from one of the pandanus trees and rolled his lit cigar up in it. He then set fire to the pandanus men's house.

Yerenowi on his way back to his men's house heard a great roar and many explosions. He at first thought it was a big wind, but then realized that his men's house was on fire and that the explosions were the crackling of the burning green pandanus leaves. He ran down to the fire yelling: "Who is burning my men's house?"

Walindimi answered him: "Friend, take it easy. I have burned your men's house."

Yerenowi asked: "Why did you do this? My men's house is not bush; it is a men's house."

Walindimi responded: "Never mind, my friend; it's nothing. Just relax. I have burned your men's house so that we two can build a real one here."

Then Yerenowi looked at Walindimi and saw that his face was covered with blood. He asked: "What happened?"

Walindimi explained what had happened between him and Yambukay concerning the ripe bananas. He said that he had left Indingai for good. He had always thought, he continued, that Yerenowi should not have to stay in a pandanus men's house. The two of them should build another.

Yerenowi said: "Never mind my objections; they are of no importance. We will do it."

The two of them got spears made of black palm which they stuck in the ground. Then they got the bast from the sago palm and made a rope which they strung between the upright spears to mark the dimensions of the new men's house. Next, they cut down garamut and kwila trees to make the posts of the new men's house. They dug the holes and erected the posts, built the frame and roofed the men's house with sago thatch. They put the two faces, of the sun and the moon, on either side of the men's house – the sun on the west, the moon on the east. Finally, they named it. The eastern half is called Wombunyeris; the western half is called Blorombir. The ground on which the eastern side is built is called Tokwapannimbir; the ground on which the western side is built is called Yokanjoy.

The men's house as a whole is called Walindimi because just as Walindimi came to Yerenowi's ground, now tourists come to see the men's house.

It should be added that the real reason that Yambukay attacked his brother was not because his brother had taken his bananas. Rather, Walindimi had seduced Yambukay's wife, Palawanpir, and Yambukay was looking for a chance to get back at him. After Walindimi had finished this men's house, he left Chambri Island entirely and went to [the neighboring island of] Aibom where he built the Kosimbi men's house right before he died.

According to this story, Yerenowi had an inherent connection with Pampanchankwi, the place where his descendant Maliwan lived. Yerenowi, a predecessor of the fully human, came up with and was thoroughly embedded in this place: he lived in a rock; his men's house, a grove of pandanus trees, was (literally) rooted here. Yerenowi married the daughter of Emosuie who was the first Chambri of all, a half man and half pig, who himself lived in a rock on top of Chambri Mountain. This delineation of Yerenowi's attributes served as an argument that he and his descendants had an indisputable claim, based on priority of occupancy, to ownership of Pampanchankwi. Moreover, since it was generally accepted that Yerenowi had no contemporaries at Wombun apart from the peripatetic Walindimi, Maliwan was also making an argument that his area was the first settled of all those in Wombun Village and thus his men's house preceded all of the others.

However, this demonstration that Yerenowi had indisputable priority of residence in Wombun by virtue of his pre-human links to Pampanchankwi carried with it the acknowledgement that Yerenowi was at the same time culturally untutored. Yerenowi, after all, mistakenly over-valued his *pliplimank*, smoking dried, wild water weeds as if they were proper tobacco; comparably, he over-valued his pandanus grove, treating this bush as if it were a proper men's house. In contrast, Walindimi had tobacco from which he made three cigars. Such a domesticated natural product itself indicated the emergence of culture from nature. Appropriately, a burning cigar was used to initiate the process by which Yerenowi's pre-cultural men's house, consisting of a wild grove of pandanus trees, became a proper men's house constructed of a variety of transformed natural products.[10]

Significantly, it was only after Yerenowi noticed that Walindimi's face was covered with blood and heard his story about fighting with his brother and leaving Indingai Village for good, that he accepted Walindimi's offer that they should together build a proper men's house. Walindimi's story made him appear to be a powerful man whose help was worth taking. He had bested Yambukay by seducing his wife and by remaining unmoved when Yambukay disgraced himself by viciously attacking Walindimi over the petty matter of a few bananas.[11] But, of perhaps greater importance, Walindimi's story showed him to be homeless – without kin, or men's house or village. Only under these circumstances could Yerenowi acknowledge Walindimi's cultural superiority and accept his assistance without becoming indebted to his and Yambukay's clan, to the members of the Wiarmanagwi men's house and to Indingai Village.

Moreover, the particulars of this case had meaning for the Chambri: Walindimi had seduced his brother's wife, taking that which brothers should *not* share; he had then been beaten by his older brother over a few bananas, being denied that which brothers should share. These circumstances could be seen by Chambri as providing Yerenowi with the assurance that Walindimi would not displace him in importance at Wombun. Walindimi's participation in the events that were the complete negation of kinship suggested that he was at least somewhat socially disengaged, that he would not put down roots.[12] Thus, because Walindimi was a knowledgeable but battered refugee, in need of only temporary shelter, as indeed proved to be the case, Yerenowi could, in Maliwan's story, accept his help.

In presenting Walindimi men's house as built by an essential and rooted Yerenowi, together with a powerful and unrooted Walindimi, Maliwan sought to establish through precedent that this men's house was *his*, that it was filled with power and that it encompassed *all* Chambri, regardless of their special ties.[13] He then extended and concluded his argument with an important assertion: "[J]ust as Walindimi came to Yerenowi's ground, now tourists come to see the men's house." In this Chambri rhetoric, for Walindimi to have come to Yerenowi's ground (rather than to some other place) to build this men's house and for tourists to come to this men's house meant that they had been attracted there, initially by Yerenowi and subsequently by his descendant, Maliwan. That Maliwan still had the capacity of his predecessor implied that he, like his predecessor, could attract other Chambri to his men's house. Thus, as the result of contemporary process and not simply through precedent, Walindimi men's house should be the appropriate focus of Chambri in general. For Maliwan to claim that he could attract tourists would bolster his contention that he should be supported because he could bring prosperity to Chambri.

Maliwan's claims to have the power of his predecessors and the power to attract were informed by two fundamental assumptions of Chambri political cosmology: Chambri assumed that in the normal course of generational succession, power became diffused and lost. Acting upon that assumption, senior clansmen, seeking to preserve their own positions of relative efficacy, would wait as long as possible to pass on to their juniors their magical knowledge which was the basis of power. Because of miscalculation and infirmities of old age, important knowledge either died with the old men or was transmitted in garbled, and substantially useless, form.[14] In light of this assumption, Maliwan's assertion that he had maintained the power of his predecessor was politically crucial. Maliwan's assertion of his power to attract followed from another central assumption of Chambri political cosmology. This assumption was that power often manifested itself in the capacity to pull people and resources into one's orbit. In this latter regard, Chambri described their society itself as having originated through a process of immigration by which individuals with specific powers were pulled to Chambri by those powers already aggregated there. As new powers supplemented existing powers, the capacity to attract additional powers increased.[15]

To summarize Maliwan's position then: he was positing that the construction of the Walindimi men's house resulted because Walindimi was pulled by Yerenowi to his ground in Wombun; in addition, he was contending that it was through the continued exercise of his, Maliwan's, ancestrally derived power that this men's house had become quite literally (in Chambri thought) a tourist *attraction* fostering economic development for all Chambri. Maliwan's argument that *his* power had produced and would continue to produce *this* sequence of events was, however, acceptable to other Chambri only under certain conditions in this highly competitive society. Only as long as Maliwan could convince others that he could continue to bring development would he receive the support that had become essential to his position as a Chambri big man. In particular, as we have said, he must ensure that sufficient numbers of tourists would continue to be pulled to Chambri and to Chambri artifacts.

Yet, what pulled tourists to Chambri was (presumably) not that they found Maliwan's magical power to attract compelling and his ancestral story about the creation of his men's house persuasive. They would, however, have been attracted by the fact he believed them to be so attracted. Given their necessarily very different view of the world, how then did Chambri and tourists encounter each other? How did the plans that Maliwan and other Chambri had for the tourists in whose hands their development was thought to reside coincide with those the tourists had for themselves during a Sepik excursion in which a visit to Chambri was only one of many stops? In short, what was the relationship between what the Chambri wanted and what the tourists were looking for?

As we will see, it was not only the idiom of ancestrality in which Maliwan made his claims, but also the system of competitive equality in which those claims were made, that the tourists would reject.

The tourists and their view of the "primitive"

Most tourists who visited the Sepik region had bought a packaged excursion from the Travel Corporation of America. This included, as part of a tour of the South Pacific, the option of four days on the Sepik river in the Melanesian Explorer. The Melanesian Explorer was a relatively luxurious, air-conditioned tourist ship which cruised at between 12 and 14 knots. It contained ample amenities: in-room plumbing and showers, a full bar, a video recorder with tapes of Papua New Guinea peoples and a library with over 100 books on the country.[16]

The brochure of the Travel Corporation of America described the Sepik River Cruise as follows:

8th thru 12th days – Tuesday thru Saturday – Sepik River Cruise: Board our cruise ship Tuesday evening and begin our journey to one of the world's most remote and fascinating areas, the Sepik River region. We cruise in air-conditioned comfort aboard the *Melanesian Explorer*. Our trip through the lower and middle Sepik visits villages such as Kamindimbit, Timbunke, and Tambanum. Off the main river, we use speedboats to travel the tributaries and the Chambri and Murik Lakes. Life along the Sepik has been virtually untouched by Western ways.

The villagers hew canoes from gigantic logs and set off on fishing and hunting trips, bringing back food, exotic feathers, shells, skins and animal bones to use as headdresses, adornments and ritual implements.

You will have time to explore the many villages, and the House Tambarans, some of which are enormous and display a wealth of art. We are able to buy magnificent ritual masks, statues and artifacts of these artistically gifted people. We will witness traditional sing-sings and get-togethers for joyous events or mourning, in the lives of these primitive people (Travcoa, n.d.: 35).

This text promised an encounter with the "primitive." Most of the tourists from the Melanesian Explorer whom we met were Americans. All were Western. Most were prosperous middle-aged professional men and women: physicians, nurses, lawyers, scientists, administrators, teachers. They sought not the "pure primitive," however, but the "primitive" just on the edge of change. (We met them when they visited Chambri by speedboat and later when we joined them on the Melanesian Explorer during one of its cruises.)

An experienced guide on the Melanesian Explorer cautioned us that in the lectures we would give in exchange for our board and room we should be careful not to over-emphasize the extent to which change had already taken place. For example, tourists interested in "black magic" should not be informed that old Chambri men had now begun to tape record their magical spells so that these spells would not be forgotten when they died. The tourists "don't mind a little change," she said, "but would hate to know that the natives are sophisticated enough to tape their own chants."

One Melanesian Explorer tourist, a woman from New Jersey, told us that her Sepik trip was "like stepping back in time, but there are modern things too." In a like vein, a physician from Chicago, in stating her reason for coming to Papua New Guinea, said that it was about as far away from her hospital as she could get, and that "it is a place which will be completely changed in ten years; one has to see it now as it really is." Another physician said that he was glad to have seen the Sepik "before," he added wryly, "people like us spoil it, as we have in so many other tourist places." Indeed, most recognized clearly that their presence as tourists was both an indication that things had changed and an impetus for continuing change.

One group of these tourists told us with satisfaction of an unscheduled visit they made to a Lower Sepik village where they came across a group of men trying to raise K4,000 to purchase what would be a collectively owned truck. The K200 they had thus far raised was displayed on a mat around which the men sat. The tourists joined in the spirit of the occasion by contributing some K60. Their names, along with those of the native contributors, were duly recorded in a notebook. Then, probably in recognition that the tourists would not be able to make reciprocal claims for their assistance, they were given two live chickens.

Because this stop was unscheduled, the tourists knew that these men were pursuing their own interests rather than engaging in a staged production.[17] They found the mixture of old and new engaging: the villagers were cooperating in a traditional way to pursue non-traditional objectives, even though they were a long way from realizing their goal. (As one tourist commented to us, "My goodness, we contributed almost a third of what they had; they'll never get to where they want to go.") Certainly in the view of these affluent professionals, the villagers appeared naive: they were sadly naive in hoping to raise the money needed for their truck[18] and charmingly naive in believing that a gift of live chickens was appropriate reciprocity to Westerners. This naivete marked these villagers as still on the edge of change and left them sufficiently open so that they would reveal their real lives to the passing tourist. (And, to their credit, the tourists were pleased that their lives and those of Papua New Guinea had touched with mutual feelings of good will.)

We were told about another encounter by two members of a group that had, before joining the Melanesian Explorer, visited the home of "the daughter of a chief" in the Highlands of New Guinea.[19] The daughter had been married to an Australian but had divorced him to return to her home territory and marry a Papua New Guinean. Now living on the outskirts of her natal village in a nice house, she had her own car in which she drove her children to school. Although well-educated, having been trained as a teacher, she was not using her skills to help her people progress. The first tourist to tell us this story was incensed by the young woman's selfishness in not helping her people advance to her own level of development. A different evaluation of this woman came from another tourist who was impressed by the attractiveness of her home, the clarity and precision of her English and the beauty of her mixed-race children. Both of our commentators agreed, though, that the sophistication of this woman relative to other Papua New Guineans must be the product of her special position as the daughter of a "chief" and as the former wife of an Australian. Although others would, and indeed should, follow in her path, she was in her cultivation still very unusual.

Another tourist we met, a physicist, apparently saw himself as a catalyst for change. He had been impressed by the accuracy of what he regarded as the largely intuitive knowledge of physical principles possessed by Papua New Guineans. He commented to us with excitement and admiration that villagers had been able to modify their traditional canoes to accommodate the additional weight and speed provided by outboard motors. Their modified canoes duplicated the configuration of a Western-designed speedboat. He was also impressed by certain internal projections in a slitgong which, he said, served to amplify the sound in the same way as did the bridge in a violin. Later, as we were walking through the village together, his dismay was evident when he encountered some bamboo scaffolding surrounding a men's house under reconstruction. This scaffolding did not employ triangular bracing. Speaking in English and describing the success of the Chinese in Hong Kong with high-rise bamboo scaffolding, he gestured toward the men's house in an effort to convince a passing youth that this scaffolding would have been both easier to construct and safer to use if diagonal supports had been employed. He believed with obvious sincerity that he could help Papua New Guineans in their further development by conveying to them an important principle of construction they had not yet discovered for themselves.[20]

Of all the villages he and the other tourists on the cruise visited, Korogo was their favorite. They said that it was the only village they had seen in which the houses were ordered. By this they meant that the houses were laid out in a geometric lattice with a wide central avenue. There were also plantings of ornamental shrubs around many of the houses. These the tourists referred to, only partly in jest, as "fomal gardens." Many were particularly impressed by a house whose roof was under construction. Three-foot sections of sago-leaf thatch were stacked neatly in piles along the length of the house, adjacent to each section of roof. The concern with efficiency that this planning seemed to demonstrate was interpreted as indicating the advent of a "division of labor," a specialization of skills and work. In Korogo, the tourists thought they had discovered a progressive community about to replicate the patterns of development of Western society. It was, in their mind, a community on the edge of modernity.

Thus, the tourists we met on the Melanesian Explorer had a relatively positive attitude toward change. Many of our conversations with them focused on the obstacles that must be overcome before change was possible. Tourists asked us whether college-educated Papua New Guineans would be able to reject beliefs in sorcery, and to persuade others to reject these beliefs. They urged us to persuade Chambri to give up the "barbaric" practice of scarification during ceremonies of male initiation. They speculated about the marvelous transformations that could be made in Papua New Guinea, a country rich in natural resources, by people of vision and enterprise (such as the Israelis).

The view that Papua New Guinea should eventually develop was consistent with the interest of these tourists in validating the system in which they, as prosperous professionals, had achieved success. However, the tourists also wanted to be certain that they had come before this rapid transformation of the "primitive" world was complete: they viewed the "primitive" as an increasingly rare prize to be witnessed and captured before it was too late. But since they wanted to be among the last to do this, they also wanted to know that they had come in time. They wished to use their money to enjoy life and see the out-of-the-way portions of the world, and they wanted assurance that these portions of the world were still worth seeing.

(Other, younger and less affluent sight-seers came to the Sepik as well. Generally in their 20s, often on long-term excursions following the completion of university studies or military service, these sight-seers considered themselves "travellers." They did not use money to insulate themselves from direct and significant experience as did, in their view, the tourists and they had a somewhat different use for the "primitive."[21] These travellers viewed themselves as unique and autonomous, with both the desire and the self-reliance to travel on their own in a place as remote and "undeveloped" as Papua New Guinea. And what they encountered there was experienced as further enhancing their already distinctive selves. [As we have indicated, anthropologists often had similar motivations.] For travelers, the encounter with what was regarded as the "primitive," that is, the exotic, the whole, and the fundamentally human, contributed to their own individuality, integration and authenticity. Correspondingly, the principal lament of those travelers who found aspects of their trip disappointing was that the people had become spoiled. The social relationships between travelers and native people had become, like those in the West, essentially commercialized. The "primitives" they had expected to engage with had, in other words, become too much like us. Those held most responsible for spoiling Papua New Guineans were the "big spending Melanesian Explorer tourists"[22] who, representing the worst commercialism and superficiality of Western society, had through their insensitive use of money fostered the commercialization of social relations throughout the Sepik. The older tourists were viewed by the younger travelers in what were perhaps Oedipal terms: the older tourists consumed and spoiled the "primitive" in such a way that it was difficult for those who were in a generational sense their children to be nourished and developed.)

The view of change held by the tourists was one of unilinear evolutionism. They believed that all Papua New Guineans were "backward, but on the road," as one man put it, to the better, more "developed and advanced" way of life, a road already traversed by those who had produced Western civilization. We found tourists generally uninterested in, and somewhat antagonistic towards, any information which challenged this particular view of historical process. Few, we were distressed to discover, would take seriously any argument we could present that, for instance, Sepik intellectual systems, forms of social organization, and political strategies for achieving eminence might be as complex, as deserving of respect, as their own.

Indeed, they resisted learning much about Papua New Guinea that went beyond their preconceptions about the nature of cultural differences. Since they assumed that all people have some form of carbohydrate as staple, they were pleased to learn that sago was eaten on the Sepik and sweet potatoes, in the Highlands. However, they were not interested to hear that men in Sepik communities were initiated into secret male cults while men in the Highlands were not, and that the presence or absence of male initiation ceremonies might relate to different ideas about what it was to be an adult.[23] The only significant differences they were inclined to accept were those between Papua New Guineans and themselves, not those between one Papua New Guinea village and another.

Thus, we came to understand that for the tourists Papua New Guineans were not representatives of complex and diverse cultural traditions. They were, rather, generic "primitives" now in transition to civilization. (In contrast, the younger travelers, preoccupied, as before indicated, with their own development, needed Papua New Guineans to remain sufficiently undeveloped to provide them with the counter-cultural experiences they believed necessary to create their unique, and uniquely Western subjectivities.)[24]

Tourists did, however, require a certain variety in the villages they visited during their five days on the Sepik. The acceptable differences between villages related primarily to readily observed aspects of material culture. Moreover, tourists were eager to acquire souvenirs of their trip, especially since they knew that the Sepik was famous for its rich artistic tradition. (It has been described as "one of the greatest art producing areas of the primitive world" [Forge, 1973: 169].) Before entering a village, they were briefed by their guide on what they would see that was artistically distinctive, including the sorts of artifacts to be offered for sale. (As we shall later see, this village-level craft specialization was partly a product of the tourist market. A community needed to offer something distinctive in order to be included on the regular route of the Melanesian Explorer. And as a consequence the circuit of the Melanesian Explorer could be seen as marking out a contemporary culture area, in that the villages it visited had constructed differing yet comparable identities.) Thus, Parambei was defined as having a beautifully constructed men's house and a wide range of reasonably priced net bags; Yentchan, several stops farther up the Sepik, was known for a delicately carved finial on its men's house and for wicker artifacts; and Chambri had the Walindimi men's house with its unusual oval windows and, as artifacts, highly polished, intricately carved, ceremonial spears.

Tourists, as well, were guided in their purchases by a readily available 43-page illustrated booklet, *The Artifacts of Papua New Guinea: A Guide for Buyers* (S.P.A.T.F., n.d.), which assured them that "any artifact from Papua New Guinea, whether it be a bone dagger or an intricately carved spirit figure, still fairly accurately symbolizes a living part of the cultural background from which it originates" (p.2). The booklet provided numerous (266) illustrations of artifacts arranged according to type and function, provenance by village and region, and degree of scarcity. Thus, next to a description of "Hooks" were four photographs with captions such as "Cult hook. Kandingai Village, Middle Sepik. Common"; or "Cult hook. May River, Upper Sepik. Very Scarce" (p. 17).

3 Parambei was defined as having a beautifully constructed men's house and a wide range of reasonably priced net bags.

In the course of the trip, the foyer of the Melanesian Explorer became filled with the newly acquired artifacts awaiting final fumigation. These were trophies of the "primitive." Conversations frequently concerned the "museum quality" of these artifacts and the most effective manner they could be displayed at home. In many ways, the interest the tourists had in the Sepik became focused on the artifacts they were acquiring. Indeed, for both tourists and Sepiks, the most significant encounters each would have with the other concerned these artifacts. We turn now to the nature and consequences of these encounters.

The Chambri and their experiences of the tourists

Because the Melanesian Explorer followed a regular sequence of stops along the Sepik, villagers could be advised by the departing guide when the next visit was planned.[25] On the appointed day, everyone at Chambri would be alert for the sound and then the sight of the powerful speedboats that conveyed tourists from the Sepik River anchorage of the Melanesian Explorer up the channel to Chambri Lake.[26] As the boats approached, they would swing out into the lake to give the tourists a glimpse of the egrets and other water birds. Then they would land near the Walindimi men's house.

At the first sound of these boats, Chambri men would hurry with their carvings to the men's house where they would add them to the hundreds left there on semi-permanent display. When the tourists arrived, the tour guide would chat outside the men's house for a few minutes with Maliwan and advise her party of some 20–30 that, since this men's house was a sacred place, they must remove their hats upon entering. Inside, the Chambri men, relaxing for a few minutes after arranging their carvings, would peer out at the tourists and comment on their sunburned and sweaty appearance, speculating as to whether particular fat and old ones would be able to negotiate the narrow cane staircase to view the artifacts on the second floor. On average, Chambri saw two groups from the Melanesian Explorer each month. Nonetheless, the tourists, loaded down as they were with cameras and dressed in safari gear, remained wealthy curiosities.

Chambri, as we have said, regarded tourism as the key to their post-Independence economic viability. By this time in their history, few Chambri were able or willing to subsist without money. Few could rely on the barter of fish for sago as the primary source of their principal carbohydrate: although it was still sometimes possible for Chambri to barter their fish for sago at markets in the Sepik Hills, the sago suppliers who attended these markets frequently insisted that transactions be in cash. (Only 15 per cent of sago transactions in 1987 involved barter.) Comparably, few could rely on such sources of apparel as the Catholic mission charity could provide at irregular intervals. Few would be willing to deprive their school-age children of education through inability to pay their school fees.[27] And, of perhaps greater importance, few would be willing for want of money to give up claims to the political respectability, if not political eminence, that came through contributing to presentations of money, an essential component, in recent times, of all Chambri ceremonies. And then, of course, few would wish to give up such minor amenities as kerosene lamps and flashlights for twisted coconut-frond torches or to forgo commodities such as sugar, canned mackerel, rice and, at least on festive occasions, beer. Many indeed aspired to acquire watches, radios, tape recorders, cameras and outboard motors.[28]

Some money did come to Chambri in the form of remittances

4   Only 15 per cent of sago transactions in 1987 involved barter.

from relatives working in urban centers like Port Moresby or in industrial centers such as the mine of the Bougainville Copper Company. However, most of the money acquired by men living at Chambri in the course of a year, some K10,000 by our estimate, came from the sale of artifacts, primarily to the tourists on the Melanesian Explorer.[29] Given the importance to them of the tourist trade, Chambri were, in fact, devoting considerable thought to what tourists were looking for in artifacts. In their speculations about what might sell, they recognized that they were in competition with other Sepiks as well as with other Chambri.

Under these competitive circumstances, success in selling artifacts was valued not only as a source of income. It was valued also as a measure of a carver's cleverness and skill. Men took pride in their capacity to appraise and anticipate the kinds of artifacts that would sell and in their ability to execute those artifacts. Indeed, one told us with pleasure that several of his recent innovations had been so successful they were being copied by others. He had been the first to make miniature carved and painted slitgongs. These sold well and others began making them too. To stay ahead of his competitors, he then decided to leave the center section unstained, although highly polished, so that the tourists could see that the stain was not covering up any defects in the wood such as cracks or termite damage. Moreover tourists and Chambri alike, he said, admired his carvings because the shapes and incised decorations were straight, clear and symmetrical.

Despite the considerable satisfaction the best carvers derived from recognition they received, even they were emphatic that the only reason anyone carved was to earn money. Despite our persistent questioning, we found no one who carved with the intention of keeping his own work or knew of anyone who did. In fact, we were informed that a Chambri might keep the work of another only if that other carver had died and his carving would serve as a memento.

It used to be otherwise, we were told. Seby Asawi, a well-educated (high school graduate) and highly skilled young carver explained: Our ancestors would "adore" (English word used) the carvings they made. They would chant over them so that their ancestral spirits entered into the carvings, making them ritually powerful. (Such, it might be remembered, had been the case with Posump and Ponor.) Now, a carver would not chant his secret totemic names over his artifacts to make them repositories of his ancestral power. True, he might use clan magic to attract tourists so that they would buy his carvings. Or he might use magic to protect himself from the sorcery of jealous competitors. But he certainly would not put his own power into something he was just going to sell.

This actual process by which carvings that were understood to regulate the world became displaced in everyday importance by objects that served the tourist trade was illustrated in the historical transformation of a spear that had come to represent Chambri in the artifact market. Depicted in the *Artifacts of Papua New Guinea: A Guide for Buyers* (p. 16), the booklet mentioned earlier, this highly polished spear was about five feet long and was made in two detachable sections so that it could be disassembled for packing; the blade had widely flaring multiple serrations; at the base of the blade was a carved face with perforated ears through which decorative cords were attached; the handle was marked with complex symmetrical carvings which culminated in a carved crocodile head. (Chambri sometimes made even more elaborate versions having multiple blades and faces.)[30] So obviously embellished was it for the tourist trade, we were surprised to discover that it had been recently derived from a ceremonial spear, named Kwandanbali, one of the most valued clan possessions of Cherubim Subur.

Each sort of spear generated and sustained quite contradictory sorts of social relationships. The ceremonial spear, regarded as a virtual person complete with social life, participated in a complex and enduring network of social relationships. The tourist spear, regarded almost entirely as an "object," served as the basis of transactions that carried no further obligations, that did not elicit future relationships. Moreover, it seemed to us that the first set of meanings was being dispelled and otherwise revised by the second. In this regard, the transformation of the Kwandanbali spear was having important and largely unintended consequences. The irony of the situation was that the transformation had been impelled, as we will see, by Chambri efforts to fulfill "traditional" obligations.

Indeed, the process of change illustrated with respect to the spear was broadly characteristic of what the Chambri were experiencing and, to some extent, shaping as they attempted to cope with and exploit the circumstances encountered during their transition from regional to world system.

Kwandanbali, Subur told us, was an ancestral spear that he controlled as senior member of the Yambusinay clan. He would activate its power under two rather different circumstances. The first was when there was a fight between any of the members of the three Chambri villages. Subur would take the spear from its rack in the rafters of his house and recite the particular secret names that activated the power of the spear and merged him with that power. He then would walk through the three villages carrying the spear, not on the main road, but in the bush in back of the houses. In this way, Subur said, he would "break the fight." (Indeed, it might be surmised from Subur's description that the power of this spear was the underlying and unseen power on which social order rested.) When Subur arrived home again, he would return the spear to its rack and kill a chicken to quiet the spear's power and to separate himself from it, lest he become sick.

Subur would also activate (and unite with) the spear on those occasions when members of Albert Tangan's clan activated their Minjinprapan ceremonial mask. This they would do to celebrate, for example, a canoe christening, wedding, or house opening. The mask and the spear were part of a ceremonial complex, once controlled exclusively by Subur's family. Subur's family had given this mask to Tangan's family after the Parambei wars. (These, referred to earlier, began at the turn of the century when Iatmul from the village of Parambei routed the Chambri with the aid of a German shotgun. The Chambri were exiled for over twenty years, not returning to their villages until the Australians assumed control of the region in the late 1920s.) During the wars, members of Subur's family had sought refuge with their trading partners on the Korosameri River. Subur's family then asked some of their in-laws, members of Tangan's family, to join them. However, Subur told us, several of the latter were then killed through sorcery by Chambri enemies from the Sepik River village of Kaminimbit. Subur's family, because they were acting as hosts, were held substantially responsible for these deaths. So when the wars were over and everyone returned to Chambri, Subur's family gave the Minjinprapan mask to Tangan's family to offset the loss they had suffered.

We must note that in compensating Tangan's family for their loss, those of Subur's family were not simply giving them an item of value. Rather, they were giving them what was in many ways a person, or that which a person became as an embodiment of power, in replacement for the death of one of their members. And, of equal importance, this transaction served to perpetuate the relationship between these two families.

Subur continued his account by explaining how this singular, powerful and valuable Kwandanbali spear with its carved faces and broad blade had become the prototype of the (often hypertrophied) spears the Chambri now produced in large numbers to sell to tourists. The first to make spears based on the Kwandanbali design for sale to tourists was Thomas Kaui. As senior member of Subur's family, he was entitled to use this design. The spears sold well: they had the symmetry, clean lines, clear carvings that tourists favored. Kaui then gave permission to all Chambri carvers to make comparable spears after his son graduated from high school. He did this, Subur said, to reciprocate for the widespread help he and his son had received in paying school fees.

In order, hence, to recompense his many creditors (and to perpetuate his relationship to them) through allowing them to make the tourist spear Kaui had seized upon a novel strategy: It was evidently based on the dual recognition that there was a tourist demand for his spears and that rights to ceremonial objects could be used to pay debts.[31] His innovation lay partly in the fact that he was *not* transferring the right to make and to become Kwandanbali itself. This remained clan property under the primary control of Subur. But he was transferring the right to make the generalized, essentially powerless and valueless derivatives.

Kaui's innovation of giving his creditors the right to make the tourist spear was, as both effect and cause, part of the process of social change in which the Chambri were engaged. In making the transition from a regional to a world system, Chambri assumptions, like those concerning the nature of obligations and the means by which obligations should be fulfilled and social relationships thereby perpetuated, were encountering altered exigencies, like those concerning the ways that money could be acquired and objects employed within a cash economy. Through this collision between aspects of the Chambri cultural system and a (substantially) recalcitrant reality, the cultural system was changed as assumptions became reconfigured and thus altered. (Marshall Sahlins has called a collision of this sort "the structure of conjuncture" [1987: xiv].) Like other Chambri confronting and embracing the social change entailed in "development," Kaui was struggling to formulate and negotiate his objectives so as to remain viable

5   Subur and friend with hypertrophied versions of the
Kwandanbali spear.

within shifting circumstances. Thus, in order to remain a socially competent Chambri in an increasingly monetized economy, he sought both to ensure his son's education as a source of future income and to fulfill his obligations to his creditors. Just as others had depleted themselves to augment Kaui and his son through contributing to the latter's education, so too Kaui was depleting himself through yielding up access to one of his clan objects. This transaction probably appeared to Kaui and other Chambri as following much the same logic as had, for instance, the transfer of the Minjinprapan mask as death compensation. Yet because the context had become that of the cash economy, such a transaction would have appreciably different consequences. The significance of the tourist spear lay not only in the fact that it was one (of many) Chambri responses to a process of change but in the fact that it contributed to and shaped those processes.

As the result of Kaui's efforts to compensate his creditors, the cultural significance of Kwandanbali was subject to change. From *sui generis*, it had become a prototype. Its meaning no longer was exclusively that of a clan-based object of power effective within a regional system; rather, its meaning was qualified by the tourist artifact derived from it, the artifact that would provide Chambri with the opportunity to develop. This shift in cultural significance stemmed in part from the fact that the spear as tourist artifact operated quite differently from its prototype. The tourist spear was an object that no longer had any essential connection with persons: no longer did it augment, enhance, embody or otherwise define them, nor they it. And, of even greater importance, the fact that the tourist spear was completely separable from those who transacted with it meant that those transactions and the social relations it engendered or otherwise affected, were also subject to change.

Kaui's effort to maintain social relations with other Chambri had involved him in a transaction in which he conveyed what was understood to be something of himself. However, as a result, it became all the more likely that Chambri would increasingly engage in transactions that did not convey aspects of the self, that did not generate significant social relationships. The tourists buying the spears were not acquiring an aspect of Thomas Kaui that would be part of an on-going sequence of relationships: they were acquiring a souvenir of a Sepik excursion. The significance that Kwandanbali did retain for Subur and others as a powerful ritual object operating in a thicket of reciprocity was in contrast to, and potentially undermined by, the increasing number of thoroughly un-entailed transactions the Chambri were having within the world system.

What more generally might be said about this transition between systems, each with its characteristic type of transaction?

On systems of difference

As we have mentioned, the Chambri were once producers and purveyors of two commodities, stone tools and mosquito bags, used throughout the Middle Sepik. In exchange for these commodities, they obtained shell valuables and a variety of art and ceremonial forms from the Iatmul. The Iatmul traded a portion of these Chambri products to the Sawos for shell valuables which both they and the Chambri used in their systems of marital exchange. Moreover, the Chambri supplied fish (and other subsistence products) to the Sepik Hills people as did the Iatmul to the Sawos, each receiving sago (and other subsistence products) in return. In addition, Chambri acquired forest products such as bird of paradise plumes, tree oil and other locally produced commodities from the Sepik Hills people in exchange for shell valuables (obtained from the Iatmul). Furthermore, much of this inter-group exchange occurred between trading partners who were bound together in long-term and often patrilineally inherited relationships of relative equality.

The village specialization and patterns of exchange created with the contemporary tourist trade were substantially different from those just described. As we have said, the tourists on the Melanesian Explorer were not seeking a direct encounter with the truly primitive; not did they wish to acquire a detailed understanding of the cultural variation existing among the Sepik villages they visited. Correspondingly, they sought to acquire artifacts that conveyed, in muted variations, a diminished primitiveness: they wanted, in other words, for their Parambei net bags to be complemented by their Chambri ceremonial spears. This encouraged the Chambri and their Sepik neighbors to present themselves so that they could be readily characterized, readily represented.[32] Although as we have seen, the idea of village specialization was not new in the Sepik, no one in the past would ever have acquired a Chambri mosquito bag, for instance, because it was a souvenir of Chambri.[33]

The Chambri were aware that their transitory encounters with the anonymous but obviously wealthy tourists were qualitatively different from those to which they were accustomed with their trading partners. Indeed, they often tried to establish more durable relationships with tourists. Sometimes they asked tourists for their addresses in an effort to become pen-pals. They also attempted to reduce the importance of the manifest inequality in wealth. As mentioned earlier, Chambri did notice that the tourists were heavily perspiring and often overweight; they joked about their incompetence in negotiating a narrow staircase or in getting out of a boat.

But these efforts to redefine aspects of the encounter between the Chambri carvers and passing tourists did not amount to much: the correspondence between pen-pals, that few even attempted, did not last long; the comments and jokes did little to offset substantial differences in wealth in this region where wealth was an important measure of self-worth.

The closest any Chambri came to establishing a relationship of comparability with the tourists was that which Maliwan established with Peter Barter, the owner of the Melanesian Explorer. Their relationship was more like that between trading partners: it was long term, based on mutual benefit and had at least the appearance of relative equality.[34] However, unlike a traditional trading partner, Maliwan delivered not stone tools but an *ethnographic experience*, the experience of buying Chambri artifacts from Chambri in the Walindimi men's house; Barter delivered not shell valuables but a *business opportunity*, the opportunity of selling artifacts to tourists. At least on the Chambri side of the transaction, Maliwan could deliver the experience of being among the Chambri only with the cooperation of other Chambri; moreover, to be granted the opportunity to sell artifacts did not itself effect the sale of artifacts. That (in the Chambri view) required both skill in carving and the successful exercise of magic on the part of each Chambri carver. What Maliwan and Barter exchanged was, thus, of far less tangibility and of far wider social interest than would have been the case in any exchange of stone tools for shell valuables. Indeed, and we are not sure what this portended, Maliwan had become a meta-purveyor of meta-objects for all of Chambri: he attempted to deliver those who wished to sell representations of Chambri such as the commercialized ceremonial spear.

But it was because his relationship with Barter differed in these specific ways from a traditional trading partnership that Maliwan was able to pursue with unusual success the traditional political objective of extending his influence among other Chambri while retaining and perhaps augmenting the ritual prerogatives of his clan. Maliwan was seizing the opportunity provided by tourists to become, with his Walindimi men's house, the representative of Chambri.[35] In this respect, the story of the founding of Walindimi that Maliwan asked us to type was both a résumé of his job qualifications and a contract with Peter Barter.

In many regards, the Chambri found it easy to accept the view, promulgated by the national government and others, that the relatively wealthy and powerful tourists would provide the basis of local development. After all, the Chambri were accustomed to a regional system in which they were neither self-sufficient nor dominant. Moreover, given the importance in Chambri thought of immigration and cultural importation, it was reasonable that their future be enhanced by the contributions of powerful others, attracted from the outside. And, with tourism, as in any matter of significance, political contention was inevitable between individuals struggling for advantage. Thus, Maliwan could assert to us (and other Chambri) that, as part of tradition, tourists must be charged admission to view the initiation he was staging for his sons: he was predictably augmenting his own prestige while showing how readily the tourists could be assimilated as a significant component of Chambri life and of their future prosperity.

Nonetheless, there were aspects of their relationship with the tourists that were, at least potentially, troubling to the Chambri. As we have mentioned the relationship between the Chambri and their trading partners had been of essential equality: it existed within a regional system of *commensurate differences*. In contrast, the relationship between the Chambri and tourists fell far short of equality, either perceived or actual: it existed within a world system of *incommensurate differences*. Whereas the interdependence within the regional system was mutual, the interdependence within the world system was hierarchical. The Chambri were of value to the tourists only because they were different and unequal. They would remain of interest only as long as they remained primitive, only as long as they remained a vanishing curiosity in the modern world.[36]

Although the Chambri no longer made objects that were significant to them because they were filled with ancestral power (carving a new Posump and Ponor would be an exception), they did take pride in their skill and sophistication as carvers. However, what tourists primarily valued in their encounter with the Chambri (and other Sepiks, as well as Papua New Guineans more generally) was not their sophistication but their "primitiveness." To be sure, the Chambri looked forward to development, but they did not regard themselves as "backward," or as "primitive" and they did not see, as the tourists did, a contradiction between development and keeping their culture strong, in remaining Chambri.

The Chambri did, in fact, recognize signs of condescension from the tourists as the following incident suggests.

Two young Chambri artifact sellers were sitting inside the Walindimi men's house waiting for tourists to come inside. One lit his freshly rolled cigarette with a disposable gas lighter. (Chambri preferred lighters that could be refilled with locally available kerosene.) The other said: "Where did you get that expensive Whiteman's lighter?"

"A tourist gave it to me."

"Yes, I know he did – I told him to. I told him he should feel sorry for you since you were a poor bush native who had to walk around with a big burning stick to light your cigarettes."

There was general laughter from those listening.[37]

Despite sporadic jokes and wry reflections of this sort, it seems to us that the Chambri only partially understood that the condescension they might sense in the tourists' relationship to them was based on a perception of the fundamental insignificance of the Chambri in the world at large. Even Maliwan, who was venturing with relative success into this expanded world, would, as we shall see in the next chapter, glimpse this perception. And he found this glimpse very troubling. Such a perception provided intimations that this expanded system might run according to rules very different from those recognized by the Chambri and their Papua New Guinea neighbors. This expanded system might run according to rules that virtually ensured that the Chambri and their neighbors could never significantly affect the outcome of the game. Moreover, we shall also see with Maliwan's initiation, further instances of the often subtle yet pervasive transformations effected on Chambri lives by this expanded system.

2

The initiation: making men in 1987

At 5:40 a.m. on October 13, 1987, Maliwan, together with his youngest son and his two wives, lay sobbing across the doorway of their house. They had spent the night before in their house singing with other members of their extended family such songs as "The brothers will lie next to each other in the ritual enclosure; we will hear them cry but will not open our eyes until they are cut." In lying across their doorway they wished to impede members of the opposed Yambuntimeri initiatory moiety from entering. The Yambuntimeri, defined as enemies in search of war captives, were about to abduct Maliwan's five older Pombiantimeri sons and take them to the ritual enclosure where the ancestral crocodile, Kwoli-mopan, was waiting to "eat" the backs of these young men. The enclosure had been built of coconut fronds next to the Walindimi men's house several days before.

The Yambuntimeri prevailed, as intended, in pulling away the youths. These youths were, in fact, already marked for transition by their sisters, who had cut their brothers' hair and affixed cords around their wrists and ankles indicating the ritual restrictions to accompany, in this case, their symbolic death.[1] By 6.30 a.m., after a half hour of intensive work, the Yambuntimeri specialists had finished making the hundreds of half-inch razor cuts on the backs and upper arms of the boys.

The specialists had tried to reduce the suffering: they had worked in pairs so the surgery could be done quickly; each initiate had been given bespelled betel nut to chew, to help him ignore the pain; and each had been lying face down on the back of a ritual companion who murmured words of support. Nevertheless, everyone recognized that this was a major ordeal. As the blood streamed, the boys writhed and moaned despite efforts at stoicism.

58

6   The specialists made hundreds of cuts on the backs and
upper arms of the boys.

And, although the men inside the enclosure sang loudly so that the women just outside would not hear the cries of pain, the women, sometimes peering through the loose weave of the coconut-frond walls, sang laments about the anguish of their children.

Although no longer obligatory, 41 per cent of males over 17 living at Chambri in 1987 had been scarified. Scarification was an ordeal that would transform and ramify: through releasing the blood that a boy[2] had incorporated from his mother in her womb, he would be made more fully into an adult member of his father's clan; through acquiring the scars that duplicated the markings on a crocodile's back, he would have its formidability and, as a warrior, he would be able to fight alongside other adult men of his clan without a child's longing to be with his mother. Moreover, the ritual procedure through which this transformation into manhood was effected would ritually energize not only the initiatory moieties of Yambuntimeri and Pombiantimeri but most of the other categories composing Chambri society.[3] It would require patriclan members to compensate in-laws for shedding the latter's blood and for terminating one aspect of their relationship; it would set patriclan members in search of prospective in-laws who would have to be compensated with bride-price so that this newly created adult could marry and provide children for his clan; it would put money (formerly shell valuables) in motion that would ripple through Chambri society, fueling additional ceremonial performances such as marriages, death payments and other initiations, again mobilizing large numbers of Chambri.[4]

After Maliwan's five sons had been cut, each was carried in near shock by his initiators from the enclosure into Walindimi men's house. There he was placed, face down on an elevated bench, above a smoking fire that would both warm and season him. Once all the initiates were inside, a member of the particular clan responsible for activating Kwolimopan's power began to strike a slitgong with the crocodile's distinctive rhythm. As the resonance mounted, he cried out: "It is enough; I am sated with blood." Then, two other members of his clan went to the now evacuated ritual enclosure: one whirled a bull roarer; the sound was Kwolimopan's voice. The other hit the ground with the stalk of a coconut frond. This was Kwolimopan's tail slapping the water. Meanwhile, in the men's house, two men of Yambuntimeri removed the transverse flutes called Wengwantlokwa from their woven bast cases and began to play them. These flutes were war prizes acquired from the enemy Iatmul village of Suapmeri during the Parambei wars. Originally blown to embody the gigantic hawk that had once terrorized whole villages, they were used by Wombun members of this initiatory moiety to celebrate a victory.

At 7.30 a.m., Maliwan brought two roosters into the men's house. He killed them and plucked a few feathers from each that would be used to apply soothing oil to the freshly cut backs of the initiates. Then he handed the roosters to the mother's brother of a member of the clan responsible for activating Kwolimopan. This man held a burning torch under their smoking feathers and carried them as censers around Maliwan, his clansmen and Kwolimopan's activators now gathered in the ritual enclosure. As he did this, he implored the crocodile to refrain from making the initiates or the men there assembled sick and from appearing in their dreams. He was here setting a boundary between the ancestral spirits and the living. He next carried the roosters, still smoking, inside Walindimi and around a carved and painted plank of black palm that had been placed in front of the house post belonging to Nyeminimba, the marriage moiety to which the men of the clan responsible for Kwolimopan belonged.[5] This plank, decorated with cordyline leaves and a cassowary feather headdress, *was* Kwolimopan. Through the medium of the smoking chicken, the boundary between the domain of the ancestral spirits and that of the living was again set.[6] Although Kwolimopan would continue to preside over the next phase of the initiation, a boundary between his domain and that of the living had to be re-established. Otherwise the initiators would become sick and the newly cut – the newly "eaten" – might suffer terrifying dreams of being pulled under the water and further devoured by the crocodile, Kwolimopan.

Maliwan then circulated throughout the men's house, shaking hands and telling everyone how pleased he was that his sons had acquired "good marks." Members of his clan brought in food for the Yambuntimeri initiators; as the ostensible conquerors of the men's house, they would for the next six days (it was said) be given anything they demanded, such as pork, beer and cigarettes, by their Pombiantimeri captives, that is, by Maliwan and his family.

While the five initiates were healing, they would be confined to the men's house and subject to only sporadically enforced and rather mild taboos. One of these, for instance, was that they must not touch their food with their fingers: they must instead use tongs.[7] Although still considered war captives of Yambuntimeri, they would be nurtured, that is protected from harm, cared for and fed, by their mothers' brothers, who in this case happened to be Yambuntimeri.

As one of the final events of the initiatory ritual in which maternal blood was let and maternal male nurtured received, Maliwan would be expected to recompense generously these mothers' brothers for both their losses and services. As he explained to us: "They will finish me because they want a large profit."

Moreover, as the sole sponsor, he would have other heavy expenses. Normally, as mentioned, a whole group of fathers from the same moiety would initiate at the same time and, thus, share many of the expenses for the food (including several pigs), beer, ritual presentations and other compensation owed those carrying out the initiation. Maliwan estimated that his total costs would exceed K1,000. That he was able to commit himself to such a heavy obligation was primarily because of his political position, as manager of the Walindimi men's house and as the business associate of Peter Barter. With Barter's help, he hoped to fulfill his traditional obligations in, what was for the Chambri, a novel manner. The novelty was in staging the initiation of his sons as a tourist attraction. This chapter is primarily about some of the consequences, both expected and unexpected, of Maliwan's innovation.

A picture in *Naven*, the classic anthropological work by Gregory Bateson about Sepik initiation ceremonies, has long intrigued us. The picture was taken in 1931 while Bateson was doing research among the Sepik River Iatmul. It seems to encapsulate many of the themes, some of which we have seen above, that are still of anthropological interest. The caption of Plate X reads as follows:

Initiation in Malingai. The novice is lying prone on an inverted canoe clasping his mother's brother who acts as a comforter and a "mother." An initiator of the opposite moiety to the novice is cutting the latter's back with a small bamboo blade. In the foreground is a bowl of water with swabs of fibre to wipe away the blood. The white and black paint on the faces of the two men is a privilege of those who have killed a man, and is worn on all ceremonial occasions. The band of opossum fur worn by the initiator is also a badge of homicide (1958).

Although the novice and the canoe on which he lies are shown dripping with blood and although the caption denotes opposition, pain and killing, the composition of the picture of initiation with the arrangement of the three tensed bodies also conveys symmetry and momentary equilibrium. Bateson seems to have well captured in this plate an understanding of Sepik political sensibility, the tenuous nature of Sepik social accord and the occasions during which this accord was likely to be most conspicuously enacted.

Bateson had wondered how social life could be sustained at all in a cultural context where males wore the marks of their homicides as emblems of honor. He wondered how Iatmul men could achieve the relations of equality that gave them worth only through engaging in highly assertive and competitive behavior. What, in other words, would check the aggression of these Iatmul men, either as individuals or as members of groups, toward those others in their own village with whom they were struggling for relative eminence? His inquiry became focused on discovering the mechanisms of internal regulation and correction that limited the escalation of male aggression, and in understanding the way these mechanisms were invoked, particularly on ritual occasions, including those of initiation.

Bateson's concerns remain of essential importance for understanding life in the Sepik, especially in a society such as the Chambri that was so directly influenced by the Iatmul. Indeed, his Plate X and caption can be seen to register the themes of even a contemporary Chambri initiation. Yet our examination of Maliwan's initiation for his sons will also reveal areas of difference. In the Iatmul case, the escalation of aggression by one side eventually triggered and was checked by sudden and exaggerated submission by the other. In the Chambri instance, the escalation was checked, not by a reversal of this sort, but by a complex evocation and balancing of oppositions. Thus, Maliwan's initiation can be understood as a ritual during which the oppositions between many of the categories that comprised Chambri society were first accentuated (as we have so far seen) and then relaxed. (Opposing categories, other than moiety against moiety, are men against women, patriclans against their in-laws, and seniors against juniors.) In this way, and reflecting the assumptions of a system of commensurate differences, the Chambri during their ceremony of initiation achieved a temporary accord by demonstrating that equality was possible between these mutually depen-

7   Gregory Bateson's Plate X, photograph of an initiation at Malingai.

dent groups either by virtue of their similarities or their distinctions.

However, Maliwan's initiation was not only a Chambri initiation; it was an initiation to which tourists were invited. Introduced, thereby, into this arrangement of intricate oppositions and balances effected during one of the most important of Chambri rituals was an audience whose relationships with the Chambri were largely premised on the assumptions of a system of incommensurate differences. Tourists assumed that their relationship with the Chambri was hierarchically ordered so as to preclude relationships of equality. Just as Chambri artifacts were, in the view of the tourists, manifestations of the inherently unequal "primitive," so too were Chambri ceremonies, especially one featuring, in the words cited earlier, the "barbaric" practice of scarification.

Encounters between tourists and Chambri during the initiation were to reflect the fact that they each, following the assumptions of their respective systems, attributed a contrasting significance to the evident differences existing between them. Some tourists were, for instance, to wonder how such a barbaric ritual, staged by "primitives," could possibly be worth as much as K10 to witness. Conversely, Maliwan was to insist that he be paid what he asked: otherwise it would be suggested that he, the practices of initiation, and, by extension, Chambri culture and the Chambri themselves were not valuable. Moreover, the structure of the initiation itself became significantly affected as tourists and Chambri interacted according to their assumptions about the appropriate relationships between them. The Chambri attempted to encompass and embed the tourists into the sequence of balanced oppositions; the tourists resisted, maintaining themselves as distinct, unentailed and – in final analysis – superior. Such an encounter within the core of the initiation itself made coming of age in 1987 a set of experiences for both initiators and initiates very different from what previously had been the case. To convey the shift in experience as well as the dynamics of the interaction between Chambri and tourists we now turn to the ritual as it unfolded.

The initiation as tourist event

Although Maliwan had sent a letter to Peter Barter announcing the date of the actual skin cutting, we were the only non-Chambri witnessing that part of the ceremony. Later that day, two Americans, traveling on their own, visited Chambri and, with our encouragement, paid K10 each to enter Walindimi. They reported to us that they were well satisfied to have seen such an authentic ritual. The day after the skin cutting, however, a group of tourists did arrive and Maliwan had his first major chance to cash in on the tourist trade.

These tourists were from the Karawari Lodge, an expensive hotel located on one of the Sepik's tributaries and operated by Trans Niugini Tours. The tourists were flown to the lodge and then taken on tours of Sepik villages by "river truck," a flat-bottomed speedboat with a canopy to protect the tourists from the sun. Far fewer tourists from the Karawari Lodge than from the

Melanesian Explorer visited Chambri – perhaps only one load of 8–10 tourists a month, at unscheduled intervals. Neither the eight tourists nor their guide who arrived at Chambri after the skin cutting knew that they would be offered the opportunity to see a remarkable aspect of Sepik culture that few Westerners had witnessed.

Maliwan immediately went out to meet them. He explained to the guide, a young Australian man who spoke Pidgin English fluently, that an initiation was going on and pointed to the sign he had posted. Written in English by one of Maliwan's young supporters, it stated: "Welcome to the Initiation Ceremony of Wombun Village, Chambri Lakes, Walindimi Spirit House." Maliwan explained further that, rather than the usual fee for entry into Walindimi of K0.50 per visitor, during the time of initiation, there would be an admission fee of K10 for each visitor or a fee of K50 for an entire group. The guide responded that he was not in the habit of paying to see things and then consulted briefly with his little group. One woman exclaimed in tones of outrage: "Ten Kina! What a rip-off!" The rest grumbled their agreement with her.

The guide then told Maliwan that they only wished to see the artifacts and asked if they were still displayed on the second floor. Maliwan said that lots were there. The group then entered Walindimi and immediately climbed the rather shaky staircase to the second floor. After about ten minutes they began straggling down with two miniature slitgongs, four spears and a mask. After those who had carved these artifacts came forward and were paid, and after the tourists had finished taking pictures of the men's house and, in some cases, the carvers from whom they had bought, the party left Chambri.

They left behind a very angry Maliwan surrounded by perhaps twenty concerned Chambri men. When we went to see what was happening, Maliwan showed us the K4 that had been pressed into his hand by the guide as he departed. He said that he had been doing this tourist work since 1973 and was not to be tricked by a young man who gave him only K4 rather than the amount he had set. Maliwan said that the tourists and the guide "think they can treat those of us in Papua New Guinea as if we are of no importance. They spend lots of money to come here and take pictures which they will sell for large amounts of money." (Maliwan was mistaken concerning the commercial value of the tourists'

8 A tourist took pictures of the carver from whom he had bought artifacts.

9   The Karawari Lodge tourists left behind an angry
Maliwan.

photographs.) He simply did not believe them, staying as they
were at the Karawari Lodge, when they claimed they could not
afford to pay the K10 admission. "If they do not want to pay, then
they can just leave," he said, with much finality.

He then asked us what we thought. We agreed that these
tourists could easily afford to pay the admission fee to see the
initiation. Yet, we did not think that the guide was trying to cheat
him since he had probably thought that because his party wished
only to see the artifacts, the usual price of K0.50 per person would
suffice. We also suggested that there should be some arrangement
so that prospective buyers who were unwilling to pay a fee of K10
would still be able to examine the artifacts. There were signs of
agreement at this point from the assembled carvers.

Maliwan was troubled. He said that the appropriate place to
display the carvings was the Walindimi men's house. However, for
the next few weeks, this was also the site for events that were an
important and expensive part of Chambri custom: K10 was not
too much to pay to see such events and, moreover, this money
should go to him to help defray some of his considerable costs in
sponsoring these events. Although no one challenged him at this

10   Melanesian Explorer tourists welcomed to the initiation
ceremony of Wombun Village.

time, it was clear the carvers were not happy about circumstances
that impaired their access to buyers.

Maliwan was determined not to be caught in this position again.
He knew that he had to separate the artifact market from the
initiation. It was neither feasible nor desirable to move the large
numbers of artifacts from Walindimi, which was, after all, a tourist
attraction in itself; the only solution was to move the initiates.
Thus, thereafter, when tourists arrived, Maliwan would send his
five sons back into the enclosure where they had earlier been cut.
Tourists could still enter the men's house and artifact market for
the usual fee of K0.50. However, if they wished to see the
initiation which was now defined as seeing the initiates – more
specifically, as seeing the cuts on the backs of the initiates – that
would cost K10 apiece or K50 for the group.

Several days later, the Melanesian Explorer arrived. Although
the guide did not know that Maliwan was staging an initiation,
Maliwan's letter to Peter Barter evidently having gone astray, she
and her party were delighted to discover that a ritual was in
progress. She agreed without hesitation to pay the K50 admission
fee and then explained to those in her charge that Maliwan was

11   The tourists photographed the lacerated backs while Maliwan posed in the background.

the father of five Chambri youths who had only a few days before received the extensive cuts necessary for them to become men. By this time, Maliwan was beaming and many of the tourists filing into the men's house shook his hand, uttering words of congratulations about how proud he must feel.

He then escorted them into the enclosure where they could see the backs of the initiates. The boys had been arranged in a row and the tourists photographed their lacerated backs while Maliwan posed in the background. Following this photographic opportunity, Maliwan arranged a performance of Kwolimopan consisting of the twirling of the bullroarer as his bellow and the thumping of the coconut frond as the impact of his tail, and had two men of Yambuntimeri again play the sacred flutes. The tourists then made their selection of artifacts, chatted with us, the resident anthropologists, and departed, well satisfied with their outing. Before she left, the guide discussed with Maliwan how the forthcoming schedule of the initiation events might fit or be adjusted to fit the fixed schedule of visits of the Melanesian Explorer.

The Melanesian Explorer would return three more times before the initiation concluded: once, as with this first visit, when the initiation was in something of a lull between important events; once for a major set of events – those of the "sixth day" – which were postponed one day for the ship's arrival; and once for the culminating events – those of the "final washing" – which were delayed at least a week.

Certainly the clash with the tourists from the Karawari Lodge indicated to the Chambri that making a commodity of Chambri culture had consequences beyond producing extra income.[8] Chambri had been aware for some time, as we have said, that the carvings they made for tourists did not have the same importance as those they had ritually activated for their own use in the past. No longer the embodiments of a person's (or clan's) social and political efficacy, their significance had both shifted and diminished to such an extent that they became "objects" whose only value to the Chambri resided in what the tourists agreed to pay for them. The encounter with the group from the Karawari Lodge suggested that a comparable process of "objectification" might be under way with respect to other and still central aspects of Chambri culture. Indeed, although this particular experience of confrontation was not repeated with those from the Melanesian Explorer, staging the initiation as a tourist event raised intimations of shifted and diminished cultural significance for Maliwan and other Chambri: what *was* Chambri culture if the initiation was becoming a performance for a paying audience of non-Chambri? What was the value of that culture if it were determined by wealthy visitors who would not pay even K10 to see one of the most important Chambri rituals?

This experience the Chambri were having of their increasing objectification provided their primary and unwelcome indication that the tourists regarded them as less than equal, as incommensurately different. Thus, as they enacted the further events of the ritual the Chambri tried to do more than establish relations of equality between the opposed groups of Chambri; they tried, as well, to incorporate the tourists into the ritual as another opposed group and thereby resist the tourists' definition of them as unequals. However, given that they were in substantial measure acting as paid performers, it was virtually inevitable that they could not successfully define the differences between themselves and tourists as commensurate.

To understand better both the intended and unintended consequences of this effort to incorporate the tourists into the structure of oppositions around which the initiation ritual was constructed, we now examine this structure in more detail.

The sixth day

The events of this sixth day marked the major transition in the initiation. Earlier in the initiation, for those in Wombun and, to some extent, in the other two Chambri villages, certain ritual oppositions, particularly those between Yambuntimeri and Pombiantimeri and between men and women, had been accentuated. On the sixth day, confrontations in the form of mock fights would be staged, first between two groups of men and then between these men and those defined as their sisters. Each confrontation would in turn be resolved into a non-antagonistic relationship of relative homeostasis: in other words, relations of exaggerated asymmetry, opposition and control that had polarized the adult community before would be transformed into relations of equality and cooperation.[9]

The newly unified community of adults would then, during the final event of the day, establish a highly asymmetrical relationship with the initiates. This would be the hazing of the initiates within the Walindimi men's house. (It was for this event that the tourists were present.) During the hazing the power of Kwolimopan would be transferred to the initiates at the same time that they would be forced to submit to the authority of a community which had become relatively unified. Following the hazing the initiates could return to more normal circumstances. Many of the taboos they had been observing would be lifted. Specifically, we were told, the initiates would be able to eat their food in the normal way, holding it in their fingers rather than in bamboo tongs.

The events of the sixth day formed a sequence in which oppositions between social categories were resolved, shifted, again resolved, accentuated and abated: all of the events must be regarded as essential components in a process by which initiates were to be transformed. The presence of the tourists as outsiders during the final stage, that is, the hazing in which a united adult community imposed its power on its youth, became part of that process.

At the first light on the morning of this sixth day, five canoes filled with men quietly set out into the lake to collect fish, waterfowl and

12   The lead men in the two canoes exchanged spears.

bird eggs. This was the bounty of the watery domain of Kwolimopan, the ancestral crocodile, invoked to initiate Maliwan's five
sons. Soon they would be joined by two more canoes, one filled
with Yambuntimeri men and the other with Pombiantimeri. The
conspicuous departure of these two canoes would provide the first
instance of opposition transformed into solidarity. The ten young
men who would form the crews made their preparations as a
single group within the Walindimi men's house. All dressed as if
for war: they painted face and body, donned elaborate feather
headdresses and strapped on cowry-shell-encrusted leg and arm
bands and belts. After having snacked together on sago and
smoked fish, they left Walindimi to engage in what was described
as a competition, a mock attack, between the two moieties. An
audience of both men and women watched from the shore and a
senior Yambuntimeri stationed on a point of land shouted directions to the young men in the two canoes.

First, the young men paddled their canoes in opposite directions, then turned and came toward each other as if to attack. But
the attack was carefully orchestrated and only apparent: at precisely the same moment, the lead man in each canoe launched his
spear (from a spear-thrower) so that it fell to the side of the
oncoming canoe where the other lead man retrieved it from the

13   The sisters waited to throw their fruit-tipped spears.

water. Their opposition neutralized through the simultaneous discharge of intentionally deflected spears, the Yambuntimeri and Pombiantimeri crews then paddled their canoes together out into the lake where they joined the others in the cooperative collection of food from the water.

Just past noon all canoes returned from the lake to Wombun. The two canoes carrying the ceremonially dressed men were in the lead; the five that had left Wombun at daybreak followed some distance behind. A large group of women, many wearing grass skirts and all decorated with body paint, shells and feathers, awaited them on the shore. There, to the accompaniment of two hand drums, they sang lyrics which translate as "blood, blood," referring to the cutting of the initiates, and "shoot him, shoot him, shoot the water bird," referring both to the game that the expedition of men had collected and to the men themselves returning from the lake.

In the front ranks of these women were two who could easily be distinguished from the others: they wore elaborate, cassowary-feather headdresses (like those of the male warriors of the incoming canoes) and carried spears. These were the sisters (one actual, the other clan) of the lead man in each of the lead canoes. As the canoes of their brothers landed, the sisters threw their spears which their brothers caught. (These sisters had been given practice the day before so that they would throw the spears high enough to be readily caught; moreover, to reduce the possibility of injury, the tip of each spear was covered by a small red fruit.) The rest of the assembled women, defined either as sisters or as mothers, showered those in the two canoes by throwing fruits of various kinds. The men immediately vacated their two canoes, leaving behind in them all the food that the entire expedition of men had collected, and proceeded the fifty yards or so to the Walindimi men's house. There they were joined a few minutes later by the rest of the men returning from the lake.

The women, described to us as having "won" over the men, gathered up the relinquished harvest and carried it in a triumphal procession to Walindimi. (The collection of twenty-five fish, eight ducks, and fifteen eggs was regarded as not more than adequate.) Singing and drumming, scooting under each other's legs in a display of intergenerational solidarity[10] they circled the men's house just as a victorious war party, we were told, would circle a human head taken in battle. Perhaps of significance in this regard, the red fruit that covered the tips of the spears that the sisters had thrown was the same kind that had been once used to represent eyes in the display of enemy skulls.

The encounter between the men in the two canoes served to negate much of the inequality and curtail much of the potential competition that had emerged between Yambuntimeri and Pombiantimeri thus far in the ritual. Although the inequality between these moieties could be regarded as balanced over time as each moiety took turns initiating the younger members of the other, nonetheless, the fact that the asymmetries were alternating created a potential for escalation in the exercise of authority and control. This potentiality was precluded in the ritual of initiation itself through the *simultaneous* and literal *exchange* of spears. The simultaneity of this exchange in which each replenished that which the other had lost would seem to avert the development of a sequence of intensified confrontation between relative equals. (It would avert the competitive sequence that Gregory Bateson had described as symmetrical schizmogenesis [1958: 175], when he encountered it among the neighboring Iatmul.) Enacted thus at this Chambri initiation were relations of *non-competitive* equality between those who, as essentially similar, were potential competitors.[11]

In what could be only a *partial* replication of the earlier simultaneous exchange of spears between the essentially similar men, each sister threw her spear at her brother, who caught it, but did not respond in kind. Moreover, the sisters and the other women then displaced the men and took full possesssion of that which they had gathered: they routed the returned warriors, captured their booty and circled the men's house as if with a captured enemy head. The women thus were acting as war victors, which in the context of initiation, meant that they were acting as the initiators themselves – as those who drew blood. But, the women were replicating only a portion of the male activities: they had thrown a spear but had not caught one thrown at the same time; they had participated in the return from the water but not the departure from the shore. Although engaged in the same events as the men, they were performing different activities. The brothers and the sisters – and the other men and women – were thus in this confrontation presenting gender as an irreducible difference, but one which could generate relations of complementarity and cooperation.

Hence, the encounter between the men in the two canoes precluded the competition that could emerge from similarity, creating instead non-competitive solidarity; the encounter between the men and the women precluded the antagonism and intransigence that could come from difference, creating instead non-antagonistic cooperation.[12] Although the differences between Chambri men and women were complementary in the sense that men and women each had a different role in the division of labor, the differences were also such that each could operate largely autonomously from the other, without being subject to coercion.[13] Indeed, occasional efforts by men to coerce women did evoke not increased submission but intransigence and possible reprisal in the form of attack on the basis of male power. (In particular, a woman could reveal aspects of her husband's secret knowledge.)[14] Thus, what was being expressed between Chambri brothers and sisters during their encounter at this ceremony was cooperation rather than, as was a possibility, conflict. At this stage in the initiation, the oppositions that had separated men from men and men from women were being resolved. Just as Pombiantimeri and Yambuntimeri were no longer polarized as competitors, so too, men and women were no longer polarized in their differences.

Into this carefully established nexus of commensurate differences the tourists were soon to enter.

The hazing

After the women had circled the men's house in triumph, carrying the food the men had collected on the water, the men reclaimed the waterfowl and five of the fish. The waterfowl would be presented to certain men, such as those responsible for activating Kwolimopan: they were the ones who had exercised their ritual prerogatives so that the initiation could occur. The fish would be eaten by the five initiates. The women, no longer acting as conquering warriors, carried off the rest of the food taken from the canoes. This, and the food they had earlier prepared, would be brought to the men's house for the forthcoming feast.

The feast for the some seventy-five men inside Walindimi enhanced the theme of equality that had been established between men in the spear exchange several hours before. Although, as before, Yambuntimeri were served prior to the Pombiantimeri hosts, for the first time in the initiation and in a reversal of the usual Chambri etiquette, the younger members of the Yambuntimeri moiety were served before the older members. Also, for the first time in the initiation, these juniors were given a portion – in this case half – of the one case of beer provided. The feast was generous and included pork – Maliwan had killed a pig – cooked fish and greens, rice, canned mackerel, watermelons, and bananas. Maliwan himself was presented with food – smoked duck and sago pancakes – by a certain Yambuntimeri who had played a strategic role during Maliwan's own initiation as a young man.[15]

On this occasion of male concord, the initiates were still treated separately from the rest. They were given special food consisting of the fish that had been caught that morning from Kwolimopan's realm and roasted over a fire in the men's house. This, as with their earlier meals in the men's house, they ate facing away from the rest of the men. Not until the completion of the hazing, soon to begin, would they resume entirely normal relationships with others.

It was after 2:00 by the time the meal was over. As mentioned, in order to coordinate the major events of the initiation with the schedule of the Melanesian Explorer, Maliwan had postponed the ceremonies of the sixth day to take place on this, the seventh day.

This meant that he earlier had to convince the Yambuntimeri initiators to delay the hazing of the initiates for a day. Thus, as Maliwan circulated after the feast, he was anxious to reassure other Chambri men that the delay had been justified, that the tourists were coming. But they were nowhere to be seen and clearly Maliwan was nervous. With what struck us as bravado, he told us that if the tourists wanted to see a rerun of the events of the morning – the departure and return of the two canoes – they would have to pay K60, in addition to the K50 to enter the men's house and see the initiates in the enclosure. Moreover, since he had recently heard that the river villages charged tourists between K100 and K150 just to see their initiates, he was of half a mind to raise his prices. Meanwhile, various men were arranging their carvings. Finally, to Maliwan's evident relief the distant sounds of the two big speedboats from the Melanesian Explorer were heard.

The tourists did arrive shortly and, as before, took pictures of the initiates posed to show their partially healed cuts. Then the initiates, together with uninitiated clan brothers – some older and some younger than they – were instructed to sit down in the middle of the men's house floor. As the tourists crowded around them, Maliwan asked us to advise the tourists that there was going to be a loud noise above them from the second story of the men's house. He did not want the tourists to be alarmed by the noise that would mark the awakening of Kwolimopan. As the four hazers, impressively ornamented in feather headdresses and face paint, approached the seated initiates, Maliwan instructed them to talk not in Chambri but in Pidgin English which it was assumed the tourists could understand.

Consistent with the emphasis on equality then current in the men's house, the four hazers represented both initiatory moieties.[16] Their public performance, earlier practiced in private, amused the Chambri audience and, periodically, even the initiates themselves. First they offered fish and sago to the initiates, but then pulled the food away and themselves ate portions. Next, they offered the initiates fish bones, fruit stalks and other inedible scraps from a platter while shouting: "You don't know how to eat; you eat just like pigs, just like ducks; you don't have any shame."

While the initiates glumly contemplated their "food," there came the thundering from above as men jumped up and down on the floor of the second story, shaking loose a great cloud of dust. No sooner had the dust begun to settle, than water was poured

14 Banana-leaf cigars set on fire were pushed into the
initiates' mouths.

through the floor, soaking the initiates and their platter of refuse, turning to mud the dust that was covering the food. The hazers walked among the initiates shouting "hurry up, hurry up" as they insisted that some of the water-soaked rubbish be eaten. (In fact, as we will discuss later, Kwolimopan's bull-roarer had been kept in this water so that the water was filled with his power.)

Betel nuts were then offered the initiates and then taken away with the words: "You eat betel nut as if you were a woman, as if you were your little sister." Oversized spatulas covered with ashes instead of the lime normally consumed with betel nuts were shoved into their mouths. Lighted banana leaf cigars, an inch in diameter and a foot long, were stuffed into their mouths and then pulled away, showering them with sparks. All the while the hazers harangued them: "You want to smoke; here, smoke! Your father is giving this to you; smoke this big one, you rubbishman. You beg for cigarettes and betel nuts all the time, well here they are; take them; are you enough for them?"

Then a large female carving was brought out and was thrust on top of the initiates with the challenge: "Are you enough to make carvings and place them in the men's house for the tourists to buy?" Large pieces of firewood, including one with embers, were pushed down on them as they were asked: "Are you enough to bring firewood to the men's house?" A broom and a large bark dustpan were pushed down on their faces with the words: "Are you enough to sweep out the men's house?" Several grass-cutting knives were pressed against them with the question: "Are you enough to cut the grass around the men's house?" Finally, the initiates were asked derisively if they had more than the understanding of their mothers – if they were enough to sire children.

All of these questions were meant to convey that the initiates should uphold Chambri custom. Chambri custom, especially as it concerned appropriate adult male roles within the men's house, was presented in a quite literal way as heavy, as not to be taken lightly. Such custom based on collective authority, an authority embodied by the four hazers (who, it will be remembered, represented both Yambuntimeri and Pombiantimeri), could be made to cover virtually all aspects of life. Thus, reference was made to a rule that men were not supposed to smoke or chew betel nuts until they had been scarified. Although this rule was normally ignored, it was presented as one that could be made binding if the collected men chose to make it so.

15 The initiates were asked if they were capable of making carvings for sale to tourists.

This assertion of collective male power had lasted about twenty minutes when one of the hazers said in Pidgin: "The law is finished now; we will stand up and the tourists will take pictures of us." Then all four of the hazers moved behind the initiates and stood in a row, facing the tourists, who were then instructed: "Clap your hands. The rule of Kwolimopan is over; it is finished now; we have completed it. OK, you can take pictures of us now. Clap your hands." The tour guide informed the tourists in English that they should applaud and had been invited to take pictures.

The tourists did applaud, and most took a picture or so – although with some reluctance. They seemed somewhat annoyed and confused at this point. The hazers had suddenly defined the performance as staged, at least in part, for tourists rather than for the Chambri themselves and this called into question its authenticity.[17] Moreover, by instructing the tourists to applaud and to take pictures of them, the hazers were extending to the tourists the same kind of control that they had exercised over the initiates: just as the initiates were not allowed to express their own autonomy with respect to activities that were usually defined as matters of individual volition – to smoke or chew betel nut – so too the tourists were commanded to express appreciation and interest. Like the novices, they were being incorporated into the structure of the event as a group brought under the authority of the collective male power represented by the hazers.

A fair number of tourists had, however, left before this point in the performance and were outside photographing the Chambri women as they chorused their support of the men inside Walindimi. The women enjoined the initiates to do as they were told with songs like: "Take it, take it; listen, listen." It was very hot inside the men's house; with the shaking of the floor, it was very dirty. The tourists were anxious about their camera lenses as the dust had poured down. They seemed to find the hazing too violent, too aggressive, too prolonged – perhaps, too primitive; one woman looked askance at the cut which had opened on an initiate's arm when he had been pushed down by a burning piece of firewood.

By the end of the performance, those tourists still remaining in the audience inside the men's house felt vulnerable, uncertain of their safety. Not only had they found the performance violent; they were no longer sure what the objectives and boundaries of the performance were. However, they were somewhat reassured when one of their number, an impressively large German man, reasserted control by overcomplying with the hazers' command to take pictures of them. First wading through the seated initiates, he then positioned his camera only a foot away from each hazer's face to take a series of extreme close-ups, capturing their ornamented heads, we thought, as if he were a photographic big-game hunter. He was, it seemed to us, transforming what the hazers meant to be commemoration into objectification.

The picture taking concluded, Maliwan sent the initiates outside into the enclosure. He was eager to clear the men's house so that the tourists could look at and purchase the carvings. Out in the enclosure, the hazers shook hands and talked with the initiates, some of whom were angry at the treatment they had received. One, for instance, was upset because several of his cuts had opened during the turmoil of the performance. He had enlisted the help of another initiate in cleaning up the blood so as not to disturb the cuts further. Looking at them, a passing hazer, in combined reassurance and disdain, said that it was nothing to be worried about.

In this initiation, and in others Deborah had seen with no tourists present, the initiates were made to appear not only ridiculous but impotent. When the initiates were told either directly or indirectly by the hazers, "You want to eat – here, eat this garbage" or "You want to smoke – here smoke this huge banana leaf cigar," and then compelled to do so, they became both involuntary agents and spectators in a collective humiliation. Escape was precluded; participants were forced to do as they were instructed, yet nothing they could do was right. They were, in other words, placed in a multiplicity of double binds in circumstances well designed to convey complete powerlessness; and the powerlessness itself was compounded in that they were unable to perform even the normal routines of life.

The hazing, however, was also a means of conveying power to the initiates. In particular, it was by having dirt and the water of Kwolimopan dumped both on them and the garbage just served, and then being required to eat of that soggy garbage, that the initiates incorporated into themselves important aspects of power – the power of Kwolimopan. As a result of this, they were released from most of the initiatory taboos. For instance, they might once more eat and scratch themselves in a normal manner, rather than with the use of tongs. In this Chambri version of what is a familiar theme of initiation throughout the world, the experience of powerlessness would seem to be an important step in the acquisition of adult status. Their domination was the precondition of their transformation from initiates into junior adults, that is, into relative equals.

What effect did the presence of tourists, both men and women, have on this ritual? Hazing, as we have just described it, would be most effective when it completely precluded any escape on the part of the initiates. It seems to us, though, that the presence of the tourists, by introducing another sort of audience, gave the initiates a partial escape from their double binds. Because the initiators were to some extent playing for another audience, the hazing was no longer a closed Chambri show.

Moreover, in part to entertain the tourists and to avoid frightening them, the tourists had been warned about the great thump that was to take place over their heads. In this warning the hazers were trying to be at least sardonically amusing. Certainly based on Deborah's and Chambri recollections of other initiations, hazing as an occasion for the display of virtually absolute power with respect to the initiates was not normally experienced or remembered by the initiates as funny. Yet on this occasion, the initiates even frequently laughed. Also there is no doubt that the incorporation of the tourists into the proceedings made the hazing shorter. Time had to be allowed for them to purchase artifacts. (As we have seen, many of the tourists thought even the modified performance was too frightening and long.) Thus, the presence of the tourists not only diluted the display of absolute power, it also partially altered the purpose of the performance and, as well, reduced its duration and intensity. The consequence, we think, of this partial leavening of ridicule was the emergence of a generally perceived element of the comic.[18]

But this comic was not characterized by a complete amiability. Although the initiates found some humor in the double binds in which they were placed, they were, nonetheless, rendered substantially powerless. And, while the presence of tourists had partially deflected from the initiates the force of the display, the tourists themselves became partial targets. They were transformed from spectator to performer and a portion of their volition (and distance) stripped from them, as they were commanded to applaud: they were required to assent, whether they had liked it or not, to a performance in which as the final act they too, as a group, had been brought under the authority of the hazers. They too had become bound by Chambri rules which denied them the right to define themselves as separate and inherently better.

Chambri rules, we must stress, did not prevent the development of inequalities in the distribution of power. We have discussed, for instance, Iatmul hegemony over those within their regional economic system, Maliwan's ascendancy over other big men, and the hazer's control over the initiates. But, unlike the hierarchies within which the Western tourists were accustomed to operate, the inequalities with which the Chambri were familiar were, in their essence, transitory. Access to power was not precluded, for example, by the enduring structures of class, caste, colonialism or neocolonialism: the Iatmul were subject to defeat, Maliwan had his powerful rivals, and the initiates became young adults and eventually hazers. (As mentioned, there was, as well, in the Chambri case an assumption of relative gender equality.) Indeed, inequalities the Chambri faced within their regional system were almost necessarily transitory because for them power in its accumulation and display was the product — both as effect and cause — of complex social relations. Thus, as we have seen, Maliwan's eminence was contingent on continuing negotiations in which he received essential support only as long as he could convince his kin, members of his men's house, his inlaws, fellow villagers and carvers that he was furthering their interests as well as his own.

(We should mention that several anthropologists have recently argued that prior to European contact relatively permanent hierarchies existed in those parts of the Papua New Guinea Highlands where intensive agriculture prevailed. See in this regard, primarily, Modjeska's and the other essays in Strathern, 1982; Godelier, 1986; and Feil, 1987. In those lowland areas of Papua New Guinea where agriculture was less important, relatively permanent hierarchical relations may have existed as well. Thus, the Carriers argue, with respect to Ponam of the Manus Province, that "prior to colonization, when the outside world was the rest of Manus, relations among Ponams were unequal, with the dominant position going to those people having the strongest control over the production and circulation of wealth within the region. However, as the outside world expanded and as the economic importance of Manus itself for Ponam decreased, islanders lost their ability to control significant sources of wealth, and

particularly wealth from outside the island, as they became dependent on the emerging national economy. Consequently, no group
of villagers was able to control wealth to the exclusion of others,
and relations among villagers became more equal" (1989: 24).
Harrison, 1985, also describes a form of hierarchy that he regards
as incipient among the Sepik River Manambu, predicated on the
control of ritual knowledge acquired through exchange relations.[19] In the case of the Chambri, however, the earliest accounts
we have provide no evidence of enduring hierarchical relations.
Indeed, Mead and Fortune's notes are filled with references to
vigorous and far-ranging competition for power among men, of
the sort we have described in this book. If enduring hierarchies
had existed for the Chambri, they certainly no longer shaped
Chambri expectations.)

Tourists, in contrast, could behave at Chambri as they often did
at home: there they occupied a privileged strata of a largely
commoditized system and their power was such that they *could*
choose largely or completely to ignore social relations. Moreover,
in deciding to buy or not to buy an artifact, to stay for or walk out
of a ceremony, they had the capacity to objectify the Chambri by
regarding them as commodities. Significantly, the Chambri effort
to engage with the tourists according to Chambri rules, that is as
potential equals, evoked an emphatic response that redefined the
Chambri as objects. Although we can sympathize with the tourists
in their discomfiture when they began to be (mildly) hazed, and
can appreciate the dramatic value of a close-up photograph of a
Chambri in ceremonial regalia, nonetheless, it seems to us that the
response of the picture-taking German tourist should be understood as an effort to re-establish superiority. It might be argued
that objectification could denote simply disconnection. Yet we
think that disconnection on the part of the rich and powerful,
especially in a context in which an overture to establish social
relations of prospective equality was being made, did constitute a
statement of hierarchical superiority.

(The illustration Bourdieu uses to contrast social systems in
terms of the different strategies by which domination is achieved
seems relevant here in understanding the different expectations
of Chambri and tourists concerning the connection between social
relations and power: "It is not by lavishing generosity, kindness, or
politeness, on his charwoman [or on any other 'socially inferior'
agent], but by choosing the best investment for his money, or the

best school for his son, that the possessor of economic or cultural capital perpetuates the relationship of domination which objectively links him with his charwoman and even her descendants" [1977: 189–90]. We might also add here with respect to the latter case that the mechanisms, even the existence, of dominance in a system based on class [and other hierarchies] may not be fully recognized or understood either by those favored or not favored by the system.)

Thus, as the events of the sixth day concluded, even though the Chambri had balanced many of the oppositions that had earlier been exaggerated, they had not been successful in their efforts to incorporate the tourists. In the events that would follow, another mode of resistance to a system based on incommensurate differences would present itself. During the last phase of the initiation many Chambri, rather than be at the disposal of the tourists as performers, tried with some success to define the tourists as simply peripheral.

The final washing

Maliwan had arranged with the tour guide to postpone the last ceremony of the initiation, called the "final washing," until the next return of the Melanesian Explorer. This was to be on a Friday: the fee was to be K60 and a case of canned fish (worth about K40). However, soon after the departure of the tourists, uncertainty became evident as to which of two possible Fridays had been agreed upon. Consequently, on the first of these Fridays, all were assembled only to disband with some grumbling by midmorning when it was clear that the boat was not coming. Hence, when the following Friday approached, most Chambri thought the final washing had already been postponed too long and, moreover, had been postponed to meet the needs of the tourists, not of the Chambri.

This stage in the initiation was an occasion of great significance to a very large number of Chambri. Numerous individuals would exercise a variety of specific ritual functions that would as well engage their clansmen and clanswomen and, in many cases, their in-laws. Substantial sums of money would be collected and disbursed and these would create, discharge or perpetuate a myriad of obligations. Large numbers of Chambri, whether as Yambuntimeri or Pombiantimeri, men or women, initiated or initiate, would participate in what would be experienced as a collective triumph. Even though postponed a week to accommodate the tourists, the performance would be very much for the Chambri themselves. Indeed, they would have a blast.

We arrived at Wombun at dawn that Friday morning to find much activity. Women were still singing, as they had been throughout the night: those women of Maliwan's family at his house were rejoicing in the successful initiation of their sons and brothers; those of the families of each of Maliwan's two wives were celebrating the accomplishment of their respective nephews. In addition, a number of women associated with the Indingai clan that controlled Kwolimopan were at the house of Maliwan's brother, acclaiming Kwolimopan's importance in the initiation.

Inside the Walindimi men's house a young Indingai man, Philip, was donning the headdress that had rested on top of the Kwolimopan effigy. As sister's son to the clan controlling Kwolimopan, it was his ritual prerogative to embody the initiatory crocodile on this day. Other men were decorating themselves with such ritual finery as tree-kangaroo wigs, bat-skull amulets, shell arm and leg bands. Soon, two other ancestral crocodiles, in charge of the water on this day of the final washing, began to cry out from a special enclosure near the lake. These were the two water drums, Posump and Ponor; they boomed as they were thumped up and down in buckets of water by a group led by Suangin. These men were decorated with muddy handprints, representing the foot-marks of the two crocodiles as they had emerged from their domain.[20]

Shortly afterward, Philip carried the Kwolimopan effigy down to the edge of the water where an arch of new coconut leaves, marking the transition between land and water, had just been erected. There, he took up his station: wearing the Kwolimopan headdress, leaning with his chin resting on the Kwolimopan effigy, he stood motionless. Beside him, shooing away flies and mosquitoes, were two women, exercising their right to ritual positions as senior female members of the clan controlling Kwolimopan. On the ground in front of them was a bowl containing cans of fish and a small bag of rice, a presentation of food from Godfried, a member of that clan. After the ceremony Philip would complete a marriage exchange with Godfried by reciprocating the gift of food with K10. Finally, at Philip's feet was a half coconut shell filled with grated coconut. This was to be thrown at Kwolimopan to welcome

16 A water drum cried out from a special enclosure near the lake.

17 A woman prepared to brush flies and mosquitoes from a
motionless Kwolimopan.

it. Throwing the coconut at Kwolimopan was a ritual prerogative of Godfried's wife.

Inside the enclosure concealing the water drums, a small tree had been secured. Into this tree a Chambri climbed to exercise yet another ritual prerogative. Motionless, in black paint and black feather headdress, he would guard Posump and Ponor: through his father he had inherited the right to be a "kink." (A kink was a variety of black water bird that slept near the water's edge in a pandanus tree and also frequently perched on a crocodile's nose, busying itself with insects until it became nervous and took wing.) A kink was thought to protect a crocodile by warning it of impending trouble.

To what was now the steady thumping of the water drums, Maliwan and his family brought out four money trees. These were palm fronds into which small cleft skewers holding bank notes had been inserted.[21] The money trees were stuck into the ground near the drum enclosure. Since Maliwan was initiating sons by each of his two wives, he would have to recompense two sets of in-laws. Two weeks before, he had invited friends and relatives to his house in order for them to contribute to this presentation. A total of thirty-five men and twenty-nine women from all of the men's houses in Wombun, from two in Indingai and one in Kilimbit had responded. Their contributions, ranging from K.20 to K10, totaled K160.[22] With the help of these contributors Maliwan had been able to affix K125 to each of the two money trees that would go to the most senior brother (currently at Chambri) of each wife. This recipient then was to divide up the money as he saw fit among those of his clan who had been designated as the principal mother's brother) the *wau* – of the individual initiates. (Maliwan told us that because the most senior brother of one of his wives was away at work and could not attend the ceremony, he had "hidden" K120 to give him when he did come back to Wombun.) The other two money trees were each of K10 and were destined for the maternal kin of each wife.[23]

After about an hour of these preparations, Maliwan asked us the time: it was 6.55 a.m. He said that the tourists did not seem to be coming. The radio broadcast of shipping news the day before had not mentioned the location of the Melanesian Explorer and Maliwan had received no message from it. Although he did not want to lose the income tourists would provide as an audience, he might have to go ahead without them. He then decided to wait a

18   Two of Maliwan's money trees.

bit longer and not begin the ceremony until 7:30. However, the Chambri by now were insisting that this be *their* performance. They were no longer willing to be controlled by Maliwan on behalf of the tourists.

A throng was already gathering around the men's house. Dancing women, soon joined by men and other women, brandished spears and in jubilation sang: "We are seeing happiness through our eyes, we are breathing happiness through our noses, we are immersed in happiness"; "the initiates have gone through pain, this is a good custom"; "you initiates have come to make me proud." Then a phalanx of Yambuntimeri men poured out of the Walindimi men's house toward the shore. There, extending almost to the motionless Kwolimopan near the water's edge, they formed two parallel lines. Feet apart, each man shifted his weight rhythmically and in unison with the others, first as he leaned to the left and hit the ground with a coconut frond broom held in his right hand and then as he returned fully upright. Almost immediately the Pombiantimeri men and women, including the initiates, began filing through the two lines. Although the Yambuntimeri men were uttering threats such as "All right, you brothers and sisters, we'll completely kill you," most in fact struck just the ground with their switches and the rest delivered only mild blows to the legs of those running the gauntlet.

The line of Pombiantimeri then passed around the still-motionless Kwolimopan, under the coconut frond arch, and stopped at the water's edge. The sisters of the initiates cut off the cords which the young men had worn around their wrists and ankles. These, as may be remembered, had been attached by their sisters the night before the youths were "eaten" by Kwolimopan, and indicated they were to observe the restrictions attendant upon their symbolic death. Then the initiates and their sisters – and in a few cases, their clan-mothers – jumped into the lake. There, amid much splashing and high spirits, the sisters washed from their brothers the mud which had been applied that morning to mark them as crocodiles.

Emerging from the water, the initiates and their sisters retraced their passage through the two lines of Yambuntimeri men, stopping by the money trees. There the initiates were presented by their mothers' brothers with new towels, new trousers and new string bags filled with toiletries – comb, powder, razor. After their sisters had dried them with the new towels, the initiates returned

19   An initiate was presented with a new towel by his mother's brother.

to the village. They were accompanied by their sisters, who were carrying the presents, by their mothers' brothers and by their mothers' brothers' wives, who were carrying the money trees.

After this, the others dispersed. The Yambuntimeri antagonists wandered up to the men's house; there they were soon joined by the kink and a very tired Kwolimopan. The time was 7:15. A great deal of intense social activity had taken place in only twenty minutes.

Meanwhile, the initiates and those accompanying them entered the house of one of their mothers' brothers. Here the money trees were placed on either side of the central post. The brother and other relatives of Maliwan's first wife plus the two initiates she had borne occupied one side of the house, while the brother and relatives of Maliwan's second wife plus the three initiates she had borne occupied the other. While mothers' brothers wives (*waiyai*) painted the initiates with red clay and placed brightly colored cords on their wrists and ankles to display their changed status as adult men, both women and men sang celebratory songs such as "Sinsi [a yellow water plant which is the totem of one of the mothers' brothers] will feed me lots of food." Finally, the initiates got into their new trousers and were presented by their mothers' brothers with an artifact marking adult maleness: this was a wooden spear that was also a bamboo lime holder. Then, escorted by their mothers' brothers and their wives, who were carrying a large presentation of food (plates of cooked rice and canned fish, coconuts, sugar cane and watermelons), the initiates, spear-lime-holders in hand, were returned to Maliwan's house. There a family feast would follow.

At 7:55, the speed boats from the Melanesian Explorer arrived. Maliwan's brother, to whom we were talking, immediately excused himself to dress up again so that he could dance for the tourists. He told us that the ceremony would be repeated. Other men went to their houses to fetch carvings. Several muttered that it was wrong for the tourists to come so late – after the ceremony had been held. As tourists gathered outside Walindimi, Maliwan's first wife emerged from her house (at her husband's request) and began dancing, bare-breasted, while holding one of her husband's large clan carvings. The second wife, wearing a bra, then emerged and the two, several feet apart, posed together for pictures. The first wife, more assertive than the second, shook tourists' hands, introducing herself as the first wife, the mother of two of the

20   The tourists witnessed a greatly truncated final washing.

initiates. The tourists then entered the men's house to purchase
carvings. This gave Maliwan time to have portions of the ceremony restaged. He wanted to make sure he could collect his fee.

The repeated ceremony turned out to be greatly truncated. It
was performed primarily by those in Maliwan's clan and by a
scattering of those with particular ritual positions. The line of
Yambuntimeri switchers was depleted and included a number of
Pombiantimeri men, augmented by women; the kink was in his
tree keeping watch, but Posump and Ponor and those activating
them were nowhere around; Kwolimopan resumed his station but
without the relief offered by those brushing insects from him. A
small group including the initiates filed through a rather indiffer-
ent parallel line of Chambri for an abbreviated washing. But, the
tourists seemed to like it. Then the tour guide called out, "Does
anyone want the backs?" and the initiates were posed to show their
scars. Finally, some tourists, asking their friends to photograph
them, posed with the initiates and with Maliwan.

Although there would be celebrations by both clan members and
in-laws throughout the rest of the day and into the night, the
initiation was essentially over. Maliwan was pleased. No one could

say that he had not generously compensated his in-laws; he had even been able to present money to the maternal kin of his two wives. He had killed three pigs and generously feasted men from all three Chambri villages. He had, he told us, spent (a very substantial) K1,545.88: his name had gone on top. And, with the book we would write about him and his initiation, he would be a big man truly to remember.[24]

Other Chambri, too, were happy. No one appeared to be ritually slighted: the grumbling by several men from Kilimbit that there should have been the evocation in slitgong playing of their ancestral crocodile Manpokkakpok was only *pro forma*. Any Chambri who had wished to participate easily found a reason to do so. At the final washing, for instance, hundreds took part: as men and women, as Yambuntimeri and Pombiantimeri, as brothers and sisters; as occupants of a wide range of particular ritual positions such as kink, as Kwolimopan and his various attendants and as the animators of Posump and Ponor; as patrikin, matrikin, or in-laws of the initiates (or of their kin). In a manner that was clearly gratifying, individuals interacted as members of virtually all significant Chambri social categories.[25] Certainly the events of the final washing became a display of Chambri in process that was performed with an exuberance Maliwan was unable, even for a short time, to contain. Nor was he able to revive these events when the tourists finally did arrive. Few, aside from those under Maliwan's direct influence, were inclined to engage in what would become by then solely a staged presentation.

This phase of the initiation appeared to be enjoyed as a glorious excess of social action, an all-stops-out performance. The Chambri experienced it as an aesthetically dazzling social complexity. If the tourists had come on time, they probably would have had little effect on such a performance of celebration. Yet, we think that Chambri exuberance was augmented because they had found opportunity to defy the tourists (and, as well, Maliwan). During the hazing Chambri had tried unsuccessfully to control the tourists so as to offset the fact that the tourists could take their ceremony or leave it. In contrast, during the final washing, the Chambri took their ceremony and left the tourists.

Regardless of whether the Chambri had found their acts of resistance or defiance effective, the tourists were an important presence during the initiation. Their presence had changed the initiation in ways both intended and unintended. The reason tourists had been invited to the initiation at all was that Maliwan needed the resources they could provide. That he had collected almost K300 in admission fees had enabled him to derive prestige by sponsoring a traditional ceremony in particularly impressive fashion. Moreover, this money from the tourists was largely unentailed: unlike the contributions, for instance, that he solicited from non-kin for his money trees, those received from the tourists carried no obligations of reciprocity beyond admitting them to a performance. Their contributions would not tie up Maliwan's own future resources.

A lack of entailment also had more general consequences. It meant that the tourists and Chambri were not mutually dependent, and hence, would always remain unequal. This realization the Chambri had found distressing and it had affected the initiation in a number of ways. In particular the Chambri were beginning to discover that the process of selling their initiations (and perhaps other ceremonies) as tourist attractions could subtly but profoundly transform both Chambri and their ceremonies. Because they were paid performers they alone could no longer determine the nature and significance of their performance. They had to deal with the presence of an alien audience and, as well, with an audience that was defining them and their ceremonies in ways they did not like.

But the Chambri also realized that the world the boys were entering was, in fact, one in which tourists were an important economic resource they must learn to use if they were to become competent adults. Indeed, this point was directly made in the hazing itself when the boys were asked whether they would be able to make carvings for sale to tourists. It was, therefore, perhaps appropriate for Chambri to come of age through an initiation, sponsored with tourist money, during which Chambri experience of coercive authority and the weight of custom was affected by the presence of tourists, and their scars were the focus of tourist attention.

That Chambri were already initiating both *under* changed circumstances and *for* changed circumstances became additionally, and dramatically apparent during the initiation. Immediately after Maliwan's sons had emerged from their ordeal, in which at least in symbolic terms they had narrowly escaped death, word came by Catholic Mission short-wave radio that another of Chambri's sons had emerged from a life-threatening ordeal. Michael Fox, a veteran with sixteen years' experience in the Papua New Guinea Defense Force, had been attacked in the Papua New Guinea Highlands while working with an exploration party led by two American mining engineers. Forced to stop their truck by a tree felled across a narrow road, the entire party had been captured by a local gang of young men, armed with bush knives and axes. All prisoners were told to relinquish their valuables and then to strip. As Michael removed his shirt, one of the assailants (presumably married into a local clan) recognized from his initiation scars that both he and Michael were from the Sepik. Because of this bond, Michael was spared further humiliation – and indeed abuse. In contrast, the two Americans were tied and then dragged naked over sharp rocks; their injuries required hospital treatment afterwards. As a result of this incident, Michael notified the Chambri that all young men should be initiated, since it had been his initiatory scars that had saved him from severe injury.

We had heard comparable talk before. Others had described the possible protection their Chambri scars might give them if threatened by assault from other Sepiks in such towns as Madang. They had also said that no matter where they might die or be killed in Papua New Guinea, they would be recognized as Sepiks and their bodies would be shipped home to Chambri.

Chambri youth were at this time coming of age in a world in which adult status had an enlarged meaning: an adult had come to be defined as one who could be effective not only *at* Chambri but also *away* from Chambri. (In fact, 43 per cent of all Chambri over the age of 17 were living away from Chambri in such towns as Wewak, Madang, Lae and Port Moresby.) Chambri had for some time encouraged their children, especially their sons, to become educated, so they would be able to succeed in these towns. Indeed, a major reason initiation was no longer obligatory was that competence as a good earner and, of particular importance, as a good remitter, itself qualified one as a fully adult clan member. (As mentioned, only 41 per cent of males over 17 at Chambri, and a much lower percentage of those away, had been scarified.) Although most Chambri would still agree that a father should initiate his sons and that all young men should be scarified, many Chambri (including two of Maliwan's just-initiated sons) told us, when we asked, that they would initiate their children only if they had enough money to throw a big party. Because scarification was unrelated to success in life in the towns, that is, unrelated to the capacity to earn money, it had become optional to Chambri: it took place no longer as a ceremony essential to making men but as one of a number of opportunities for a father to display his affluence. Moreover, the marriage exchanges that had such an important part in an initiation could be replicated in the context of education: rather than be compensated during an initiation for having provided over the years food, clothing and nurture, a mother's brother might be recompensed for his contribution to his sister's son's school fees.[26]

Thus, when Michael Fox and others stressed the importance of a traditional initiation in preparing men for life in the towns, they were redefining the significance of scarification. From their perspective, the importance of initiation was not primarily that it transformed young men into full clansmen, freed from their mother's blood and filled with the power of Kwolimopan, who were able to create and maintain a density of social connections; rather it gave urban dwellers a visible cultural affiliation that might protect them from capricious attack. It is to the Chambri experience in that urban world, including their perception of the alternatives the urban world provided to life at Chambri, that we now turn.

3
The town

Until rather recently, the Chambri experienced the small coastal town of Wewak, the Provincial Capital of East Sepik Province, in terms of transition. From the 1930s through the 1950s, Wewak was a point of departure for the labor migrants on their way to the plantations of New Britain and New Ireland; or it was a place of religious training for the Catholic Mission catechists before they were stationed throughout the Sepik.[1] However, by the early 1960s, Chambri began to travel to Wewak for other purposes and for longer periods of time. They came to supervise their children who, having completed the limited schooling available at Chambri, were attending mission schools in Wewak; or they came to watch out for their kin who were receiving treatment at the Wewak hospital.[2] In order to provide housing for themselves they eventually rented from indigenous landowners a small area adjacent to one of the main roads. Here they built the makeshift houses that formed the nucleus of what became the Chambri Camp.[3]

By the early 1970s, Chambri began to travel to Wewak in ever increasing numbers, usually staying with those kin or co-villagers already there, living in Chambri Camp. They came primarily to earn money to take or send home. But they also came to see what town life was like. Women who came to sell fish might stay several months before returning to Chambri; the men who accompanied them or those who came alone might look for jobs and stay longer.[4] They built houses or additions to existing structures for themselves from whatever was available – bush materials, scavenged pieces of sheet metal and even cardboard – and squeezed these in as they could.

And, although few had intended to stay very long and none had long-term claim on the land, the Camp came to look and function

21   Chambri camp came to look and function like a Chambri village.

like a Chambri village, with plantings of fruit and coconut trees under which chickens, ducks, and the occasional pig foraged. Chambri Camp became increasingly crowded but was never a slum: outhouses were built on the periphery; separate bathing places for men and women were cleared along the banks of a nearby stream; and yards were swept and trash burned. Men met in the three, modest but functional, men's houses which, significantly, were named after the first men's houses in each of the three Chambri villages. In fact the residential pattern at the camp replicated that at Chambri with migrants from Kilimbit, Indingai and Wombun living in their own respective sections of the camp. These had the same spatial relationship to the coastal range and ocean as had the three Chambri villages to Chambri Mountain and Lake.[5]

Even though this residential pattern persisted in Chambri Camp with migrants and visitors usually continuing to stay with or near kin and friends from their village of origin, Chambri in the Camp came to describe it as the fourth Chambri village. Indeed about as many lived there as in any one of the home villages.[6] And, furthermore, many of those living in the Camp eventually considered it their home and did not plan to return to Chambri at all, except perhaps for brief visits.[7]

For virtually all Chambri, regardless of whether they were living in Wewak or Chambri, part of the significance of life in town was its contrast to life at Chambri. It was largely in terms of this contrast that Chambri visualized, experienced, and appraised their ideas and aspirations about development. As we shall begin to see in this chapter, it was also in terms of this contrast that those differentially placed, by generation, gender and competitive success in the system of commensurate differences, wrangled with each other about the appropriate relationship between tradition and modernization, about the meaning of being a Chambri in a changing world.

Chambri – both men and women – found wandering around Wewak exciting, especially when they were dressed in nice clothes and accompanied by several Chambri friends. The tradestores were well-stocked with clothing, mattresses, radios, tape recorders, pots, pans, and repair parts for stoves and lamps; the supermarkets had cases of canned fish, stacks of 25-kilo bags of rice, frozen food, cold soda, and take-out fried food; the bars served cold beer, and for recreation provided dart boards and sometimes pool tables; the outdoor markets were held daily and offered produce from throughout the province. On the waterfront, gangs of men unloaded cars, containers, heavy construction equipment, and other cargo brought in on Japanese, Taiwanese, and Australian ships.[8] Chinese, Filipino, and Australian entrepreneurs, American and German missionaries, and tourists (mostly travelers) from all over the world were to be seen on the streets. And, there were other Papua New Guineans – a few from the Highlands or perhaps from Rabaul, but most from the various villages of the Sepik. As they circulated in little groups they were looking at each other as well as at the sights of Wewak.

Although there was ordinarily only minimal interaction between these Papua New Guineans, such as an occasional greeting in Pidgin English, most knew each other, often by name, and certainly by village or region of origin and by area of residence in one of the equivalents to Chambri Camp scattered throughout Wewak. (These were behind the markets, adjacent to the dock, along the beach front near the hospital and army barracks.[9]) Encounters among those who were socially peripheral but not

socially irrelevant to each other were charged with excitement
stemming from a sense of freedom, potentiality and adventure.
Such a sense was most palpable at night as young men, and
increasingly young women, wearing their most sophisticated out-
fits, congregated to drink and dance at the Sepik Club or another
bar, or at some temporary dance ground.[10] Although liaisons
occasionally occurred, more typically the efforts by a young man
to impress a young woman from another group provoked a fight
between the young men of both groups. (In an instance that most
Chambri found amusing, a young Chambri man asked a woman
from another village to dance and when she refused, he kicked
her in the rear: his performance as seducer and fighter was
regarded by even his friends as seriously flawed.)

Life in town was often exciting; it was also frequently hard.[11]
Only 17 per cent of those adults living in the Chambri Camp had
regular salaries.[12] Most of the other men and women in the Camp
considered themselves carvers or basket weavers and relied for
their survival on income earned from sales. Yet, only 57 per cent
of those who tried to support themselves in this manner in fact
made any sales at all in the course of a year: their average yearly
income was K199.[13] Hence, 43 per cent of the artisans, that is, the
carvers or basket weavers, or 42 per cent of all adult inhabitants in
the Chambri Camp, had *no* income.

Moreover, if all of the money earned by those in the Camp *had
been* evenly distributed among all the inhabitants, a family of four
would have had available only about K1,315 per year to support
life in a place where virtually all the necessities of life had to be
purchased. We conservatively estimate the annual cost in Wewak
for a family of four to meet minimally such essential needs as
shelter (rent paid to the land-owner), water (purchased from the
town), food, tobacco, betel nut, clothing, and school fees would be
K1,316. And this amount would be barely enough, provided the
family had only one child in elementary school and engaged in no
traditional exchanges, contributed to no church offerings and
partook of no pleasures of town such as drinking an occasional
cold beer, or buying a child a flavored ice.[14] Simply put: given the
presence of kin, no Chambri at the Camp actually starved;
however, many were frequently hungry. They eked out a living
somehow, depending for food at least partly on smoked fish
occasionally sent from Chambri, green mangoes gathered from
trees belonging to others and small marsupials killed in the bush at

the edge of the Camp. Moreover, many had to rely on remittances from kin farther afield in Papua New Guinea.

In these circumstances, those in need frequently made claims on those who had an income, whether from wages, artifact sales, or remittances. To deny a claim was to risk creating a grudge which might then lead to sorcery and illness.[15] Consequently, it was very difficult for anyone to accumulate: windfalls tended to be converted into beer that was immediately shared and consumed; displays on ritual occasions were minimal and redistribution prompt.[16] As one Chambri told us: "It is the custom here in town that whenever anyone is up, everyone comes around and asks him for credit; that is how everyone is made equal." Although certain Chambri at the Camp were influential, by virtue of their knowledge and judgment, no one was able to control sufficient resources to be a big man. (Maliwan's accomplishment in raising and disbursing over K1,500 for the initiation of his sons would be unheard of for anyone living in the Camp.)

In the view of most of those still living at home on Chambri, the principal reason that Chambri should live elsewhere, rather than helping their kin at home with subsistence and ritual tasks, was to earn money (or prepare through education to earn money) so they could remit. However, as we have indicated, even those Chambri in Wewak with reasonably good incomes found it difficult to accumulate; moreover, many did not earn enough money to support themselves, much less to remit.

The following translated letter from a young Wewak migrant, only sporadically working as a laborer, to his parents in Chambri illustrates both the expectation they had that he remit and his difficulty in doing so.

Dear Mama and Daddy
Hello and good night to both of you. It's been a very long time since I have written to you both. Also, I received the message you sent me. Concerning the money you want, I will send it in August of this year. About Christmas, I cannot say when or if I will come. But, I really mean that I will send the money to you, although I cannot say how much I will send. And don't think that I'll come for sure at Christmas. That's all now, except that I was happy to receive your message. Say a big hello to Timothy and Albert. So, that's all.

Moreover, in recent years, an employed Chambri migrant farther afield in places like Madang or Port Moresby would receive letters of appeal not only from those at Chambri but also from those in Wewak. From the perspective of Chambri at home, those in Wewak had become largely useless as sources of money and, as well, were deflecting to themselves money that should have gone to Chambri. Thus, to the physical hardships of life in Wewak were added the frequent rebukes of those at home who accused unemployed migrants of being shirkers and parasites.

Life in Wewak and in other towns was more than hard; it was, at times, dangerous. There was a widespread perception that crime, particularly in the towns, was rampant.[17] The Chambri experience of crime, as both perpetrators and victims, was probably roughly typical. During the six months of our research in 1987, in Wewak alone, three Chambri were arrested for two separate thefts, one robbery at knife point, the other burglary, and three Chambri suffered attack: one rape, one stabbing, and one death as a result of beating.

When those Chambri no longer new to the town and its excitements reflected on why they remained in Wewak they recognized that if they were to return to Chambri Island, they would have plenty to eat. Indeed, they talked nostalgically of the times when the eggs of ducks and other water birds could be gathered in handfuls; of low water times on the lake when fish could simply be scooped up into a canoe. (During one trip to Chambri from Wewak we had with us a young Chambri boy who had visited his home village only once before as an infant. That late afternoon, the Sepik tributary that led to Chambri Lake was filled with fish, thrashing in the water, gulping air. The lead man in our canoe repeatedly thrust his spear at the surfacing fish, harvesting at least thirty within as many minutes. As ducks and egrets exploded into flight around us, others in the canoe pretended to shoot them with paddles held as shotguns or discharged their slingshots after them. The boy was entranced. For someone who had grown up on the frequently short rations of Chambri Camp, this was an unfamiliar vision of abundance. For us, it was a vivid picture of an original affluent society.)[18]

Those Chambri remaining in Wewak recognized, too, that one would be safer from criminal attack in the home villages than in Wewak. And this was so even though at Chambri there were occasional acts of vandalism and confrontations between youths of the different villages.

As we shall see from the following two cases, at least some of

those who had become committed to town life, despite its recognized deprivations and dangers, were so committed because it
enabled them to escape the constraints of the village. Part of the
attraction of life in town was, then, that it provided an escape from
some of the competition and coercion characteristic of the system
of commensurate differences. Indeed, the same circumstances of
development that were allowing Maliwan to pursue novel strategies for enhancing his stature as a Chambri big man were
providing other Chambri, especially young men and women, with
the opportunity to evade the power of big men. However, it is
important to note that virtually all of those seeking reprieve from
what, according to their particular perspectives, were negative
features of traditional Chambri life, still considered themselves to
be thoroughly Chambri. They were bound to other Chambri by
complex and continuing histories of interaction and they found in
them the sources of their identity as persons.

On why young men and women do not like living at Chambri

We frequently asked Chambri residing in Wewak why they chose
to remain there. The reasons Rex Kamilus gave were typical. Rex,
twenty-eight years old at the time of our interview, had gone to
Wewak in the late 1970s to complete correspondence school. His
father then came to Wewak for medical treatment of a serious
illness contracted at Chambri. Following his discharge from the
hospital he remained in town with his son. Soon afterward, in
1980, Rex's youngest sibling died at Chambri and the rest of the
family joined those already in Wewak. It was evident to all that
someone at Chambri was ensorcelling members of the family.
Rex's mother soon insisted that they all move to Madang in order
to get even farther away from the source of danger and this they
did. Then, in 1986, in order to sell artifacts, the mother and
several of her children went to Rabaul, where they have remained.
Rex and his father stayed in Madang to watch out for the youngest
daughter who was still in school there. Rex did not like Madang.
He was attacked by a Sepik, a "wanted criminal,"[19] with a hatchet
and was hospitalized with serious gashes to his scalp and face. (The
criminal was later killed by the police.) After Rex recovered from
his wounds, he left his father and sister in Madang and returned
to Wewak.

Rex preferred life in Wewak to that in Chambri because in town "you are free to walk about; you are the master of yourself." At the Chambri Camp, "youth" experienced "freedom." In contrast, he said, people at home practised the "ancestral custom of killing people by poisoning [ensorcelling] them." When we asked him to elaborate, he said that if, for example, he tried to seduce a young woman at Chambri and her father found out about it, he would be likely to ensorcell him or to hire someone else to do it.

He continued by telling us that the big men at Chambri consistently prevented the younger men and women from holding all-night dance parties to modern music because they thought that such occasions encouraged young people to choose their own sexual and marriage partners. Big men liked to arrange marriages for everyone. (Indeed, Rex was right: the arrangement of marriage alliances was central to Chambri politics.) He described a recent debate that took place at Chambri concerning these parties. All of the older men sat on one side of the men's house, opposing the dances as new and pernicious, while all of the younger men sat on the other side, supporting them as new and desirable. The young men lost and the dances were discontinued.

Not only did Chambri big men wish to protect their political interests by controlling Chambri youth, Rex continued, they tried to maintain economic power by opposing any economic development they did not control and by pulling down others who were trying to get ahead. Rex himself had hoped to improve the artifact business at Chambri and had discussed his ideas with the big men in the Walindimi men's house. He recommended that they deduct K1 for every K10 from artifacts sold in order to have money available to repair or improve the Walindimi men's house. No one agreed to this. (Rex's proposal, of course, would have been regarded by Maliwan as a direct meddling in his affairs.) Big men, Rex said, wanted to stay in charge. (An older woman listening to Rex turned to us in agreement. She noted wryly that Chambri was an island full of stones, and stones did not change.) Rex hoped that changes would occur when these big men died. They would be replaced by younger men of his generation who, because they were not inclined to become big men, would not be "jealous" of others and discourage their accomplishments.

Rex believed that young men would – and should – continue to leave Chambri as long as the big men there prevented them from entertaining themselves and destroyed anything they tried to build up. And, of course, as the illness, death, and subsequent flight from Chambri of his own family showed, it was not only young men who were (thought to be) the objects of sorcery.

A similar perception of Chambri as a place to leave and avoid was presented by Gabriella Apak, a woman of twenty-nine with two illegitimate children.[20] She had been living in Wewak for seven years, supported largely by remittances from a brother working in the Bougainville copper mine. When we asked her why she did not return to Chambri, she at first said she was foolish for not doing so since Chambri was a much better place than Wewak. Everything in Wewak must be bought and one must have money simply to survive. Why then, we persisted, did she not return? Lowering her voice, she revealed that she and many other young women did not go home because they would be expected to marry old men whom they did not like and would be ensorcelled if they refused. When big men at Chambri were rejected, they would, for instance, place a bespelled object on a path frequented by the woman who had thwarted them; when she stepped over it, its magic power entered her body and she became sick and died.

Gabriella then told us that she had been warned of this danger in a recent dream. She dreamt that a man from Wombun came to the house of one of her female friends at Indingai and said: "Here is some betel pepper for Gabriella. When Gabriella wants to chew betel nut, give her a little of this." She also described the man in her dream as holding the pepper, which was huge, at the level of his crotch. Gabriella knew that this had been a "real" dream, one which predicted forthcoming events, so she went to two other Chambri women living in the Camp to discuss it. They told her that she should avoid taking betel pepper from anyone. They also suggested the identity of the man wishing to ensorcell her. He had already given another woman who had refused to marry him poisoned betel pepper. As his intended victim bit into it, a bespelled leaf had emerged. Fortunately, she had the support of her father and brothers who had not wanted her to marry the sorcerer. They helped her to counteract the magic by gathering the youngest coconuts from the tallest trees, boiling the nuts and then washing her with the resulting liquid. This enabled her to be cleansed of the poison she had consumed, but it had been a narrow escape.

Profiting from her dream and from the example of this young woman, Gabriella did not intend to return to Chambri as long as this man desired her, lest she be doomed either to become his wife

or to die. Nor, since she already had children, did she much wish
to be anyone's wife: her position was as good as that of most of the
married women she knew at the Camp.

Like other Chambri women, Gabriella sought to achieve worth
primarily through reproductive closure – by reproducing those
who had given her life. In particular, a Chambri woman usually
preferred to marry in such a way that her daughter's daughter
would eventually assume the social position of the woman's
mother. The woman would thereby have caused her own existence. However, any children Gabriella might bear, regardless of
how or whether she was married, would be viewed as adequate
self-reproduction, that measure of self worth for a Chambri
woman.

In contrast to women, Chambri men sought to achieve worth by
competing with other men in terms of relative power. As we have
seen in Maliwan's initiation, a significant measure of a man's
power was the capacity to repay, primarily by staging elaborate
ceremonies during which he compensated his in-laws, those who
had provided life for him and others of his clan, especially those
who had provided his mother and his wife. Through his own
marriage(s) and those of his clan members a man became
immersed in complex obligations that gave him the opportunity of
achieving political eminence. He did this by showing he was at
least the equal of his male contemporaries, as well as his predecessors, in his capacity to pay his debts. Gabriella's father and
brothers were, however, troubled that she was not married.
Although her illegitimate children were welcome as members of
her clan, she herself was a wasted political resource: she had
generated neither bride-price nor in-laws. Perhaps one unstated
reason Gabriella had for choosing to remain in Wewak was the
realization that her male kin would be delighted to have her marry
as important a man as the potential "suitor" of her dream.

It should be noted, though, that even a powerful man was not
likely to wish to marry a woman against her will. She might, for
instance, disclose to his enemies secret magical spells he had
inadvertently revealed, perhaps while sleeping. Thus, women at
Chambri, hearing of Gabriella's fears, denied that she would be in
serious danger if she returned to Chambri.[21] Many said that the
real reason Gabriella and other young women remained in Wewak
was because they were too lazy to fish and gather firewood. One
told us resentfully: "They say we smell of fish; they like to walk

around town smelling of perfume; they prefer to be supported by others rather than working hard themselves."

The sorcery that Rex and Gabriella feared came from flouting the will of big men. Yet they did not object that big men had the capacity to ensorcell, either through their own direct efforts or the efforts of those they employed: indeed, this capacity was by definition an attribute of big men. (For example, one young Chambri man, admiringly described his father as a big man, by referring to him as the "poison snake of Chambri.")[22] Nor did they find it surprising that big men wanted to remain in charge. Nevertheless, they thought it best to leave rather than have to deal with these predictable and thoroughly traditional forms of coercion through sorcery. Thus, for Rex and Gabriella, development meant that juniors (and others) could, if they chose, evade the degree to which they were controlled by powerful seniors. And this was so in spite of the fact that they felt pressure to redistribute to those equally impoverished camp residents. Rex and Gabriella were certainly not indicating, though, either that Chambri life was fundamentally flawed or that they wished to cease being Chambri themselves.

Of course, it might be suggested that they were not in an economic position to repudiate Chambri life or identity. However, even those whose economic circumstances would have enabled them to live entirely apart from other Chambri and to break completely the ties that bound and coerced did not choose to do so, whether they lived in Chambri or Wewak. As we shall see, social entailments so constituted the sense that Chambri had of themselves as persons, that they could be abrogated only by becoming a very different sort of person.

The twisted histories of a successful migrant

When a highly successful Chambri like John Illumbui, a university-educated accountant employed in Port Moresby, came to Wewak he was a conspicuous target for Chambri who had claims on him for redistribution. Indeed, John had stayed away from Chambri Camp for eight years because he was afraid to evade, and thus wished to avoid, the torrent of requests he would receive for money. When we met him in Wewak he and his wife had just come to the Camp in order to celebrate the first communion of his sister's daughter. John told us that meeting the demands of Chambri in Wewak would clean him out and, although he had not visited Chambri Island in twelve years, he could not afford to do so on this trip.

On the night of his arrival, John held an all-night beer party for the older men of the Camp. He began by thanking them for all the help they had given him. It had been this help that had enabled him to become a success. They responded that he was indeed acting as a young Chambri should by showing gratitude to the senior men of the community with this little present of beer and by promising to repay them all for their considerable help. This way, they continued somewhat darkly, no one would be angry with him. Several then made more specific statements about the help he must repay: one said that he had come to see John and given him baby presents when he was born; another enumerated the names of those who had died since John had last visited, implying that contributions to death expenses would be in order. John nodded dutifully to each reminder.

One older speaker did reflect briefly that by the time visiting migrants were able to leave Wewak for their Chambri villages, they had no more money because people at the Camp had begged it all: indeed, the reason there were no businesses on Chambri Island was that migrants never had money left over to help their relatives there. However, aside from this revealing but anomalous statement, the litany of personal claims continued throughout the night.

Near the end of his visit, John told us that his stay was costing him at least K150 per day. In fact, he had that morning missed his plane and joked that his savings would be finished by the time he could leave. His Chambri wife added (in English): "These Chambri will finish you up entirely if you have any money." We then asked John directly why he helped his relatives. He replied that they were his family and would become angry if he did not. When we persisted by asking what would happen if they became angry, he said (also in English): "They would kick me out of the family and if I did anything big they would not come and no one would see it." Thus, despite his Western education and business activities, in short, despite a life that most Chambri regarded as epitomizing the potentialities of development, he located himself, with only moderate ambivalence, very much through reference to, and entailment with, other Chambri.

Before he could leave Wewak, John, to his regret, acquired new obligations. He became enmeshed in a collective history composed of claims and counterclaims that linked him, his life of relative affluence in Port Moresby and his future relationships with Chambri to the time when post-war labor migrants were first returning home, bringing with them the promise that the future would be filled with new opportunities.

On the final afternoon of John's visit, a community court was convened at the behest of his wife, Sisilia, primarily to bring charges against her elder sister, Mariana. The testimony established these facts: Mariana had gone to Port Moresby to help Sisilia with her children. While Mariana was helping with the children she and John had an affair and John agreed to take her as his second wife. Discovering these plans, Sisilia evicted Mariana from the house. Mariana returned to Wewak. On the occasion of this visit the two sisters met again after two years. They were still angry with each other.

The court, attended by perhaps fifty interested Chambri, was under the very competent direction of an elected committee composed of a representative from each of the three sections of the Camp. The committee stated that anyone with a grievance connected to this quarrel between Sisilia and Mariana should air it: there must be no grudges left hidden that might manifest themselves in sorcery and sickness.[23]

The court case was defined as primarily concerning women, and indeed, coalitions formed around the two senior women who had become involved. Sisilia sat with John's mother, Nessaria; Mariana sat with her (and Sisilia's) mother, Yandi. Sisilia attacked Mariana for wanting to marry John and for having insulted her and her children in nasty and threatening letters and phone calls. Sisilia also said she was afraid of the threats themselves because what an older sibling said was likely to come true. Mariana insisted that she must be paid for all of her hard work in taking care of Sisilia's children. Yandi was angry that Sisilia and John did not help her more with money; Nessaria was worried that her son, John, would get sick because Yandi had bad feelings about him.

The court soon decided that even though it would be appropriate for a younger sister to enter into a marriage already established by an older one, the opposite arrangement (for reasons that were experienced as compelling but that no one could clearly define)[24] would be profoundly contrary to Chambri custom. Sisilia was then entirely within her rights to expel Mariana from her household. Mariana and John would simply have to accept this. However, it was also decided that John and Sisilia should send Yandi more money.

Additional testimony was then given about a sizable sum of money which had gone astray. After Mariana returned from Port Moresby, John sent K120 by postal money order to Wewak to be used to "straighten the name of Mariana." Hearing of this, Mariana claimed the money at the post office and spent it all. She explained to the court that she had understood that this was compensation sent her for the insult she had suffered in being evicted by her sister. However, as the court was informed, this money was not intended to go to Mariana but to Lucas Yangim. Lucas was to use K20 of this amount to cover his travel expenses between Wewak and Chambri; he was to use the remaining K100 to settle a debt, primarily owed to his older brother, Yorondu, that would bring to an end a convoluted sequence of events, dating back to the late 1940s.

Shortly after World War II, Yandi, Mariana's mother, had married Willard who proved unable to pay a bride-price for her. Then a man named Ambun returned home upon completion of a work contract. He looked so fat and sleek that Yandi wanted to marry him. Her father, brothers and several others with an interest in Yandi's bride-price were in favor of this: they had received nothing from Willard, and Ambun at least appeared prosperous. However, when Yandi went off with Ambun, the rejected Willard complained to the European patrol officer. The officer arrested Ambun on adultery charges and jailed him in Ambunti. There the court fined him A£20. Ambun languished in jail until Yorondu, one of those who had wanted Yandi to leave Willard, paid the fine.

Yorondu intervened in this case because Yandi's mother was a member of his family. Because bride-price payments had never been completed for Yandi's mother, Yorondu and his brother Lucas were supposed to receive the bride-price that Yandi would fetch. It was at least in part to improve his prospects of getting a bride-price from Ambun that Yorondu got him out of jail.[25] However, the fact that Ambun could not pay his own fine did not bode well concerning his capacity to pay a bride-price.

When Ambun's family in fact paid only a portion of Yandi's bride-price, Yorondu's and Lucas' claim (augmented by the sum used to spring Ambun from jail) descended yet another generation to become a lien on the bride-price of Yandi's first daughter, Mariana. Mariana, however, at least prior to her affair with John, had shown no interest in marrying anyone. She preferred instead the freedom that life in Wewak afforded her.[26] Thus, the money John dispatched to Lucas, to "straighten the name of Mariana," was destined primarily for Lucas and Yorondu. It was intended, really, as a quasi bride-price: by paying for the use of her sexuality, John hoped to legitimize sufficiently his relationship with her to avoid the danger of sorcery that might arise from the rancor of these senior men.

It was the opinion of the court that, since the first payment had gone astray and since grievances had grown with the further passage of time, John must send another and larger payment, of at least K200. These various verdicts reached, representatives of each side placed betel nuts and a K2 note in separate bowls. The two coalitions lined up and the bowls were exchanged between them. Then everyone, except Mariana, shook hands. She ran off with an angry expostulation at her sister. People said to let her go; maybe later someone could talk to her.

John was not likely to send K200 any time soon and no one we spoke to really expected him to do so. He was also not likely to deny his obligation to send the money. As we have said, Chambri could not repudiate the claims other Chambri made on them without repudiating their essential identity: it was other Chambri, John had explicitly told us, who provided the context that gave a person's deeds significance.[27] One way, however, to regulate these claims which were multiple and extensive, given the twisted histories that linked all Chambri in this largely endogamous society, was to distance oneself from their source. To live at Chambri Camp as Rex and Gabriella did was to evade the claims by big men who wished to control their lives to a very high degree. To live in Port Moresby, as John did, was to buffer the claims of those who wished his remittances. (Another migrant living in Port Moresby went to even greater lengths than John to modulate his relations with ever-demanding Chambri. He had come to Wewak on business and, without telling anyone of his visit, left a packet of money with the Catholic Mission to be given to his kin. Only on his return to Port Moresby did he send word of what he had done.)

Forever Chambri?

Although, as John Illumbui's case illustrated, it was possible to remain a Chambri *in absentia*, most Chambri adults, including those in Wewak, believed that becoming Chambri, that is, recognizing relations and claims as compelling and constitutive of self, might well depend upon having lived there, at least for a time.[28] Consequently, Helen Pandu, who had herself visited Chambri only once in her seventeen years of living in Chambri Camp, reacted with consternation when her eight-year-old son asked her visiting brother *what* Wombun was. Not only did the child fail to recognize it as one of the three Chambri villages, much less as his own village, he did not even know what sort of entity it was. Helen immediately removed her son in mid-term from his Wewak school and sent him back with her brother to Chambri. He was to remain there, she told us, until he knew where everything was and what everything looked like.

Indeed, when we moved from Wewak to Chambri, we were immediately impressed by how much better grounded children there were in what all Chambri parents would recognize and value as traditional culture. For example, the day after we arrived, a delegation of neighborhood boys and girls took Frederick up Chambri Mountain for a view of the lake. In the course of this ramble, they showed him numerous rock dwellings of ancestral and other spirits. Arriving at the outcropping overlooking the lake, they recounted in some detail the story of the spirit that still lurked beneath where they stood: angry that her voice had been captured inside a flute blown during initiation, she had trapped within her rock and then eaten an entire class of newly cut initiates. Frederick's young instructors knew they themselves were members of the men's house in which the initiation had taken place and that they were among the descendants of those related to this ill-fated class. Pleased with Frederick's interest, they informed him proudly that they knew lots more stories because they frequently visited the old people who liked to tell them. For these children, unlike those at Chambri Camp, the very landscape of their daily lives constituted and displayed their social and cultural identities.

The identities formed in these ways were so indelible that in over fifteen years of research, we have met only one adult Chambri who said he rejected his identity as a Chambri, including those claims other Chambri might make on him. As his case indicates, though, this redefinition of self and repudiation of claims were only partial and were a source of considerable disquiet to him.

One morning, early during our stay in Chambri Camp, Godfried, in whose house we were staying, came into our room and said with evident disapproval that Martin Gawi had come to talk with us.[29] We emerged to find a young man, in his mid-thirties, dressed immaculately in white. Speaking in excellent English, Martin introduced himself as a musician who performed evenings at the bar and dining room of a local hotel. He had just come from an all-night jam session with some Filipino friends who also frequented the hotel. On our part we introduced ourselves as American anthropologists who had been working among the Chambri for a long time. Deborah jokingly said that she had become a woman of Chambri. Then we plunged into an hour-long conversation like no other we had ever had with a Chambri.

Martin told us that he did not really consider himself still to be a Chambri because: "It doesn't provide me with any benefits. You know how it works, when you have something, you have lots of friends; when you have nothing, everything closes down."

"Even your family closes down?" we asked.

"Yes, even your family. Genuine feeling is missing in a family; the only ones who really care about you are mothers: they give and give and enjoy giving."

Martin then said he would provide us with an example based on his recent experience in a West Sepik jail. The "worst of the incarceration" was his fruitless waiting for someone in his family to raise his bail. Even his wife (who had a job in Wewak as a nurse) was unwilling to provide his bail and finally Martin had to "borrow from a complete stranger" a sum of K200. This sum he was now paying back. Yet, in contrast to the way his kin had treated him, Martin had just the previous day borrowed money from his employer in order to bail out his brother, jailed for drunken fighting.

We learned later from other Chambri that the trouble culminating in Martin's incarceration in the West Sepik Province had began several years before when he was employed in the East Sepik Department of Public Works. He had eventually been fired from this job for frequent misuse of funds. Two such instances were of particular concern to the Chambri. In the first, Martin had contracted with men in his home village of Kilimbit to repair the airstrip there, promising them K700 for their work. The men had engaged in this work with enthusiasm, pleased both at the prospect of these wages and at the possibility that with a functional airstrip more tourists might come to their end of the island. There was even discussion that Martin might be able to provide government funds for a tourist hotel to be built in Kilimbit to rival Maliwan's Wombun tourist attraction. In the second project, Martin, again promising K700 for the work, had arranged for the men of Indingai and Wombun to enlarge a channel from Chambri to the Sepik River, a channel often impassable for the tourist speed boats during the dry season. In both cases, the work was done but Martin, it was claimed, simply pocketed the money, spending it on himself. After leaving government service in the wake of vociferous Chambri complaints, he began a construction business in the West Sepik, borrowing money from locals in order to buy a car, a truck, and other equipment. When, according to our Chambri sources, it was discovered that no actual business existed, he fled to Port Moresby, one step ahead of his angry creditors. After about a year there, he was arrested and sent to jail in the West Sepik for fraud.

In our conversation, Martin only alluded to these events, referring to them as "my downfall." He did describe in some detail his time in Port Moresby, saying: "All people suffer in their lives, but when I was in Moresby, I suffered terribly." For a time he had no place to live. He went to the house of his wife's brother – John Illumbui, in fact – who, having heard of Martin's misdeeds toward Chambri said, according to Martin: "Don't waste my time." Martin continued: "He would not have anything to do with me. I wandered around in dirty wet clothes for many nights, talking to prostitutes, who seemed like my friends." Finally, he applied and was admitted to the National Music School, "because I had some interest in music but mostly because I wanted a roof over my head and some bread from the government."

At the music school he was taught to write his own music and he did in fact compose a number of songs. One song written simply for the commercial market was about "desire" and was in Pidgin English. His other songs were a "matter of self-expression," and were in English because he found that language more suitable than Pidgin for expressing his feelings. Among these latter songs was the romantic "I Want You To Be My Girl." (This song included the lines "I want to settle down with you; I want to live my life with you.") One was the searching "Can Somebody Please Tell the Truth." (This included the lines "Sometimes I wonder what the hell I am doing in this world; Can somebody please tell me?") And one, written for a benefit for Solomon Island cyclone victims, was the empathetic "Let's Help Each Other." (This included the lines "Let us eat, drink and be merry, for we don't know what tomorrow has in store; If our brothers fall on the way, let us stop and help them along.")

We talked about the considerable difference between his songs of self-expression and traditional Chambri songs, which, aside from often stylized laments, were recitations of clan ancestral names, places and powers.[30] Chambri music did not seem to be a source of inspiration to him, although certain events of his own Chambri past did affect him, particularly as they suggested that this past was forever behind him. In fact, his favorite composition, which he thought might "reveal too much about myself," was the reminiscent, "Childhood Days," a song we thought nicely captured some of the everyday experiences by which children became Chambri:

Verse: Walking up the rocky path together.
            Pumping little lizards with small bows and arrows.
            Playing as I like in the trees and in the lake.
            Having spearing contests on the mountain trail.
Chorus: Those were my childhood days.
            But, they're really gone forever.
            Living in another time.
            Oh, what a sad story this is.
            Wish I was back in my childhood days.
Verse: Hunting birds along the mountain path.
            Getting eggs in baskets two at a time.
            Eating local fruits from season to season.
            Playing soccer games without no rules.

When we told Martin that no other Chambri had expressed to us his sense of the past as irrevocably lost, he agreed that his experience was exceptional and had distanced him from other Chambri. Moreover, he had suffered disgrace in their eyes. "I have," he said, "lost status since my downfall." He elaborated: "When I was young, I always got everything I wanted; in school I was smart but as soon as I got out in the world, I tumbled."

At the time of our conversation, Martin was out of jail on bail, his court case was still to be resolved. He said that he had lost all ambition for himself, and only wanted "peace." He regretted that he had "never been happily married" because he had never been able to "really talk" to his wife. Although his wife had two years of high school she did not use her education and that, Martin thought, was equivalent to never having had it.

He continued in his expressions of resignation to his changed circumstances by saying he had recommitted himself to Christ. He had remained a Catholic because the Catholic Church, more than any other, provided "order." If he were to pursue an earlier ambition of going into politics, it would be to help him express his "vision" for people "to live in a good house, have clean clothes, clean body, good food and the capacity to educate their kids."

Martin did, in fact, soon decide to stand as one of five candidates from the district that included Chambri Island for election to the provincial parliament. In designing his strategy, he realized that, apart from the Chambri villages, he was not well known in the district and that he had only enough money for one campaign trip. He therefore decided to distinguish himself among his opponents by the length and quality of his platform statement. Whereas his rivals distributed fliers describing their entire plat-form in three or four brief (Pidgin English) sentences, e.g., "I will help youth employment," Martin intended to distribute copies of a thirteen-page typed document describing in detail his position on development. He hoped to arouse sufficient interest during his single campaign sweep so that voters would subsequently peruse the document; he hoped that even those unable to read would be impressed by the extent of his thought. The document (here translated from Pidgin English, but preserving his format and emphases) began as follows:

Dear all brothers and sisters,
Greetings to you all, to the old people, the mothers and fathers, the young men and women and the children. And may God bless you all.
I am one of your candidates and I wish to speak to you about WHAT IS MY VISION, THE ROOT OF MY BELIEF CONCERNING:
1.WHAT KIND OF DEVELOPMENT THAT ALL OF US MUST WORK HARD FOR.
2.THE TRUE STRAIGHT WAY OF LEARNING WHAT KIND OF DEVELOPMENT THAT PEOPLE REALLY NEED AND MUST HAVE IN ORDER TO MAKE THEIR LIVES GOOD AND EASY AND GIVE THEM HAPPINESS AND COMFORT.
3.WHAT KIND OF LEADER IS SUFFICIENT TO BRING ABOUT THIS TRUE DEVELOPMENT.

The document amplified each of these points in turn, arguing overall that "human development" must be defined as the capacity for each person to realize basic needs. These needs were listed in his platform as follows: food, clothes, a good house, good health, education for children, a means to earn money, a means to save money, respect for elders, law and order, a transport system, a good communication network, the practice of liking each other, good water to drink, the practice of working hard, humility, good leaders. Each of these needs was then discussed separately. For example, under the heading "Good Health" Martin explained:

Good health develops if we eat well, sleep well, exercise, refrain from chewing betel nut and smoking too much and take medicine when we are sick. Every house must have a first-aid kit which will enable us to take care of all small illnesses and cuts. The Health Department must write a little first-aid pamphlet to distribute to everyone so that they will become aware of how to take care of themselves. We must become our own doctors when we have small illnesses. We cannot have many people wasting time by going to the hospital and making our hospitals over-crowded. Finally, we must have enough health centers and aid posts to serve us all.

Martin stated in his platform that only through the efforts of a new kind of well-educated leader could such goals be achieved. Present leaders thought only of themselves and not of development; they had no real plans. Moreover, the work of government and business had become complex and required an understanding of English. It was now time to elect "young blood" as leaders. However, older men must continue to advise the younger. A good leader did more than follow his own ideas: he must listen to the genuine concerns of the people. A true leader was not concerned with bringing honor to his name; he was a servant of God, more afraid of God than of other men; he was to speak out against bad customs and to lead by example.

Martin also knew, however, that he would not win the election on the reasonability of his platform alone. He believed that voters were decisively affected by magic that could attract them, as might a magnet, to a particular candidate while blinding them to that candidate's defects. Although he was having his father work magic for him at Chambri, he was afraid that his rivals had access to more effective forms than he. Moreover, as a candidate, Martin considered himself to be the target of sorcery and his life to be in danger: he told us, for instance, that he had refused the offer of magical help from a particular Chambri, fearing that the magic proffered was actually intended to disable him.

Martin was sustained at this time by his belief in God and by reliance on the teachings of Dale Carnegie, whose book, *How to Win Friends and Influence People*,[31] he had acquired in Port Moresby. Drawing on what he had learned from this book, he said: "If you could make people feel important, then they would do anything for you." His plan was to approach all the sorcerers working for the other candidates and explain to them what must happen if development was to occur. He would then say: "You are a good man, a man of intelligence and a man of power, but you have been using your power in the wrong way. You must use your importance for important things."

He told us that even if he did lose, he was going to leave Wewak and go home to Chambri where he could become "re-educated in our good traditional ways." (Significantly, he first learned during this campaign, while inquiring about the magic he would need as a candidate, that the extensive paraphernalia always on display around the central post of his father's house belonged to a major ritual complex controlled by his own clan.)

Martin came in last in the election: he never did become much known outside of Chambri and even there he was, because of the enmity he had created earlier, not given much support beyond his own family. Although he argued that he would bring develop-ment, most Chambri thought that he was interested only in advancing his own interests. Nor did he go home to Chambri to live. When we last spoke to him, he had returned to his job in Wewak as a musician and had begun to give guitar lessons. He admitted rather wryly that he had forgotten just how many mosquitoes there were at Chambri; and he acknowledged, too, that he had grown accustomed to the comforts – "the little bags of sugar" – of the town.

About a month after the results of the provincial election were announced on the radio, Chambri were again listening intently to the results of another provincial contest. District by district, the names were announced of the relatively few children who had been admitted to grade seven on the basis of a nationally adminis-tered examination. The parents of the four (out of forty) Chambri chosen were elated because their children might yet acquire sufficient education to qualify them for well-paying jobs in town:

these would be jobs of the sort that both John Illumbui and Martin Gawi had gotten.

However, most Chambri thought that John and Martin had used the opportunities provided by development to move beyond Chambri in quite different ways: John had affirmed his ties with Chambri by remitting to them; Martin had negated his ties with Chambri by extracting from them. More than a failed remitter, more than simply a corrupt government official, Martin was a betrayer. Chambri expected that those in government, including Chambri, would frequently fail to deliver on promises and would intercept government funds for personal use; but they also expected that Chambri in government would channel funds and benefits and a portion of their gains to other Chambri. By providing government projects that appeared to benefit the Chambri, that is, appeared to further their development, but instead benefited primarily only himself, Martin had duped them. He used his government position, they thought, not to provide a conduit from the government to them, as a Chambri politician should, but to provide a conduit from them to himself. As someone who turned against his own people, he was likely at least periodically to be viewed and to view himself as a non-Chambri.

Nonetheless, not even in this extreme case were the Chambri and Martin free from a yet continuing history of mutual entailment: his father and a scattering of others had supported him in his political campaign; Martin had expressed pride in furnishing bail for his brother and had relied on his father's magical help. And, although his sense of self was much more individualistic – certainly more subjectivistic – than was usual for Chambri, many of his images of happiness and success still referred to Chambri. (It may be recalled that he wanted a wife to whom he could express his inner feelings.) On occasion he saw himself back in his kin group, learning kin lore; at other times he saw himself immersed in a Chambri community, albeit a community that his political vision had helped change.

Alternately detached from and engaged in Chambri affairs as well as alternately enjoying the stimulation and recognition provided by the heterogeneous acquaintances met through his work at the hotel and craving the peace and order of a quiet life without ambition, Martin appeared the most psychologically complex, certainly the most articulately introspective, Chambri we knew. Perhaps our most telling image of him was from the occasion that brought John Illumbui to Wewak, the first communion of his sister's daughter. While John and his sister – Martin's wife – were tying K2 bills to packets of pork for distribution in celebration of the event, Martin, seemingly unconcerned with arranging for a counter-presentation, was sitting in the corner with his youngest daughter, rehearsing "Moon River" on the guitar. This was to be played later as dinner music for the Western guests at the hotel.

We have suggested that the contrast between life at Chambri and life in town provided the basis for Chambri to visualize and appraise the possibilities that were following from development. The perceptions Chambri had of what development should be, or should not be, varied, as we have seen, according to their particular circumstances. Thus, for Rex, Gabriella and others in town who sought to evade the coercion of Chambri big men, development meant a welcome freedom. Members of the senior generation living at Chambri, however, saw the freedom of those in town as enabling them to avoid useful work and to absorb remittances which otherwise would have supported, for instance, the important ceremonies on which big men based their political reputations. Opinion was, to be sure, less divided on someone like John Illumbui. Although, as we have seen, some criticized him for withholding resources, most Chambri, both at home and in town, regarded him as embodying one of the desirable possibilities that development offered. Yet, despite the disagreements over whether the lives of Rex, Gabriella, and John represented changes for the better, no one disputed that they were still thoroughly Chambri, still entirely embedded in twisted histories with other Chambri.

Although Rex, Gabriella, and John may have wished to evade or buffer certain of their obligations to other Chambri, they had not indeed repudiated the system that generated their entailments and thereby determined their identity. Thus, for example, when John told the senior men in Wewak that he was giving them a party because he owed what he had become to them, he was acknowledging as fact that theirs was a relationship of mutual dependency. He was affirming that the processes of development and the life he had come to lead in a distant town had not created incommensurate differences between him and other Chambri.

By comparison, Martin was the only Chambri we knew who had thought about himself even briefly as a non-Chambri, who had in actuality rejected ties of mutual obligation and had acted as though the differences between him and Chambri were so incommensurate that he owed them nothing at all. But even he, the most Western of the Chambri we have known, was still held within the Chambri ambit by his continuing perception that Chambri, the source of his memories of his childhood days, was the center of efficacy, order and significance.

This chapter has been about the ideas and experiences of development that have compelled various Chambri to leave home in search of what they viewed as a changed and better life. Few have, in any sense, gone very far. In the next chapter, we turn to the effects these ideas and experiences of development have had on those who chose to remain at home.

4
Western representations at home

None of those Chambri living in Wewak and beyond whom we have described was free from the pull of the society that provided each with elements crucial for personal definition. John Illumbui acknowledged explicitly the strength of the pull; Martin, despite his efforts to cultivate a subjectivistic individualism, never could entirely deny it. They were, as were virtually all Chambri, inextricably involved in twisted histories, in recursive relations of entailment, that tied them to those living and dead at Chambri Island. That the links of entailment led back to Chambri Island was not, however, just because until rather recently all Chambri had lived there. It was also because the ancestors from whom Chambri derived major aspects of their personal identity were literally grounded at Chambri. As "The Story of the Founding of the Walindimi Men's House" has already demonstrated with respect to Maliwan and his long-dead predecessor, Yerenowi, Chambri viewed their relationships and powers in terms of, and as stemming from, those of their ancestors.

Hence, it was only *with* other Chambri that the entwined relationships that located and constituted the self could be satisfactorily enacted[1] and it was *at* Chambri that the social relationships of entailment originated and had the greatest density. Furthermore, only at Chambri itself could the relations with the ancestors and their powers be established. (Individuals away from Chambri relied on relatives at home to mobilize ancestral support for them.) Thus, regardless of whether Chambri were residing at home, intended to visit home, enjoyed being home (some, like Martin, had missed their "little bags of sugar"), or felt that their lives were in danger at home, Chambri Island, people and place, remained their essential reference point, and the basis for individual and collective viability.[2]

Chambri were, as well, adamant that Chambri Island remain their primary reference point. As one middle-aged man told us: "All Chambri *must* eventually return home." Even in death and regardless of misdeeds, he continued, Chambri were always "children of Chambri." Chambri dying away from Chambri Island "must" be brought back so that they could be buried with their ancestors and so that their mourners, that is, those already at Chambri and those who would return for their funerals, could, at the very least, express regrets to them that they had died away from home and (as the case might be) alone. Buried at Chambri, they would themselves become part of an ancestral presence that would persist as the ultimate source of connection and efficacy for living Chambri.[3]

Yet, while pulled to the people and place of Chambri as the enduring source of identity, those such as Rex and Gabriella might, since pacification and the advent of the towns, also be sent into flight because they were vulnerable to coercion by elders attempting to establish reputations as Chambri of power – as big men.[4] Their impetus to escape from what they experienced as the negative aspects of tradition was sustained and shaped by largely Western representations, those of "freedom" – essentially, freedom of choice – and of "youth" to which Rex had referred.

In this chapter we will further explore these representations of freedom and youth that did more than simply send individuals in flight from Chambri. We will show how these representations were coming home to Chambri in ways that portended change in the system. Our focus will be on an internal negotiation at Chambri itself, between youth and their seniors, between those distinguished, as were initiates from hazers, by their different positions in the system of commensurate differences. How did those youth at Chambri who directly encountered the system of traditional inequalities, in a way that Rex and Gabriella did not, respond to and employ these new ideas of freedom and youth? And what implications for the shape of future political activity at home did this confrontation between generations raise?[5]

We will now see in the life, death and burial of Nick Ambri, a young rock and roll singer who had been living at Chambri, an intergenerational conflict, difficult, if not impossible, to resolve. Moreover, we will also suggest that the full implications of the new ideas had not, as yet, become manifest.

Nick Ambri, a Chambri James Dean

We first heard about Nick in Wewak from Kenut Manjintimi, a teenaged Chambri friend of ours who lived near us in the Camp. Although Kenut liked listening to our tapes of American rock and roll, he insisted that the music of his favorite Chambri musician, Nick Ambri, was as good as could be found anywhere. (The only musician he liked better than Nick was Stevie Wonder. Kenut's near-blindness made him identify strongly with Stevie Wonder to whom he wrote a letter, counter-signed by his teacher to attest to its veracity. In the letter he explained his medical situation and asked for a pair of dark glasses comparable to those Wonder wore.)

Rex, telling us earlier of the repressive actions of Chambri big men, had also mentioned Nick. It was over performances of Nick's Yerameri Drifters Band that the big men had instituted a ban on all-night dances. (The name of the band suggested a double alienation. To that of the drifter was added that of the exile: Yerameri was the bush road leading to the settlement on the Korosameri River established years before by Wombun villagers when they fled from Iatmul raiders.)

Chambri youth in Wewak, we discovered, frequently sang Nick's songs, sometimes to the accompaniment of cassettes they had made of him and his band. His songs blended traditional and modern elements: the lyrics set to string-band music consisted of a brief Chambri phrase repeated over and over, yet they were concerned with themes of love and rebellion. The following eight songs (in translation) were the entire corpus of Nick's music:

1. Come here. [This was addressed to his girl friend.]
2. Father, mother, I don't belong here.
3. Mama said slow down. [But he did not listen.]
4. Mama said so. [But he did not listen.]
5. She follows me when I walk about. [This referred to the devotion of his girl friend.]
6. You're too loud. [This was what the big men said about his music.]
7. You don't want to wait for your boy friend. [He was trying to convince a woman to reject the man arranged for her as husband and to accept him.]
8. Bernadette. [This was the name of his girlfriend, later his wife.]

It was clear to us that the power for Chambri youth of these songs of love and rebellion came in significant part from the circumstances of Nick's own life. Whereas many young men and women had fled Chambri, as had Gabriella and Rex, rather than be subject to arranged marriages or other forms of coercion, Nick, after attending vocational school in Madang for a year, had chosen to remain at Chambri and challenge his elders. He had, we discovered, defied his father by marrying Bernadette, the woman of his own choice. His subsequent and lamentable, although in Chambri thought quite predictable, death epitomized for these young Chambri the problems they faced as youths living at home. Consider, for instance, the following (translated) passage from the eulogy written by three of Nick's friends, who were also members of his band, and read aloud, outside the Walindimi men's house, at Nick's funeral: "Nick was a man who liked his friends. He was a man who fought for the rights of all young men and women. Mainly he helped his mates through all kinds of trouble. He was a man who was not afraid to face the problems that met him."[6]

Our most vivid account of Nick, his circumstances and eventual death was provided at Chambri, some six months after his funeral, by a young man, Theo Pekur, in answer to our question, "What kind of man was Nick Ambri?" The coherence of Theo's response, certainly relative to other accounts we heard from him, strongly suggests that the events of Nick's life had been told, retold, pondered and discussed. Indeed, in the course of answering our question, Theo provided something of a youth manifesto. Evidently, Nick's life, as Theo and his friends had come to understand it, embodied and clarified their sense of themselves, their problems and the possible solution to those problems. Theo's text that follows (which we have transcribed and translated) is, we believe, a revealing exposition of the perspectives Chambri youth had about what their lives were and about what their lives should be.

Nick was my best friend. My mother and his mother are sisters belonging to the clan of the black cockatoo. Nick and I were born on the same day and, because of this, we were in the relationship called "one play [age mates]." We were born in 1960. A great many people were born on that day: Herman Kaui, Robert Ason. Robert was born first. Pat Yambunapan, the one now married to Camilus Kaui, was born slightly later. But she grew faster and was ahead in school. Nick also started school before I did. He was in Grade 6 when I was in Grade 5. I saw my baptism record at the Father's house and it was right next to Nick's.

The day before he died, Nick called a meeting of all the youth. It was a Wednesday when he called us all together. He told us that we should start a sago business and sell sago to make money for the youth. But then he said: "Never mind, that kind of business is too much work. Let's start an artifact business and sell carvings to tourists for K5 and K10 and earn money this way." Then he said: "Never mind, what we have to do is various small jobs around the village to earn money." Then he said: "It doesn't matter. I am going away alone, and if I come back I will look at you as if I were a tourist."

All of us thought that this was very strange talk. So we thought we'd go into the men's house to practice our guitar songs for church. When we were there, Nick said to us that we should take care of his string band because he was going to leave us. One boy asked him why he was saying all of these crazy things. He answered that he was not lying to us, that he really was going away.

Nick then went home and told his wife that the next day he planned to cut the posts he would need to build his house on his own land. [Because of the enmity of his father, Nick was temporarily living with his father-in-law, away from his own clan land.] He awoke the next morning very hungry and went to his mother who gave him the head of a fish. She had given the tail of this fish to Nick's father earlier, before he left for [the Patrol Post of] Pagwi. She wasn't thinking. She should not have given Nick part of a fish that his father had eaten.

After eating, Nick, his mother and several of his sisters went in his father's canoe to the clan land around the back of Chambri Island towards Aibom. Nick [because he had married against his father's wishes] had been forbidden by his father to use this canoe, or to use clan land, or anything else belonging to his father. He was, however, allowed to come inside his father's house to visit his mother. They moored the canoe and cut the posts. Nick's sisters carried them back to the canoe. As they were doing this, Nick went into the bush to cut wood suitable to make carvings. Some think that it was at this time that a spirit met him. His mother [later realized that she] saw in the distance a small man with red flowers in his hair, swinging a hatchet toward Nick and knew that this was not a real man, but a devil-man activated by magical power.[7]

After Nick returned to the canoe with the carving wood, he told his mother that he did not feel well. His mother said: "Why not? You didn't work that hard."

His sisters had walked home on the road after putting the posts in the canoe. He and his mother got into the canoe to paddle it home. Along the way, he told his mother that he was feeling very hot and wanted to cool his body. But they had arrived at a place where magical crocodiles live and his mother advised him not to enter the water there. He had with him a yellow hard hat, given him by a relative who had worked at the

Bougainville mine, which he used to scoop up water and dump it over his head. He was very thirsty and drank a lot of water.

Nick decided to get out of the canoe at the beginning of Wombun and walk home. His mother continued in it. He walked as far as the Kamanimbit men's house, where he entered the lake to cool himself. Still thirsty, he opened a green coconut and drank its milk.

Arriving at where his mother left the canoe, he began to lift out the posts, but felt too sick and told his brother that he couldn't complete the job. Instead, he went to the house of his father-in-law where he knew his wife would be. He told his wife that he was very cold. She helped him put on shoes, socks, long trousers, a T-shirt and a coat.

He then went to sleep. When he awakened, he saw a can of fish that his wife had bought. He told her to open it because he wanted some. She said that she had purchased it to take with her when she went to the bush to make sago. He told her: "Never mind, I want to eat it now. I am going to be leaving you now." So, his wife opened the fish, and got four plates so that the whole family could share it. Nick said to her: "Put three plates back. We will all eat from one plate." He put each of his daughters on a knee and the one plate of fish in the center between him and his wife. They all ate the fish from one plate. After he finished eating, he said that he would like to sleep some more.

About midnight, he got up and began to act crazy. He was trying to box as if there was a man there to fight with. Then he shrank back, crying: "Don't hit me! Don't hit me!" He did the same thing again, until he began to shake all over. When he stopped shaking, he clenched his teeth and was unable to talk. They tried to get a spoon into his mouth, but couldn't.

Father Dwyer [a visiting Catholic priest] was spending the night at Chambri. We asked him to help us by taking Nick to the aid post at Timbunke [a mission station] in his speedboat. But the Sisters there could do nothing for him. They sent him to Wewak in an ambulance. He was admitted to the hospital and seemed to get better. He told Kony [a hospital orderly originally from Wombun], who had been sitting up with him, that he should go and wash. When Kony was away doing this, Nick died. It was about midnight.

Rather than putting his body in the morgue, Kony brought it to Chambri Camp where people mourned and sang over it all night. The next day Kony and others took the body home to Wombun. They had radioed Chambri on the mission wireless about what had happened. People found out at the market on Saturday. As soon as they heard about the death, the market broke up. Everyone just went home.

A boy from each of the villages returned to Chambri with the body. As soon as it came, people from the different villages performed different tasks: Indingai took the body from the canoe; Kilimbit played Nick's string band music. Then his body was carried into the Walindimi men's house and a church service was held right outside. Afterwards they carried the body to the house of his father-in-law where everyone mourned. Finally, they took him to the house of his father and mother. The house was filled with people – too many to put the body down, so they held it up in the air. Very soon the body began to smell and so they carried it to the graveyard and buried it. People who went to the graveyard were careful not to wear shoes or sandals or anything to which earth might adhere, lest Nick's spirit come back with them from the graveyard.

Nick was a good man. He gave people betel nuts and betel peppers. At parties for the youth, he would cook food and generously distribute it to everyone. He was not afraid to defy the big men when they told him whom he could or could not marry. He told the big men that we should be allowed to marry whom we choose because we are young lives.

His father was responsible for his death. His father didn't want him to marry Bernadette. One night when Nick's father and others were drinking, Nick's father promised that Nick would never marry Pombank's daughter [Bernadette]. But Nick insisted that he marry her because he already had made her pregnant. [Pombank, a church leader and catechist, insisted that the marriage take place.] Nick's father won't remain alive long now. Nick will fight back from the grave.

There was a big meeting after Nick died at which two pigs were killed, one by Peter Pombank and the other by Nick's father. These pigs had been magically treated. All the big men of all three villages were invited to come and eat. The food would stick in the sorcerer's throat. Nick's father ate and he was all right, but this was only because he must have hired someone else to do the sorcery. He killed Nick, all right.

In Theo's view, a special bond, that of best friend, existed between him and Nick largely because they were of precisely the same generation. The other special source of solidarity between them derived from their matrilateral relationship: their mothers were clan sisters. Indeed, it was through emphasizing the relatively inclusive generational and matrilateral ties, that young men and women throughout the three villages of Chambri could acquire the commonalty which linked them as youth, as "young lives." And this was so despite the fact that they belonged to over thirty distinct patriclans.

Moreover, Nick's deadly confrontation with his father had been engendered in part by the system of competition existing between these distinct patriclans. Any senior man with political aspirations would seek to gain renown as the leader of a powerful clan by displaying and augmenting his power through skillful manipulation of marriage relationships. As an essential component of this strategy, he had to coerce or otherwise control his children so that they made the marriages which furthered his alliances and interests as clan leader.[8] For Nick and those of his generation, Western concepts, such as those that defined modern personhood at least partly in terms of freedom to make choices, served to exacerbate their resentment at being controlled by their senior clansmen. These concepts also provided them with an ideological justification for resisting that control. In addition, the Western concept of "youth" itself became adopted as a useful term to denote those who found Western representations, especially those of freedom of choice, compelling. (Such a definition of youth gave rise to the logical possibility envisioned by one of our Chambri friends in his forties, that "old people can be youths.")

These Western representations, again especially that of free-dom of choice, were presented to Chambri in contexts ranging from Catholic Church teachings about the freely entered "Chris-tian marriage" to popular literature, music and advertising about the importance of fulfilling desire and romance. Thus, in this latter regard, a typical advertisement in a Papua New Guinea newspaper or magazine might be for the very expensive Nissan 280ZX. Depicted with two attractive Papua New Guinea women draped on hood and trunk, the Pidgin English caption (translated) stated that "it should be acquired by everyone who wishes to have a good time"(Mathie and Cox, 1987: 17).

Not only Chambri in town but also those living at home were thoroughly familiar with these publications. Indeed, many young men at Chambri pinned sexy photographs such as bathing-suit advertisements to the walls near the sleeping areas allocated to them by their fathers. Sometimes they added a text to these pictures, also clipped from magazines. For example, in one display of fifty or more photographs, a picture of several young Asian women in bikinis had affixed to it, by way of caption, a clipping with the words: "At what age did you first have sexual inter-course?" Another, of a woman sitting astraddle a man's lap, had scrawled on it, in Pidgin: "Look at the two of them!" (Young women also clipped pictures from magazines, although they did not post them. One showed us her collection, which she kept in an old school notebook: it consisted of white women, posed in romantic settings such as rose gardens, wearing formal, frilly dresses – frequently bridal gowns. She had underlined several of the captions, including: "With the rustle of silk and the hint of tulle, you will be the envy of all single girls. Make sure you choose the dress of your dreams on your wedding day.") Thus, from the point of view of Chambri youth, Nick's decision to risk alienation from his father by marrying the girl to whom he had himself been drawn, the girl he had himself chosen, was not at all peculiar.

However, decidedly peculiar and certainly the most perplexing to the Chambri of Nick's actions (and probably an early symptom of cerebral malaria) was his promise that if he returned it would be to gaze at them as though he were a tourist. It should be remembered that Chambri were troubled when, during Maliwan's initiation, the tourists objectified them by regarding them as commodities to be chosen or not, to be taken or left. Nick's vision of himself as a disconnected tourist, one who came and went exactly as he chose, without significant involvement or interaction, would be, thus, for the Chambri, an image of alienation and revolt, extreme to the point of virtual incomprehensibility. (It would be an image that surpassed any Martin in his alienation was able to construct.)

Yet, we should also note that Nick's image of himself as a disconnected tourist *was* consistent with the images of choice presented in the Western representations to which youth were responding. (We will return to this point later in thinking about the Chambri future.) Although Nick and his friends were probably unaware of it, the representations of modern personhood focusing on choice that now prompted Chambri youth to defy their seniors were in fact a product of the tourists' own class-based system of incommensurate differences in which Chambri were defined as inherently unequal.

Regardless of whether they regarded Nick as having been truly driven to the point of tourism or not, his mother and sisters sympathized with him, thinking that his father had gone too far.[9] Thus, they supported him in his plan to leave his father-in-law's house and build a new house for himself with clan-owned materials on clan land. This was both a refusal to capitulate to his father who had rejected him, and a reaffirmation of himself as a loyal clansman, despite all that had happened. Not only did his mother and sisters help him cut the posts, his mother gave him a portion of a fish that the father had left. In this latter regard, Nick's mother's wish to help him may have backfired for it led her to transgress an important taboo, a taboo reflecting cultural recognition of this intergenerational tension. Father and eldest son must not share food or eating utensils lest the father get sick. Thus, to judge from Theo's account, the mother's action in sustaining Nick with food to the detriment of his father's vitality may have caused the father to activate the devil-man.

Because it epitomized the intergenerational conflict inherent in Chambri patrilineality, Nick's death was upsetting not only to the young Chambri who shared his particular life circumstances, but to all Chambri. Older women (comprising most of those present at the weekly market which disbanded with news of Nick's death), who, after all, bore sons for clans not their own, were much more concerned for the welfare of their sons than for the political standing of particular clans: they would find Nick's death an attack on them as mothers.[10] Older men would recognize that in his efforts to create a strong clan, Nick's father had, by ensorcelling his son, negated the very principle of clan unity. He had, moreover, reversed the appropriate relationships between the living and the dead by introducing into the world of his deceased ancestors, committed to his support, the spirit of his dead son, committed to his destruction.

Theo's account portrayed Nick as very different from his father. Nick was the leader of a new social category, Chambri youth, which defined itself as united through the structural principles of matrilaterality and shared generation that subsumed particularistic clan loyalties. They were united through interest in earning money to support their activities including those of their rock and roll band. And, of most importance, they were united in their insistence on controlling their own marriage choices. However, in defining their interests as opposed to those of senior males, especially concerning control over marriage choices, these youths were not denying the importance of social entailment. Nick, for example, despite defiance of his father's wishes, was living with his in-laws, maintaining close relationships with his mother and sisters and working to re-establish himself as clan member in good standing.

Hence, while Nick and others of his generation were powerfully affected by Western representations that defined youth in terms of desire, romance and freedom of marital choice, they also remained immersed in social networks which still defined them as *Chambri* youth. Yet, because the disagreement between youth and senior men was substantial, because it focused on an area of great importance to both, and because it was taking place at Chambri itself, Nick's death would remain an unsettled and unsettling preoccupation. To this extent at least, as we will see in the following description of Nick's final burial rites, Theo was right: Nick would fight back from the grave. The antagonisms between generations that his death had made manifest would not be stilled with his burial. Nor had the implications of those Western representations that had inspired his intransigence run their full course.

The final ritual for Nick to "finish a worry"

In November 1987, some six months after Nick's death, a final ritual, the *tsem mijanko*, which meant "to finish worry," was staged. (This was held immediately after Maliwan's initiation; for reasons later to be explained, there was an intentional overlap between them.) As the name suggests, the events during the several days of *tsem mijanko* were meant to resolve grief and conflict. During this final ritual, the relations and sentiments that had been brought forth by Nick's life were to be evoked, culminated and dissipated in a process whereby Nick was deconstituted into the elements which had composed him, including the ancestral power he had incorporated during his initiation. Nick's *tsem mijanko* was, in other words, intended to finish worries by running back through the social and cosmological processes that had produced and been produced by him. In the ceremony Chambri youth made evident that they and Nick's music had been essential constituents of Nick's life.

In brief, the ritual would begin with the mourners, hair shorn and covered with mud, grieving over Nick's personal effects and over a mask containing his spirit. The ritual would end with the mourners, by that time bathed, dispersing these personal effects into the river, bringing the mask into the men's house so that Nick's spirit could be installed there and then engaging in a series of terminating presentations of money and food. Hundreds (as with Maliwan's initiation) would enlist in a ceremony which coalesced a plurality of interests defined by a plurality of relationships. Taking part would be Nick's extended family on both his mother's and father's sides and many of their kin including in-laws; Nick's wife and her family; those who had assisted as *tsambunwuro* in Nick's initiation and in the initiations of his other clansmen; all those of his men's house; those of the eight clans who had ritual prerogatives connected to the playing of a complex of seven flutes and a hand-drum; those of the Yambuntimeri and Pombiantimeri initiatory moieties; senior men from the three villages; Maliwan and the new initiates and their patrilateral and matrilateral kin; and many more, including two anthropologists. And, perhaps of most relevance for the future, young men and women would participate, not only as kin of various sorts, but as youth.

Indeed, anyone who wished to take part in Nick's last rites could do so and in a variety of ways. Such a Chambri ceremony would almost necessarily be inclusive. The ritual was about the social reality that was Nick and, given the ramifying nature of Chambri social relationships, virtually everyone was, or could easily claim to be, connected with Nick.[11] Because Nick, like other Chambri, had been constituted through a complexity of social relationships, so too the process by which he was deconstituted would elicit a comparable complexity. (In this regard, the construction of Maliwan's sons as men through initiation could be seen as at least a partial mirror of the deconstruction of Nick through his last rites.) The ritual was, as well, politically tangled for it provided far more than a measure of the sponsor's efficacy. It also became a context in which various people, including youth, made assertions about their own efficacy by laying claim to a role of special importance in having constituted Nick.

Significantly, through engaging in a ritual that defined efficacy as the capacity to affect social entailments, the youth were subscribing to and endorsing the Chambri system of commensurate differences. By asserting in this context that they were a group to be reckoned with at Chambri, by claiming Nick as their own within a ritual that was largely about the social entailments which had constituted him, the youth were *not* responding according to the logic of commodities, that of objectification and socially disembodied choice, which had engendered the Western representations of choice to which they were drawn.

In the following account of the *tsem mijanko*, it is important to note that the mourning for Nick took place in his father's house, as would have been the case if there had been no enmity between them. The central post of the house had been decorated with flowers and other foliage. In front of this was a small shrine consisting of a low table on which had been arranged a cross, a picture of the Virgin Mary, a plastic bag containing Nick's shoes and other items of apparel, and some of his personal effects including one of his prized possessions, a World War II artillery shell. This was filled with flowers and foliage associated with his clan. Above the table, attached to the house post, was a *mwai* mask provided by Nick's mother's brother and containing his spirit.[12]

The display also included items for his last journey: a shirt and a string bag containing necessities such as a comb, soap, powder, betel nuts and peppers, lime powder, and tobacco, all of which Nick's sisters had provided. For their part, his in-laws had contributed two large washtubs filled and surrounded with food: coconuts, watermelons, bags of rice and sugar, large bunches of bananas, cans of fish and clusters of betel nuts.

By mid-afternoon when we arrived, the house was already packed and still filling. Most men and women paused on entering to have their hair cut and have mud rubbed on their faces and bodies. They then took their seats around the periphery of the room. Nick's female kin, the usual principal mourners on such an occasion, were already gathered before the central shrine. His wife, sisters and clan sisters, his mother and her sisters and clan sisters, and his mother's mother had for several hours been caressing his effects, laying their heads on the table, wailing and singing dirges.

Nick's mother sang: "You must come and get me. It is not good if I stay and you are gone"; "You can't leave me. What will I do when I see your age mates?"; "Everything we gave to him must be destroyed and discarded tomorrow. He is not coming back." A sister sang: "You stayed a long way from your father and mother [referring to Nick's living with his in-laws] and then you worried about them. You came home and died." A matrilateral aunt sang: "It was the first time that you broke the taboo [placed upon him by his father concerning the use of clan property] and then you died." These latter songs were only some of the explicit references made during the ceremony to the circumstances of Nick's death.

Outside, a more temporary and different sort of shrine, a *sirilkam*, had been constructed by Nick's father and clan brothers. In many regards, this shrine was Nick's effigy. About the height of a man, it consisted of a center of coconut fronds and totemic plants significant to Nick's matrilateral kin. To these had been added the various implements marking Nick's adult economic and ritual status: his fish spear, pig spear, spear thrower, canoe paddle and, from his initiation, his spear–lime holder. In addition, there was a coconut-leaf broom and a woven food basket, representing his adult obligation to sweep the men's house and carry food there.

Very early the following morning, this shrine would be (and was) dismantled with the objects distributed to his clan brothers. At the same time, the fronds and other plants would be removed, tossed into the air, to "free Nick's spirit." The clan brothers would then burn the fronds and totemic plants and, in the resulting fire, cook bananas and sago to be eaten by Nick's female matrilateral kin – his "mothers" – when they returned at dawn from washing the mud of mourning from their bodies.

Thus, in these among other ways, Nick would be deconstructed in death: the objects that defined him economically and ritually as an adult, as a full member of his father's clan, would go to members of this clan; the contribution from his matrilateral kin of the totemic power and food that had nurtured him would be returned by his clan to his "mothers."[13]

On this second day there was again ritual within Nick's father's house. Women continued to mourn throughout the afternoon and night around the shrine containing Nick's effects and the *mwai* mask. Men, however, who had been sitting on the peripheries of the house, began drifting away in late afternoon. Most headed to the Walindimi men's house where they awaited the arrival of a set of seven transverse bamboo flutes and a hand drum. These, constituting Waykumbunmank and her family, would when played manifest the primordial power, the force-field, that characterized and maintained Wombun village.[14] (Each of the three villages had a comparable, although distinct, set of seven flutes and powers.) Others joined the men already assembled in Mindimbit, the small men's house at the farthest extreme of Wombun. There Waykumbunmank and her family were played and their powers thus activated. Next, the flutes and drum were carried by a procession of Pombiantimeri men to the small men's house near Nick's father's house, where they were again played for about twenty minutes, and then to Walindimi, where they would be played all night. These men – who belonged to the moiety responsible for initiating Nick – transported them from one men's house to another along with bundles of the firewood that would warm and illuminate the participants during the all-night performance in Walindimi.

The next morning as dawn was just breaking we arrived at Walindimi to find that, although the flutes and drum were still playing, most of the men had just gone to wash the mud of mourning from their bodies. About an hour later and after a night of mourning at the Ambri house, a throng of women passed the men's house on their way to the shore. They were carrying many of the objects from the indoor shrine including the cross, the plastic bag with Nick's shoes and some of his clothes, the string bag with travel necessities, the artillery shell filled with flowers, the *mwai* mask and assorted decorative foliage from the display. In addition, they carried three six-foot-long sago and coconut loaves.

The women laid these down at the shore under an arch of young coconut leaves (again, this arch seemed to mark transitions, as it did during the initiation). The some twenty who were the principal mourners – Nick's wife, sisters, clan sisters, "mothers" – helped one another remove the cords they had worn on their wrists and ankles since Nick died. Then, swimming out into the lake, they released the foliage and the cords to be carried away by the current. The rest of the women joined them and all washed off the mud of mourning.

After emerging from the lake, the principal mourners carried the memorabilia and the long loaves *into* the Walindimi men's house. The *mwai* mask was carried by Nick's mother's sister, who led the procession to the bench belonging to Nick's clan. There she put the mask down while the other women did the same with the objects they held; then, after a brief pause to allow Nick's spirit and its power, contained in the mask and in the objects, to be restored to his place in the men's house, the women picked up the mask and other objects to return them to the shrine in Nick's father's house. Thus, Nick's matrilateral kinswomen, who had brought him into the world, relinquished their claims on him. As they filed out of Walindimi, one gave the man acting as the head of Pombiantimeri a long loaf of sago and coconut bread and a basket of smoked pork, saying that these were for Waykumbunmank.

The rest of the day was devoted to presentations involving both men and women. First, members of Nick's clan presented K140 to four of their in-laws who had contributed the food on display next to the household shrine. They also gave K50 to the senior woman of Nick's mother's clan with the expectation that she redistribute it

22 Nick's *mwai* mask was placed by his mother's sister in the men's house.

to the other principal mourners of that group. The in-laws, in turn, reciprocated by giving Nick's clan the *karanaplanpinar amtar*, "the food for the head of the man who died." Placed next to the shrine at the central post, this was the only food of all that given to Nick's clan that its members could eat – the rest would have to be redistributed. Fortified by this food, members of Nick's clan continued in their distributions. They gave K5 to each of the several Pombiantimeri who had assisted by cutting the hair of the mourners. They gave sandwiches made of flat sago leaves with a chunk of pork as filling to several key Pombiantimeri. Because these *tsambunwuro* had been centrally instrumental in making Nick and other members of his clan into men by lying under them during the bloody cutting of their initiations, they had with Nick's death suffered a loss for which they had to be compensated.[15]

Finally, all those men who had helped at the time of Nick's death were invited to a feast at the Walindimi men's house. Three pigs were provided for this occasion. One of these, a wild one, had been killed by Nick's best friend, Theo, with the help of some companions. They had carried it into the men's house on the previous day, announcing that it was being contributed in the name of the Kilimbit youth. Three washtubs, each with a tag to which K6 was attached and on which was written the name of the recipient Chambri village, were filled with the cooked pork along with rice, sago, tins of fish and betel nuts. These were then carried from Maliwan's house into the men's house where, to the periodic accompaniment of the Waykumbunmank flutes, the guests ate heartily.

This feast was also understood to be a way of discovering who had ensorcelled Nick: whoever refused to partake of or who choked on the pork would be revealed as the guilty one. However, in the view of those suspecting Nick's father, the test was poorly constructed since, as a host, he would not be allowed to sample any of this food. Indeed, a rival of his for clan control objected strongly and publicly to Nick's father's role as host by carrying a tub of his own into the men's house. His tub was filled with canned fish and topped with betel nuts, to which K20 was attached. He said that this tub was for Kilimbit, and that he would shortly bring in other tubs for the other villages. He asserted that Nick's father, because he had disinherited Nick, should not be able to claim the prestige that accrued to the host on this occasion. Neither should he be able to avoid the test that would reveal or clear him of guilt. Perhaps because his political move, that is his claim to Nick, came too late in the ritual proceedings to be fully effective, he allowed other senior men eventually to quiet him.

This was not the only potential source of contention that the senior men were to encounter. Shortly afterwards, they met with a delegation of the young men who insisted that they be allowed to stage an all-night dance to the performance of Nick's music. Nick, they asserted, would have wished it so. As Nick's friends, companions and, in some cases, fellow band members, they claimed the right to speak for him. They prevailed: permission was granted and the party took place that night adjacent to the Walindimi men's house.

On the following and culminating day of the ritual, we arrived in the early afternoon at Nick's father's house to find virtually all of the young men of Chambri gathered outside. Wearing their most stylish clothes, many in sun glasses, they were listening to cassette recordings of Nick's music, performed by him and his band. Some with their own cassette radios were making their own recordings.

Soon, women emerged from the house, carrying the *mwai* mask, the artillery shell – now filled with hibiscus flowers – and the other

23   Nick's memorabilia were placed on a small raft.

memorabilia that had been brought back after they had washed at the shore. The flowers, one of Nick's mates told us, were chosen because they were appropriate to Nick's moiety and because Nick had been "a young man who liked to decorate himself." The women carried, as well, several baskets of food and a plate of rice and pork. Filing in quiet procession through the village, past Walindimi, they arrived again at the shore. There, they laid the *mwai* mask and the artillery shell on a cloth on the ground. The rest of the items, including the hibiscus flowers and the food, were placed on a small (two by three foot) raft, made for the occasion.

While Nick's wife, mother, and mother's mother remained on the shore weeping, six women of Nick's clan – three sisters and three father's sisters – swam with the laden raft out into the lake. There they capsized the raft, sinking or dispersing its load into the current. As they swam back to shore, several dived under the water to listen for sounds of the watery realm: they listened for the voices of ancestral crocodiles and other powerful spirits of the water and, especially, for the cries of Nick and of their other dead kin, who might be hungry for sustenance. To these dead kin, the women must respond that the food just capsized was for Nick alone. Finally, as one of the last acts in the ritual transferring Nick

24　Nick's wife and other relatives remained on the shore weeping.

from the living, one of the women remaining on shore vigorously and repeatedly rinsed out the empty artillery shell that had contained the flowers representing Nick and his youth. Then, the reassembled women picked up the *mwai* mask and the shell and returned to the Ambri house.[16]

There they devoted themselves to preparing the small sago packets that would comprise the final distribution of food. At the other side of Wombun, another group of women were similarly engaged, preparing for a comparable sago distribution that would conclude the initiation of Maliwan's sons. Maliwan had decided to postpone his distribution to coincide with that for Nick in order to show that Nick and the initiates were "brothers"–that all were young men.

In these recurrent ways attention had been explicitly drawn to the circumstances of Nick's death as a young man. The lamentations of several of the women, the donation of a pig by the youth of Kilimbit, the conflict in the men's house about who should sponsor the ritual, the lifting of the prohibition on all-night parties, the playing of Nick's music and the cooperative arrangement that the sago packets for Nick and the initiates be distributed at the same time were periodic reminders that Nick's death had aroused unusually wide and persisting concern.

But the ritual had, nonetheless, been performed: Nick had been appropriately mourned, the social relations that had constituted him had been elicited and then dissipated, and Nick had been placed among the ancestors. Many questions remained, however, not only about the cause of his death but about the effect of his life, particularly as it concerned Chambri youth and their increasing insistence that they be allowed to establish their own entailments. Most generally, Chambri were wondering whether these youths at home would eventually come to act in the manner of their seniors, to embrace at Chambri the patterns of authority that they were repudiating and, if not, what would they become?

At the moment, the freedom that Chambri youth wanted was to choose some of their own entailments within a system of pervasive entailments. They certainly were not seeking a freedom that could allow them to choose to have no entailments at all. Thus, when in his delirium Nick spoke of returning to Chambri as a tourist, as one primarily obligated only to himself who could, therefore, come and go, buy or not buy, take Chambri or leave it, as he chose, everyone knew something was very wrong.

But if the Chambri would reject tourists as providing for them a model, might the logic of commodities nonetheless insinuate itself into their system through the attraction the commodities themselves might exert on the Chambri? There was no doubt that Chambri youth would love to have cars such as a Nissan 280ZX or to be married "with the rustle of silk and the hint of tulle." Yet for them and for Chambri of any generation the primary significance of such objects and their cash equivalents was that they could be used to demonstrate what was essentially a social efficacy, to mark them as successful *within a system of entailments*: they wished to be successful as Maliwan had been during his initiation when he had generously compensated his in-laws, other claimants and participants; or successful as John Illumbui had been during his visit to Wewak when he had staged an all-night party for the senior men and had dispersed K150 a day to his in-laws and others.

Thus, no Chambri we knew, whether youth or elder, would suggest that freedom and choice be used to extract oneself altogether from relationships and entailments. However, the commodity logic of freedom and choice, engendered as it has been by certain sorts of economic relationships, has not always resulted from the freedom to choose. Commodity logic has come unbidden in circumstances where survival was possible only through selling one's labor as a commodity. Fortunately, at the moment, with their fish-rich lake and otherwise intact subsistence economy, the Chambri were not under such a degree of pressure. Thus, they could flirt with Western representations, using them for their own purposes, within a system in which their fundamental identity was not, as yet, class based.

In the next two chapters we examine the Chambri encounter with other Western means for defining the world. We turn now from a consideration of Western representations to one of Western modes of representation: those of literacy and of the state.

5
The written word

Many of the Western representations concerning development were conveyed to those at Chambri in newspapers, magazines, and religious literature. They were compelling, in part, because they appeared in written form. As such, these representations could be readily consulted and discussed. Moreover, they were imbued with appreciable intrinsic authority because writing was *itself* the mark and the means of development.[1] The ability to read and write, at least in Pidgin English if not in English, had in fact become for the Chambri (and for many other Papua New Guineans) a fundamental component of development.[2]

Indeed, literacy was a national priority, one of the central objectives of the nationally determined school system, for it was regarded as essential to the development of a united and effective Papua New Guinea state. Only if Papua New Guineans were generally literate, it was thought, could they develop a common national culture that would unify them. (Government policy accorded with Anderson's [1983] perception that it was through common cultural experiences acquired from such media as nationally circulated newspapers that peoples were able to perceive of themselves as a citizenry.) And, only with the support of a relatively united public – a citizenry – could the Papua New Guinea government hope to operate as a modern state, a modern state that could exercise authority sufficient to formulate and implement national policy. Literacy thus would enable the state to represent Papua New Guineans in a double sense, that of speaking for and to them. In other words, literacy would enable the state to represent them in defining their interests and to represent their interests to them. To return to the statement with which our book began, it was part of national educational policy designed to further development that Angela was told about development and was instructed to write about it.

Because written representations were generally recognized as powerful, literacy came to have a central role in advancing quite different political perspectives. In particular, there were significant differences between national policy and local opinion about the sort of development that literacy might implement. This was so especially concerning the distribution of power. From the perspective of the Papua New Guinea state, literacy was valued, as mentioned, because it provided the state with the opportunity to develop authority sufficient to subsume its peoples in order to represent them as citizens. Significantly, literacy was, in this regard, a means of implementing a system of incommensurate differences, based in part on differential access to and control of state authority. However, as we will see in this chapter and the next, the Chambri, both as individuals and as a collectivity, refused to allow other Papua New Guineans to speak for, otherwise represent, or subsume them. From the perspective of the Chambri, literacy was valued, in major part, because it provided the opportunity, as did development more generally, to pursue with greater effect their largely traditional interests: for instance, they valued written accounts – documents – because these enhanced the authority of particularistic claims and perspectives within their existing system of commensurate differences.

However, as we shall also see, since the patterns of authority that literacy conveyed were designed to subsume the autonomy of others, these patterns would prove difficult to contain within this system of commensurate differences. One Chambri, our assistant in fact, began to construct a representation which he called a Chambri Bible. It would encompass all Chambri within a document and would bring, he thought, power and prestige to him and, through him, to them. The nature of, and Chambri response to, his effort raises again some of the questions concerning the politics of ethnographic representation that we considered in the Introduction and to which we will return in the Conclusion.

Literacy within a system of commensurate differences

We had long been aware, as have other anthropologists in Papua New Guinea and elsewhere, that our informants were likely to present a particular view of events in order to enlist our aid in furthering their local political objectives.[3] Yet only recently have we recognized that much of our use to the Chambri lay not in our possible command of wealth, educational and employment opportunities, or access to government services, but rather in our capacity to inscribe and thus memorialize, in effect, to make tangible and substantial, individual lives and accomplishments.

During this most recent fieldwork, we were virtually besieged with Chambri requests to create documents – typed documents – that would bolster special interests. Far more than in the past, Chambri were seeking to take better advantage of the sources of validation that lay outside their own immediate system. We were, for instance, often asked by Chambri struggling to find employment to document their educational and work experience. Each of our research assistants in Wewak and in Chambri wished a letter of recommendation from us for future use; other Chambri brought tattered letters of recommendation for us to retype in more presentable form, not realizing the importance of the original letterheads and signatures. One of the more enterprising and better educated brought us a hand-written letter, describing in the most glowing terms his Papua New Guinea work experiences with a Western-based mining company. He assured us that this was an exact copy of the letter of recommendation the mining engineer had given him – the original, unfortunately, had been substantially eaten by cockroaches. Encountering grammatical errors, we asked him whether he wished us to type the text as written or to make corrections; he laughed unrepentantly, instructing us to "straighten the bloody English."[4]

Much of the Chambri interest in literacy, however, focused on their internal political relationships. Individuals frequently brought hand-written (in Pidgin) family histories for us to type: they wished us to give their version of the past the appearance and status of a printed document. Because ancestral precedent was highly important for the Chambri in conveying contemporary rights, much political activity took the form of making claims and counter-claims about whose ancestors did what. (Maliwan's assertion that his ancestor had founded the Walindimi men's house was, we have seen, prompted by such considerations.)[5] Consequently, the more authoritative a family history appeared to be, the stronger a particular political position. The following is an example (in translation) of one such history:

The story of the ancestors: Mepir, Mepiro, Yarus and Kuimampi

A long time ago the ancestor Mepir, his sister, Mepiro, and Mepir's two children, Yarus and Kuimampi, lived on the island of Kabano. The name of Mepir's wife is forgotten. They lived on two areas of Kabano called Lampari and Mambus. When they lived there, they never saw the face or body of friends; nobody lived close by; everyone lived a long way off. When Mepir and his wife died, it was on Kabano. They had three children by this time, Yarus, Kuimampi and Mambus. After their parents died, the three children began to think about finding a new place to live. One brother, Yarus, went to Warmpuk. Kuimampi went to Chambri. Mambus stayed on Kabano. And now, we who are descended from these ancestors are many in number, living on Chambri, Warmpuk and Kabano.

We were asked to type this by a man preparing to press claims to land in case one of the several mining companies prospecting in the area discovered gold in any of the places settled originally by his ancestors. This document was designed not only to be convincing to such outsiders as the officials of a mining company or government land-court, but also to be effective against the inevitable counterclaims of Chambri and their neighbors.

Given such prior experience with Chambri requests, we were not surprised when Aron, a Chambri in his mid-thirties, invited us to his house because Kapiwon, his father and the most powerful man of Kilimbit, wanted his family history recorded. This history, as we had expected, demonstrated the genealogical centrality of Kapiwon's family (and, hence, the merely derivative contributions of other families) in the settlement of Chambri.[6] Aron's request fulfilled, our help was then commanded in another more unusual, but again thoroughly political, matter of concern to Kapiwon.

Aron said that his father was distressed because two other Chambri, Yarapat (see below) and Wasi, had received medals from the Queen and he had not. Kapiwon, he explained, was a very important man of Chambri who deserved a medal and a little present because he also had worked for the Queen: Kapiwon's father, Kindui Yukindimi, was the first *luluai* (government appointed headman) of Kilimbit.[7] Kapiwon had helped his father communicate with the European administration by translating between Chambri and Pidgin English. The reason that Yukindimi was appointed *luluai* was because his ancestor originated from Chambri. Neither Yarapat's nor Wasi's father had been appointed *luluai.* In fact, Yarapat's ancestors did not even come from Chambri: they came from Milae, a community on the other side of Chambri Lake. Kapiwon also deserved a medal, Aron continued, since he was a second NCO, a captain or a lieutenant, for the Japanese during the Second World War. Some of his generation got pay and presents from the Japanese during this time but he did not. Kapiwon, moreover, began the work of building the church on Chambri; in addition, it was his power, augmenting that of the Bishop, that persuaded God to bring two new species of fish to Chambri Lake so that the people would enjoy a greater variety of food. He also gave the land on which the Kilimbit airstrip was built. Nowadays he kept Kilimbit, and sometimes all of Papua New Guinea, a good place to live. He helped councilors settle disputes. He had provided the powerful rituals that enabled Michael Somare to remain Prime Minister of Papua New Guinea for such a long time;[8] indeed, Somare's recent failure to form a government was directly attributable to his failure during the last election to solicit Kapiwon's ritual assistance. Finally, Kapiwon, as a curer, made Kilimbit a healthy place to live.

Aron concluded his recitation by saying that his father wanted us to write a letter to the Queen requesting a medal in recognition for these achievements. We agreed to write such a letter to the British Embassy in Papua New Guinea. Aron suggested as well that, given Kapiwon's war-time service, we write to the Japanese Embassy and to several, specified, Papua New Guinea politicians, including the present Prime Minister.

A few days later, Yarapat, in pursuit of his own political objectives involving literacy, summoned us as recorders to a meeting area near his house for what would prove to be an impressively orchestrated and politically astute performance. He wished, he said, to help us in our work of writing a book about Chambri culture by showing us the ritual activities through which he regulated the annual cycle of high water and low water in Chambri Lake. Significantly, he chose to instruct us on this essential "public service" (terms used) at a time he knew a crowd would be gathering nearby to hear an important court case. Arranged for our edification and for all to see were a number of his important ritual objects. Each depended for its efficacy on the recitation of secret names. Some, such as a *mwai* mask that *was* Saun, Yarapat's principal ancestor, and several flutes that spoke with Saun's and other powerful ancestral voices, would provide

Yarapat with ritual potency; others, such as a canoe paddle and two blackened clay pots would be used to perform the particular ritual tasks of controlling the level of the lake.

Yarapat outlined a portion of the procedure he would follow to bring about seasonal change. To the recitation of secret names, the appropriate pot must be filled with water and placed over a fire in his men's house. The direction that the water spilled when the pot boiled over would indicate the duration of low water. (Low water was the time of greatest plenty, as described in Chapter Three.) The other pot and the paddle were used if the season of low water were shown to be too short. Yarapat then would probe the bottom of the lake with the paddle to find where the water was deepest; water taken from this spot would be boiled away in the second pot to bring and prolong, through ancestral intervention, the time of low water.[9]

After giving us this preliminary explanation, Yarapat went to change clothes. In a few minutes he returned, wearing a coat and tie and carrying the copies Deborah had given him of her PhD thesis and her monograph, *Sepik River Societies*. He first instructed us to find a passage in each referring either to Saun or to Yarapat; this done, the monograph with a marker at an appropriate passage was added to his display of ritual objects and the dissertation, still opened, remained in his hands as a prop.

Then, flanked by clansmen, each in his best European clothing, and in front of an audience composed of those gathered for the court case, Yarapat sought to define himself as Deborah's Chambri host. Addressing her throughout as "sister," he welcomed her to Chambri as if she were a new arrival, as if common knowledge about her and her work did not exist. His speech, tape-recorded by Frederick at Yarapat's request for inclusion in our book, consisted largely of questions which Deborah answered one by one: What country had Deborah come from? When did she first come to Papua New Guinea? How did she first hear about Chambri? How long had she lived at Chambri? Had she found Chambri life good? When would she be returning to America? When the speech was over, Frederick was instructed to take a picture of Deborah and Yarapat shaking hands. Finally, Yarapat and two of his clansmen performed some of the exoteric portions of the chants which must accompany the rituals with paddle and pots to expel the water and so bring the dry season. (What Yarapat wanted could be considered a meta-documentation in that we had

25 Still holding Deborah's dissertation, Yarapat and his
clansmen performed chants to control the water level.

recorded for inclusion in our forthcoming book reference to the
previous books in which he had appeared.)

Apparently not fully content with the documentation thus far of
his identity as a man of knowledge and power Yarapat then told us
that when we next returned to Chambri, we must bring a very
large camera. With such an instrument we could encompass in a
single image all of his ceremonial paraphernalia, all of the ritual
actions employing these objects, as well as the product of those
actions such as the running of fish that took place during the
season of low water.[10] Then, the demonstration over and our
assignment for the future made clear, Yarapat carried his various
objects back to his house, changed clothes, and returned to
dominate with complete assurance the proceedings at the court
which had been pending during this display.

We can readily see, thus, how in this competitive Chambri world
where male reputations were subject to continual attack and
required continual bolstering, the Chambri would invest anthropologists with the political role of memorialization. To recapitu-
late, many of our activities, some undertaken at Chambri initiative,
some at ours, such as typing family histories, writing to the Queen,
documenting Yarapat's ritual capacities and responsibilities,

recording the events and expenditures of Maliwan's initiation, were significant to Chambri men primarily because we were thereby substantiating their reputations, their claims of power, in a system of commensurate differences in which all, at least potentially, were equal and, thus, rivals. Written documents along with photographs and tape-recordings became comparable in their political importance to such objects as the flutes, clay pots, *mwai* masks (and the Queen's medal) in this sense: all testified to, and were durable manifestations of, the power that a particular man controlled.[11] (We are certain that not all Chambri found our activities in these regards to their liking. Although we provided documentation to anyone who asked, the substantiation of the claims of one individual would necessarily diminish those of another.)

Godfried Kolly's Bible

The Chambri interest in literacy was to take an additional and, for us, an unexpected turn. As an unanticipated consequence of our field work, the Chambri came to have their own transcriber of ancestral stories, their own indigenous ethnographer. More specifically, in the course of serving as our research assistant, Godfried Kolly sought to establish himself as a man of knowledge and power by collecting and compiling traditional Chambri stories. Addressing not only the Chambri concern with the documentation of power but also their concern with the rapidly changing circumstances of their lives, Godfried worked to preserve and compile ancestral precedent. This was to be a source of both continuing strength and truth in the developing world. However, as we shall see, in attempting to create an authoritative document that would represent tradition for all Chambri, Godfried was presenting himself, at least in the eyes of other Chambri, as authoritative arbiter of what the Chambri fundamentally were. Moreover, if he had succeeded in creating his Bible, he would then have threatened to transform from within the system of commensurate differences: by winning the competition so absolutely he would place himself above all others.

Godfried had worked with Deborah during and after her first trip to Chambri, primarily as her motor-canoe driver and one of her research assistants. In the latter capacity, he had collected basic information on such subjects as clan affiliation, men's house membership and migrational histories. From the early 1980s he had been living in Wewak. When he learned of our plan to live for a time in Chambri Camp, he arranged for us to stay in a room in the house he occupied with his family. We all assumed, and rightly, that he would again be working with Deborah (and, this time, Frederick). It was clear, however, that he was no longer interested in collecting routine data. We therefore initially suggested that he tape-record his autobiography: that would be suitable work for one with his anthropological experience and with his relative seniority.

Much taken with this idea, Godfried prepared by first writing in Pidgin an account of his life. (This included a description of a religious vision which we present in Appendix A, in its entirety as he asked us to do.) He then read his Pidgin English account into the tape-recorder. Delighted in our turn by these written and oral texts and by his evident interest in both writing and recording, we suggested he keep the recorder and continue to document what he and others considered "matters of importance." (We were careful not to be too specific in our charge to him.)

Godfried agreed that this would be suitable employment and immediately set to work with energy and concentration. Rarely without his clipboard and tape-recorder, he started by focusing on the Chambri myths he knew; but soon he was recording and transcribing myths elicited from others.[12] Of particular interest to us were the commentaries that he began appending to his transcriptions. In these he drew analogies between the Chambri story at hand and a Christian story. To facilitate these comparisons, he had us purchase for him a book of Bible stories. Moreover, included in the manuscripts he presented us every day or so were other forms of commentary including his lists of what was "good" and "bad" about Chambri life.[13] (His corpus eventually contained several hundred pages.)

Eventually he told us, as, apparently, he had told various Chambri earlier, that these manuscripts (including the commentaries) were to be the Chambri Bible. Godfried had, by compiling, explicating, and evaluating the activities and practices of Chambri ancestors, created a Bible that would serve as a guide to contemporary Chambri life. The Chambri Bible would not only contain truths to be taken as seriously as those of the Catholic Bible but truths quite literally identical to those of the Catholic Bible. As an example, and one we will return to, Moses *was* the same as the

26   Godfried Kolly worked to preserve and compile ancestral precedent.

Chambri ancestor Yambukay. Moreover, Godfried's Chambri Bible, filled, as it was, with accounts of Chambri ancestors, would also be the Chambri history.

In creating this Chambri Bible, Godfried was, as mentioned, addressing the circumstances Chambri were facing in a changing world. Older men, in particular, were concerned that Chambri youth were balking at arranged marriages; they were also troubled that young men were not learning the Chambri myths. Consequently, they feared that these repositories of Chambri tradition, wisdom and power would soon be forgotten. In fact, virtually all adults were worried by changes that had taken place in Chambri life, both at home and in the towns, because they felt that, for youth especially, good Chambri customs were being replaced by bad imported ones, that is they were being replaced by Western representations of how life should be led.

In addition, at least the entire generation of Chambri who had grown up as Catholics faced the epistemological problem of reconciling two sources of truth, each regarded as irrefutable. Finally, Chambri wanted to maintain and consolidate what they regarded as their position of religious leadership in the largely Catholic Sepik. Chambri, after all, had provided catechists to other

Sepik villages and still had the largest, most elaborate church building in the Middle Sepik.[14]

By recording Chambri stories in enduring and consultable form, by resolving the difference between Chambri and Christian stories and by providing a Chambri Bible that could be read not only by the Chambri but by their neighbors, Godfried was engaged in an activity that many Chambri, as we shall see, found eminently worthwhile. However, as we have already suggested, some of the opposition Godfried eventually was to encounter stemmed from the fact that others wished to deny him the prestige and access to power that would come to him from completing such an encompassing project. Furthermore, because actions of Chambri ancestors established important ritual and political prerogatives, any rendition of their activities that purported to be authoritative was likely to be strongly contested.

At least partially aware of these difficulties, Godfried sought to establish his authority as indigenous ethnographer through frequent reference to his religious visions in which he claimed to have directly communicated with Christ. It should be mentioned that Godfried, along with many other Chambri, had been strongly influenced by the charismatic movement within Catholicism.[15] Certainly Godfried's visions (and those of others) were of great interest to Chambri, who had come to expect that both Chambri ancestral and Christian powers would have an active role in their daily lives. However, Godfried also claimed – and this seemed an innovation – that the Chambri life which incorporated ancestral precepts and powers *was* the Christian life: in his view, the Chambri were originally true Christians. Correspondingly, as we will see below in the texts from his Bible, he believed that powerful Chambri ancestors were equivalent to biblical characters: indeed, all Chambri ancestral power was God's power.[16]

That he saw this Chambri past as a Christian one was a special perception, but one that other Chambri, as we will also see, found intriguing and plausible. Certainly other Chambri already accepted the belief that there was a fundamental compatibility between ancestral and Christian ways. All had been affected by the attention to and tolerance toward indigenous religious beliefs and practices that Western priests had displayed since the reforms of Vatican II. Consequently, Chambri listened with interest but not apparent surprise to Godfried as he provided to a bemused Polish priest a lengthy exposition in which he claimed that Chambri primal ancestors were the original "Christian family." (The priest had come to provide Christmas services.) In so doing, Godfried was speaking to the priest as an equal, as one theologian to another.[17] It mattered not to Godfried that the priest embodied Western power, right and truth.

Yet, other Chambri would eventually object when they sensed that in conjoining Chambri and Christian stories and practices, Godfried was not simply augmenting the authority of one by that of the other. By asserting their essential identity, he was, as well, introducing a different and a far more peremptory authority into the heart of the Chambri system. However gratifying it might be for Chambri to establish parity between their truths and those of Westerners, and, by implication, between themselves and Westerners, such an endeavor carried with it significant perils.

From Godfried's Chambri Bible:

The Story of the Promise Stick, Named Kwolimopan, that God Gave to Yambukay[18]

A long time ago, when only the pig named Emosuie and the man named Yambukay lived on Chambri Island, God gave a promise stick to provide for the Chambri people. We call this promise stick Kwolimopan, which is the name of a crocodile. God made this animal the king of the water. God gave the promise stick to Yambukay. God told him that the stick had the power of the Holy Spirit. This stick would bring the food of the water and the other things of the water to the people. When the people had no fish, God said you must put the stick in the water and pray to Father in Heaven asking for fish, crocodiles and all the food of the water to come to you. And God gave the song [which consists of the phrase]: "I am the spirit crocodile Kwolimopan" [followed by a string of esoteric names of Kwolimopan].

After he finished this song Yambukay would put the stick in the water and everything in the water would come and Yambukay would say: "That's it. I have been given the fish of the water." When Yambukay received this stick from the hand of God, God told him: "When you want to put the stick in the water, you must refrain from eating fish, meat, and crocodile and everything else of the water for six days. After six days, you can make yourself a bit of food and you should wash your hands. You can also eat fish, smoke, and chew betel nut. If you follow this law I have just given you, you will be able to receive from me what you have asked me for. And if you follow my law, you will find the food you have asked for after the sixth day."

Later God told Yambukay about initiation. When you cut skin, you must take this promise stick and stand it up in the middle of the men's house. The next day you must cut skin. After you have finished, you must promise that you will forbid the initiates from eating with their right hand; they also must eat with tongs and only eat greens. They cannot eat fish. After six days, you can cook a little soup, and let them drink it and wash their hands and then they can eat normally. They must stay in the men's house for six weeks. After six weeks, they can go outside into the water. When they want to wash in the water, you must place the promise stick near where they will be. This way, they will get the strength of the Holy Spirit. I will go inside them all.

Explanation: At Chambri, this promise stick still remains. It marks Jesus. And this way of cutting skin is the way we mark baptism, holy communion and confirmation. At the time we cut skin and wash, we get the strength of the Holy Spirit. Nowadays, we still follow this custom and this promise stick remains, which we call Kwolimopan. All the people use it when they cut skin. This stick which marks Jesus remains with me in my house. And this story of the Kwolimopan stick is the same as the story of God giving Moses a stick and a stone with the Ten Commandments. We at Chambri have the same thing which God gave to our ancestors. No man made this Kwolimopan stick. God himself gave it to Yambukay. Godfried Kwolikumbwi wrote this. It is for the reasons that I have given that all the people of Chambri call the Kwolimopan stick, the king stick.

The Story of Tun

This story is a true story of something that happened at the time of the fourth generation of the fathers and ancestors of Chambri. At this time, there was a man who lived alone on an island called Lukwe . . . He was the kind of man to attract all the women and copulate with them. Women on the way to and from the market would stop their canoes at his island and give him food. He would copulate with them all – there was not one that he missed. The women would also give him most of the good food that they got at the market . . . [The men, suspecting something, hid an observer in one of the canoes who reported what Tun was doing with all of their wives and daughters. They sent word to Tun that there was an important meeting requiring his presence at the Yangaraman men's house.] In the morning, the men started to cut grass at the same time that Tun arrived. As Tun walked through the village, the men slashed his legs with their knives, saying: "Sorry, you good man. I cut you." Tun replied: "That is all right; you complete your work. I will just pass along the road here. I have no complaints." And it was the same as he passed all the men. They all cut his legs. He fell down near the Yangaraman men's house when the bones of his legs were cut through. They buried him near the place where the Indingai graveyard now is. After they buried him, many men from the Sepik River came during the night and took his flesh away, back to their own villages. Some men of Chambri did the same thing.

They wanted his power to attract women. They made a big soup with his blood and they drank it. That is the end of the story of Tun. When you open your Bible and read the story of Jesus, you will see that Tun is Jesus because he was crucified and died near the place where the church now is.

To summarize the central elements in Godfried's synthesis: the story of Kwolimopan concerned the power that God gave Yambukay in the form of a stick-like effigy (see Chapter Two) to use on behalf of all Chambri. The stick, which contained the Holy Spirit, enabled Chambri to invoke and control the ancestral crocodile in which God had invested power. This power would, if the proper incantations were performed and taboos observed, provide fish and other food from the water, and impart to initiates the strength of the Holy Spirit in a way equivalent to baptism, communion, and confirmation. This stick denoted Jesus and was the same as the staff and tablets God gave to Moses. The story of Tun was about a man who lived in the fourth generation, had remarkable power to attract women, allowed himself to be killed and was eaten by those wishing to absorb his power. This man was Jesus.

To understand the analogies Godfried established between Kwolimopan and Jesus, Yambukay and Moses, and Tun and Jesus, we must remember that for the Chambri, essential identity was determined through access to ancestral power. In a fundamental way, Chambri men *were* their totemic powers. Their identity stemmed from their capacity to effect action and that, in turn, rested on their esoteric knowledge which enabled them to embody their powerful ancestors.[19] (Thus, Yarapat *became* Saun, when he invoked the power of his *mwai* mask to control the level of water and the running of the fish.) The analogies – indeed, the equivalences – that Godfried drew between Chambri and Christian characters were based on his perception that each was essentially the same because each incorporated substantial portions of the same power. In Godfried's view, ancestral power was God's power, the power of the Holy Spirit: God did, after all, both create Kwolimopan and give Yambukay the means of activating, that is, becoming, that power.

Although from the Western perspective Tun, the great fornicator, would seem to be quite different from Jesus, the celibate, from the Chambri perspective they were comparable as both were obviously men of power:[20] Jesus was able to work miracles and Tun was able to attract – to "pull" – women from other men.[21]

(That they happened to manifest their power in somewhat different ways was not of much interest to Godfried when we discussed this analogy with him.)[22] Moreover, both Tun and Jesus had comparable deaths that marked each as powerful. Frequently in Chambri accounts, powerful men were killed only when impossibly outnumbered and, even under these circumstances of unavoidable death, they often maintained the semblance of control by making their enemies the present of their death.[23] After the death of such men, others might ritually incorporate their flesh in order to obtain a portion of their remarkable power.

In his effort to construct a Chambri Bible like the Christian Bible, Godfried wished not only to establish equivalences between Chambri and Christian characters but also to create a Chambri history comparable to the Christian one. Typically in his stories, as with his location of Tun's feats in the "fourth generation," Godfried attempted to establish the temporal sequence of Chambri characters and events. (The "first generation" was defined as that of the first Chambri, the autochthonous half-man, half-pig Emosuie.) His efforts to construct a Chambri history must also be understood as a response to one of the central dilemmas of Chambri life. Chambri, as we have previously indicated in Chapter 1, were convinced that the loss of power over time was – or at least had been – virtually inevitable. A written history that both salvaged and reconstructed the past would circumvent the process of forgetting by which access to power had been steadily diminished.

Chambri, as might be remembered, thought that power was likely to be lost with the passing of each generation because men were always reluctant to pass on to their sons their most powerful names – the names which were most effective in establishing identity with an ancestor: to do so would diminish their own access to ancestral power and so hasten their social as well as physical decline. Senior men realized, though, that if they did not eventually transmit their names, their inevitable physical deaths would separate them forever from the living insofar as their sons would be unable to embody them as ancestors. Consequently, men did not wish their names to die with them; nevertheless they tried to retain exclusive knowledge of them as long as possible.

But many old men, it was believed, delayed too long, either forgetting their names in the confusion of old age, or dying before they had transmitted them. Because of miscalculations of this sort,

Chambri said that many names had been lost every generation. Indeed, those lost were the most important names, those most likely to be kept as long as possible. Consequently, the Chambri assumed that in the course of social life, access to the ancestors and their pool of power had become impaired. While the amount of ancestral power remained essentially constant, the availability of that power had been steadily diminishing.[24]

Hence, among those people who were in fact preoccupied with the danger of forgetting, literacy had a special significance; it meant retaining power. Godfried's project then of creating the Chambri Bible was generally welcomed, particularly given the perception that loss of traditional knowledge was likely to increase with the captivation of youth by Western representations and with the widespread emigration that resulted in many growing up away from Chambri. However, Godfried's effort actually to produce a Chambri Bible modeled on the Christian Bible encountered difficulties. Although he had little trouble convincing others that the characters and activities of Chambri history were comparable to those of Christian history, that, for example, Jesus was Tun and scarification was baptism, his efforts to enlist the help he needed were continually frustrated. It was, in part, Godfried's ambition to represent Chambri history in a form as complete and authoritative as that of the Christian Bible that undermined its success.

The indigenous ethnographer meets with the big men

Although Godfried had been able to collect a number of stories from Chambri while in Wewak, he was delighted to accompany us to Chambri where many more still retained extensive mythological knowledge. Kosemp, an elderly non-relative with room in his house where Godfried could stay, became his first major inform-ant at Chambri.[25] Godfried soon discovered that Kosemp con-sidered the stories he had already collected in Wewak to be seriously flawed. Characters, for instance, were often misidentified by species and proper name: someone described as a crocodile with a particular name and set of descendants was actually, according to Kosemp, a python with an entirely different name and lineage. Moreover, actions described as occurring in particu-lar areas of Chambri at the very moment of settlement had occurred in quite different places and at much later times. Godfried, shaken by these revelations, checked the stories he had collected with his father, Yorondu. Yorondu described them all, including Kosemp's renditions, as ill-informed rubbish. He then gave Godfried yet other accounts. Adding to Godfried's growing sense that Chambri history was indeed difficult to delineate was the reluctance of many to cooperate with him: some powerful men simply refused to tell him any of their ancestral stories at all or, if less overtly intransigent, told him only the most generally known of them. Finally, Godfried became sure that many of those who appeared to cooperate with him were intentionally presenting him with incomplete or incorrect versions.

After a month of struggle, Godfried decided to confront these problems directly by inviting the big men from the three Chambri villages to a meeting at his men's house. Godfried began the session by informing an audience of some fifteen senior men that he was collecting traditional stories so that the Chambri could retain and revive their ancestral precepts and vitality. He wished their assistance in this endeavor. Holding up the Christian Bible, he explained to an approving audience:

The Yambukay stories [which belonged to Godfried's clan] and the other good stories must be collected and made into a Chambri Bible where all could see them. It is important to collect these stories now because lots of the youth are fouled up on lots of matters. The bad customs of the youth and the elders need to be corrected by the good stories of the Chambri Bible. There are many new customs which spoil Chambri . . . lots of rubbish, copycat [word used] customs including those of buying and selling food . . . all ways of white people who buy everything with money.

Godfried then brought the members of his audience up to date on his work by enumerating the histories he had already collected. He specified points of confusion and areas of omission and again asked for their cooperation.

All agreed that Chambri youth were woefully ignorant of proper Chambri ways and that Godfried's work in collecting the stories and recording the history was important so as to prevent further loss of ancestral knowledge. There was an additional and well-applauded observation that the document Godfried planned to assemble would confirm the position of Chambri as a center of knowledge on the Sepik, comparable in this respect to Rome.[26] Then the discussion ranged through a set of related questions: What was the position of the Chambri relative to those in the world at large, especially to those in the West? What was the position of Chambri clans relative to each other? How, beginning with Adam and Eve in the Garden of Eden, had Chambri come to be settled? How long in terms of generations had Chambri been inhabited? What had been the relative order of settlement on Chambri by the founders of various clans?

Godfried presented and explained his calculation that Chambri had been settled for seven generations. But then, after some discussion, Aron asked a perplexing question: since Adam and Eve lived well before Jesus, and Jesus had been dead nearly two thousand years, where in this course of events did these seven generations of Chambri history fit? During the ensuing silence, Godfried searched in vain through his collection of Chambri stories for an answer. Finally, a local catechist came forward. God, he said, had told Adam and Eve to have lots of children; some of their descendants were sent to Chambri, others, including Abraham and Jesus, were sent elsewhere. This position seemed acceptable for it established the differences between Chambri and others – again, primarily those in the West – as commensurate: all were descended from the same ancestors and all therefore had comparable rights to claim fundamental ancestral powers and prerogatives. (To be sure, this Chambri effort to articulate their own mythic history with the Christian mythic history in order to arrive at the "truth" about what "actually" happened, may strike some Western readers as doubly naive; nonetheless, according to Chambri beliefs about the nature of ancestrality, their speculations were entirely reasonable.[27] These speculations were, in addition, prompted by a Chambri insistence that they remain autonomous actors in a system premised on potential equality.)

There were a few historical embellishments. For instance, they agreed that Chambri ancestors must have helped construct the Tower of Babel prior to their departure for the Sepik and that people had the power to live longer in those early times than at present. Then the attention shifted to the much more divisive question: where and in what order had particular clan ancestors settled on Chambri Island?

All agreed with Aron that, if this history of the founding of Chambri society by waves of immigrants were to be a proper guide for the conduct of present and future generations, "it must be told correctly, starting from the beginning without any jumps and be collected from those to whom the stories belonged." Nevertheless, few were willing to accept as true anyone else's story of ancestral deeds. Kosemp, for instance, vigorously contested one account of

Chambri settlement that relegated his ancestor, Kwimembi, to the subordinate position of a fairly late arrival. Using a wealth of corroborative detail about Kwimembi's diverse activities, specifying, for example, all the sites where Kwimembi in his travels had built houses,[28] so that the extent and precision of his knowledge could not be easily denied, Kosemp reminded all that his ancestor was necessarily among the first to live on Chambri: it was Kwimembi, after all, who had taught the Chambri to eat sago rather than sun-dried mud. Kosemp then offered a general challenge to the others by demanding to know "who is sufficient to tell *me* who the first on Chambri were?" Another made a comparable claim of ancestral significance by asserting that his ancestor had originated the practices of warfare. Others followed by hinting darkly that they alone knew and were entitled to tell the truly primal stories, stories far too important to reveal in this context.

By this point, the meeting had the form of a Chambri debate with men competing for eminence by bragging about ancestral accomplishments and by alluding to esoteric knowledge.[29] Although the meeting had begun with agreement that the stories should be made public, it was now clear that, however eager these men were to hear the stories of others, they were unwilling to reveal anything but the most general features of their own. Indeed, one explicitly warned Godfried that he could collect no stories of importance in such a public place. And, he wondered, did Godfried intend to collect as part of these stories the secret names of the ancestors?

Godfried responded by saying that only the "little" names – the esoteric ones – would be in the book of stories he wished to make available to all. The esoteric Chambri names would be written elsewhere. Likewise, he said, the powerful names of Israel were not in the Christian Bible; these names were not given out but were kept in a special and dangerous book in Rome, available only to select priests.

Finally, after his guests ate of the rice and canned fish he had provided and the meeting came to an end, Godfried talked briefly to those present of his future plans. He would move permanently back to Chambri, build himself an "office" and continue to devote himself to collecting and transcribing Chambri stories.

Godfried left this meeting well satisfied. He told us that people finally understood and supported his work. He admitted that problems remained, yet he was confident that his project had the cooperation of the big men who would help him by freely giving him their stories and by reaching an agreement among themselves on such matters as the sequence of ancestral settlement on Chambri. And, while recognizing that his project was a major undertaking, he had no doubts as to its importance and feasibility. When he finally got the history right and finished his book, the old men, like Kosemp, would acknowledge that what he said was true and the young men, like Kosemp's son, could learn what it was that was true.

Godfried's confidence proved misplaced. To be sure, the big men at the meeting had agreed that ordinary mechanisms of socialization might well no longer be adequate to ensure the transmission of the knowledge necessary to provide natural and social order and that it would be highly desirable for Chambri to become the Rome of the Sepik. Nonetheless, these big men did not subsequent to the meeting tell Godfried their stories in any detail, much less reveal any of their esoteric secrets. No one wished to relinquish either his knowledge, or his reputation for knowledge, to other big men, to the population in general, or to Godfried who, if his project were completely successful, could become the most knowledgeable and, hence, the most powerful Chambri ever to exist. Such a person would be intolerable since he would transcend and thus subvert the system of commensurate differences.

Godfried did not, however, give up on his project: he managed to gather some additional information from sources such as Kosemp, his father and other members of his men's house; and he continued to struggle with the intellectual difficulties that had prompted him to call the meeting in the first place. These difficulties persisted in part because, as an *indigenous* ethnographer, he was engaged in a pursuit without Chambri precedent while still following Chambri cultural assumptions.

Although using literacy to create that which had never before existed at Chambri, that is, a comprehensive and authoritative written history, Godfried still very much accepted the Chambri assumption that their myths constituted an accurate – a true – history. This meant that in the course of his project he had to deal with the fact, in a way other Chambri did not, that these clan-based accounts not only were often esoteric and thus difficult to collect, but were, as well, fragmentary and inconsistent. Most Chambri dealt with disparity between stories by citing their own clan stories – their own incontrovertible truths – as evidence that other ancestral accounts were false. Yet, while Godfried did accept his own clan stories as fundamentally true, he was reluctant simply to dismiss, as other Chambri would, conflicting or incongruent stories as completely riddled with lies and misconceptions. In order to construct a Chambri history that focused on more than one set of clan ancestors, a clan history that was *comprehensive*, he had to find a way to utilize at least aspects of the stories others told of their ancestors. (Again, this was a project seemingly feasible only with literacy.) He wished to believe that these stories were substantially accurate and could, with some adjustment, be incorporated or subsumed into a larger picture.

Part of the challenge Godfried faced, then, was to develop logical criteria for accepting, rather than political criteria for dismissing, a conflicting account. For instance, he eventually suggested that two stories locating apparently the same event on different islands in Chambri Lake might each be correct if these separate islands had, at the time of the event, been joined as a single island. Differing accounts of the settling of Chambri, he also argued, could be shown as consistent if the actions described were adjusted relative to each other so that some took place, for instance, in the third generation and others in the fourth.

Conceivably, as the result of this project Godfried (and others) could come to question their assumption that Chambri myths were historically accurate. If, for instance, Godfried were unable to develop criteria adequate for distinguishing the relative truth of disparate accounts, he might conclude that all were wrong, or equally inaccurate, and that one could never know, at least through such accounts, what did happen and what the nature of ancestral precedent was. However, at the moment, the epistemological basis of the system of commensurate differences remained intact. Although Godfried, in his efforts to collect and use all the available accounts, became unusually aware of, and perplexed by, the extent to which they differed, he was still, as an indigenous ethnographer, convinced of the essential and absolute truth of his intellectual system. Thus the capacity of literacy to subvert Chambri faith in their own traditions, and in turn undermine Godfried's objective of making ancestral precedent more compelling, was still to be recognized.[30]

In the beginning of this chapter we stated that Godfried's attempt to write the Chambri Bible had caused us to re-examine our own role as ethnographers among the Chambri. Should we conclude from what we have seen to be some of the potential consequences of literacy[31] that any attempt to write about the Chambri would be hegemonic: that to do so would deny them *their* capacity to speak in multiple voices, as potential equals, for themselves? Are we, as exogenous ethnographers, claiming the same relationship of power to the Chambri that Godfried was claiming, for example, to Kosemp: would our role in representing Chambri to the world be comparable to Godfried's role in representing Kosemp's ancestor Kwimembi to the Chambri?

We will return to these questions in the Conclusion, where our answer will be both "yes" and, in a way we think makes it important that we do write about the Chambri, "no." As God-fried's attempt makes clear, all claims to representation are political. Yet, representations are politically important not only depending on who represents whom, but also depending on what is said, to whom, and in what context it is said.

However, before we can adequately distinguish our enterprise of representing the Chambri to the first world from Godfried's project, we must discuss the Chambri response to circumstances in which the power to represent could indeed have led to loss of their collective autonomy. Thus, in the next and the last chapter, we examine Chambri relationships within the nation-state of Papua New Guinea, including, in particular, Chambri relationships to the state itself. Chambri resistance to the state, like their resistance to such other mechanisms of control as representations, objectifi-cation and class, will clarify what was crucially at stake when they tried to shape and control the changing mechanisms of authority they were encountering in a developing world that was increas-ingly shaped by the first world. Our final position may appear somewhat paradoxical. We will argue that it was precisely because we, unlike Godfried, were from that first world that it was important (at least at this historical moment) for us to represent the Chambri to that world, provided in so doing we elucidated the meaning and importance of Chambri resistance to representation and other mechanisms of authority.

6
Negotiating with the state

Although Godfried was evidently the first to propose compiling a Chambri Bible, the manner in which he presented this project was entirely familiar to other Chambri. It was common – indeed expected – for Chambri men to present their particular political objectives and accomplishments as constituting "public service" (to quote Yarapat). Such statements did not, however, strike Chambri as in any way hypocritical, lamentable or other than inevitable.

Because the Chambri viewed all power as stemming from the same (clan-based) ancestral source, they regarded an individual's efforts to pursue his own interests, and his efforts to regulate society and nature, as comparable activities: all such (essentially male) activities were fundamentally political as all testified to a person's control of his ancestral power. This meant that the Chambri were unlikely to conceive of public service or public interest for its own sake. Under these circumstances in which all projects were understood as having important components of self-interest, a frequent objective of rhetoric was to convince other men that a given project would bring benefit to them sufficient to offset the prestige accruing to the successful sponsor.[1] Thus, for example, Maliwan managed to convince most of the men of Wombun that enhanced artifact sales would justify their support of his men's house.

Chambri did not, though, see their society as simply the product of individuals engaged in the competitive pursuit of their own self-interest. Rather, Chambri saw this competitive pursuit of their own self-interest as taking place within a context in which mutual and fundamental dependence was recognized and accepted. As Chambri frequently said: "One man is not enough to make the right things happen." Only if individuals conjoined and coordinated the specific powers of their various ancestors could a *system* of regulation adequate to control the world – both social and natural – result.[2] To illustrate the individual competition within the context of mutual dependence: the competition for prestige came when men strove to elaborate the relative importance of their part in this system. It was at this point that they might or might not be able to enlist the support of others. And even very powerful and persuasive men often had difficulty in convincing very many to support their projects.

Godfried's enterprise, while neither unusual in its presentation nor in its failure, was remarkable in its audacity. He wanted people not only to use their power to support him but, in effect, to deed him much of that power by entrusting him with their ancestral stories. (Hence, he could perhaps be seen as attempting to employ a new technology to exercise power by controlling the "discourse of truth" [Foucault, 1980: 93].)[3] Inevitably, other Chambri balked. To relinquish power to another would be to diminish both their own identity and viability. We doubt that either megalomania or a revolutionary vision impelled Godfried to ask the impossible of the Chambri big men. More likely, in his effort to create a true Chambri analogue to the Christian Bible that was to be an instrument of written authority and centralized control,[4] Godfried became, as we have suggested, an unwitting proponent of an alien form of authority. This was a form of authority implicit in the church and in its mutually supporting structure, the state. He was, in other words, led by the logic of his project to introduce and promote, in the very center of Chambri life, a hierarchical sociopolitical organization based on the relinquishment of power by the many, within which the Christian Bible operated.

In this regard, the Chambri intransigence to Godfried's proposal becomes additionally instructive. It not only reflected a clear recognition of internal Chambri politics; it also indicated the logic of their response to the national state of Papua New Guinea and to its non-Chambri citizens.

The Papua New Guinea state, independent since 1975 and based on an Australian parliamentary model, sought to exercise control over some 700 linguistically distinct groups. Its legitimacy and claim to efficacy rested on a proposition that the Chambri (and many of the diverse others) found very difficult to accept: in its most fundamental concepts, that of citizen and public interest, the state was premised on the relinquishment of power, on the ceding of power to a higher authority. (Significantly, because the Chambri perceived both Western missionaries and colonial administrators as largely outside their realm of competition, they had accepted the authority of the Christian Bible and, at least in the earlier years, that of the colonial state. In neither case did the Chambri regard themselves as having ceded power to another, much less to another like themselves.)

Central to the idea of the democratic state (including that of Papua New Guinea) was the definition of citizens as formally equal and the definition of public interest as that shared by all citizens.[5] This formal equality and shared interest were, in part, understood to be the product of individuals having granted substantial power to the state. In return, the state, with its superior power, would represent its citizens, protect (and define) their interests, adjudicate their differences and guarantee them equal protection for the exercise of individual (but still state-defined) rights. Under these conditions, a "good citizen" was one who cooperated with the state, accepting the fact that power had been ceded and centralized, by showing forbearance in the exercise of his/her own rights and tolerance toward the exercise of individual rights by others.[6] That the concept of citizen with a set of inherent rights was an essential part of political rhetoric and ideology[7] did not, however, mean that individuals actually were forbearing and tolerant, or that the state actually did extend full citizenship to all within its boundaries, or that individuals actually held interests in common. Of particular importance in these regards, and a point to which we shall return, was the existence of a contradiction: although the state defined all citizens as formally equal, there was, at the same time, both an institutionalization and a substantial acceptance of relatively permanent social inequalities such as class.

The Chambri, in contrast, who coordinated but did not relinquish their powers, found no compelling reason to believe that individuals necessarily, that is, in the absence of specific social connection, had particular rights, responsibilities or common interests.[8] For the Chambri, rights, obligations, and interests – indeed worth – were produced and shaped by social relationships: these entailments did not exist antecedent to those social relationships. Conversely, in the absence of relationships that entailed, individuals could not know what to expect of each other except enmity or indifference. (It was, however, true, as mentioned in Chapter Three, that youth found the freedom from entailment to be an exciting aspect of town life. It was exciting because of its possibilities, including those of danger, which as we shall see below sometimes proved fatal.) Yet, if relations of entailment could be established through, for example, a regular exchange of gifts and services as between trading partners, then there was the basis for individuals to grant each other the rights, responsibilities and shared interests of equals. (Attesting to the fact that relations of entailment were sufficient to establish relative equality was the fact that particular Chambri were linked by trading partnerships with individuals from groups recognized as both more powerful and less powerful.) In other words, the Chambri were likely to assume that the differences between individuals would be sufficiently commensurate that negotiations of entailed equality were possible.

Thus, in contrast to the context of the state in which citizens were defined as formally equal yet social relations were characterized by such persistent inequalities as class, the Chambri did not *assume* equality, but were always open to *negotiate* relationships of social entailment and equality. (Indeed, it seems to us that Papua New Guineans frequently sought common ground, including similarity of interest, that indicated at least rudimentary entailment. As we mentioned in Chapter Two, Michael Fox was told by one of his assailants that he would not be hurt because his scars marked both of them as from the Sepik, and, moreover, as subscribing to Sepik definitions of manhood. So too did a Chambri working in the Highlands of New Guinea explain to us that his friendship with a man from Mount Hagen stemmed from their sharing the same Sepik River drainage system.)

The primary Chambri frustration with the tourists, hence, resulted from the tourists' rejection of their overtures to negotiate relationships of relative equality. The tourists did not encourage long-term social relationships that would encompass the differences between individuals and groups. It was not that the Chambri and the tourists were different and initially disconnected that bothered the Chambri; rather, they were troubled by the fact that there seemed to be no way in which they could establish *even the basis* of negotiation, entailment and potential social equality. The differences remained painfully incommensurate.

Correspondingly, the Chambri were reluctant to accept the fact that the relationship between them and the state was based on incommensurate differences. Although delighted that the state had sufficient power to protect them, for instance, from enemy attack, the Chambri were distressed when they had difficulty influencing, or entailing the state. They were not able to involve the state in negotiations that would result in transactions as potential equals.

Below we will examine a series of cases illustrative of the relationships the Chambri were having within the context of the Papua New Guinea state, both with other groups and with the state itself. We shall see that, when dealing with these other groups and with the state itself, the Chambri were unwilling to yield to the state as adjudicator, to grant it superior authority.

Negotiating with neighbors: our farewell dinner at Aron's

Near the end of our stay we were given a particularly concentrated exposition of Chambri views and strategies concerning the most effective ways to deal with their non-Chambri neighbors. That we would soon travel back through Papua New Guinea to America brought up questions about Chambri and the outer world; that our departure was imminent suggested that our help, or at least our advice, be enlisted immediately. Thus, one December morning, Aron came to our house at Indingai to reaffirm our mutual entailment.

Bearing an enormous stalk of bananas, weighing at least fifty pounds, he said that now he was making good on a previous promise to help us with a *few* bananas. After asking whether we were sure we had accurately recorded the history (genealogy) of his family (see Chapter Five), he requested that we make a book of this information, just for him and his family and not for the public. He then expressed sorrow that we would be leaving Chambri in January and he asked what else he could give us. Thinking of foodstuffs other than bananas, we indicated that we particularly liked chicken cooked with greens and coconut milk. He said he would serve us this for a farewell dinner the following week.

The conversation then turned to the possibility that on our next visit to Chambri we might find gold-mining operations under way on Mount Garamambu, on the edge of Chambri Lake. We had previously told Aron and other Chambri that if large-scale gold mining were begun in the area, the cyanide likely to be used in gold extraction might well leak into their lake, killing their fish. Such an accident, we said, had already happened elsewhere in

Papua New Guinea when a barge containing drums of cyanide
had sunk in the Fly River. Aron and everyone else had found this
prospect most alarming. Now, as we visited with him, he sought
our advice about an idea he had to circumvent the danger of
contaminating Chambri Lake. Rather than risk having cyanide
leak into Chambri Lake, he said, it should be pumped directly into
two (specifically named) lakes on the other side of the mountain
or, perhaps, into the Sepik River. If pumped into the Sepik, then
the channel leading from the Sepik to Chambri Lake must be
altered so that the cyanide remained in non-Chambri waters.
Thus, in a completely unselfconscious way, Aron talked about
protecting the Chambri by pumping poison into the fishing areas
of their neighbors. Further examples suggesting that the Chambri
were quite oblivious to the "rights" of their fellow "citizens" were
soon to be brought to our attention.

Arriving at Aron's house on the day appointed for our dinner
we were pleased to find his children in hot pursuit of squawking
chickens. Several other guests were present, including Aron's
father, Kapiwon, and Kapiwon's in-law, another Kilimbit big man
named Pekur.

Our relations with Pekur had become somewhat strained.
During our previous field trip, he had discovered that Deborah's
Sepik River Societies contained several maps drawn by Yarapat, an
Indingai rival. Pekur had derided these maps as seriously incomplete, and insisted that we record his view of the primal Chambri
boundaries in our next book. Upon meeting us shortly after we
had arrived in Wewak on this visit, he demanded a copy of "his"
book, containing "his" map. Because we had not in fact included
his account in our most recent book, we simply replied, as was the
case, that the book was still at the printer's and we would give him
a copy when it became available. (This incident provided us with
perhaps our sharpest reminder that it was we as anthropologists
who ultimately determined what was to be represented in our
ethnographies.) Our response did not satisfy Pekur and he insisted that we give him, as we had given Yarapat, a copy of *Sepik River
Societies*. Having no copies with us, we could only promise to send
for one in America to be shipped air mail. Pekur was to rebuke us
for this unfulfilled promise virtually every time we saw him: he
again broached this topic at Aron's.

Deborah apologized for the delay of the book and offered to
buy him a copy of it when we passed through Port Moresby. Pekur

only grudgingly accepted this apology, saying that she had wasted his time and that he needed the book for a meeting of the land commission in late January.

The land commission referred to was to settle the territorial disputes between the Chambri and the Mensuat, a Sepik Hills people currently living on Peliagwi, an island adjacent to the Chambri village of Kilimbit. There had been periodic clashes between the Chambri from Kilimbit and the Mensuat over the hunting of crocodiles in the channel separating their settlements during the season of low-water. Pekur, and the other Kilimbit men gathered at Aron's, wanted the Mensuat to vacate immediately (what they claimed was) Chambri territory and go back to the Sepik Hills, where they had come from. Moreover, as Aron's wife was quick to point out, the Mensuat in their present location on Peliagwi were no longer willing to work hard: now that they had ready access to the fish of Chambri Lake, they were no longer eager, as they once had been, to process sago beyond their own needs in order to barter it with the Chambri for fish. Under the present circumstance, Mensuat women were willing to produce surplus sago only for cash sale, and at high prices.

All of those present at Aron's insisted that the Chambri had full ownership of Peliagwi because the Chambri ancestors had first settled there. Irrefutable proof of original occupancy by Chambri, we were told, lay in the fact that contemporary Chambri held control of the masks and ritual paraphernalia discovered or constructed by those first residing on Peliagwi. Also, Chambri had detailed knowledge about the lives of those first occupants, including the names they had given to various areas of Peliagwi. Pekur said that Deborah's book, which contained ancestral stories about the first settlers in Chambri Lake, would demonstrate to the commission the extent of this Chambri knowledge.

We replied that several copies of this book were already in Chambri hands. Pekur insisted that he must have *his* copy and pantomimed for us all what was clearly to him a gratifying scenario of a highly effective negotiation. Rising, he showed us how, book in hand, he would saunter up to the land magistrate. Then, after a strategic pause in which he waved the book for all to see, he would throw it down on the table in front of the magistrate. Then, while turning on his heel to leave the room, he would assert: "It is all there." The magistrate could only reply: "Yes, Pekur, you win." Moreover, Pekur continued, the Mensuat would be caught off guard when the case was brought before the commission. They had thought the matter was settled when, after recently meeting with the Chambri to resolve difficulties over crocodile hunting, all had shaken hands and chewed betel nut. Pekur resumed his seat to approving nods and smiles from Aron and the others at what was perceived to be an excellent strategy.[9]

Perhaps to appear no less keen than Pekur on confrontation, Aron followed by saying that he had often thought of putting a chain across the channel and daring the Mensuat to pass over it. This would undoubtedly provoke a fight which, Aron was confident, the Chambri would win. Fear of yet further violence might well induce the Mensuat to move back to their own land. Then Aron made a telling comment: he said that the Mensuat had been ignoring traditional land claims by following the ways of white people.

In this reference to white people Aron had, we think, two related matters in mind. First, he was referring to the policy of the Australian Colonial Administration which, in the late 1950s and early 1960s, had sought to bring remote groups under more complete control by persuading them to move closer to centers of government. Accordingly, the Mensuat had been encouraged to move from the Sepik Hills to the lake so that they could have better access to medical services, schools, and the labor market and so they could become members of the local government council, vote, pay taxes, be included in the census and be effectively policed. In other words, they had been encouraged to move so that they could become citizens with the same rights and responsibilities as the other citizens in Papua New Guinea.

Second, in Aron's view, as the result of colonial interference, the Mensuat were not only living where they had no right to be. They were, having made this move, also continuing to follow the ways of white people by relying on state-protected equality to establish their relations with their neighbors: through their recourse to a system of hierarchical power, they were acting as white people because they denied the necessity of generating and maintaining social entailments with the Chambri. This the Chambri found unacceptable because it placed the Chambri under a double disadvantage. It suggested (as did Chambri encounters with tourists) that the Chambri were not worth negotiating with and, in addition, it jeopardized Chambri access to the staple of sago. With at least talk of using force, the Chambri intent was to push them back into a position in which they would have to re-establish exchange relationships with the Chambri.[10]

The Chambri very much wanted the land commission to rule in their favor since they hoped then to be able to enlist the support of the police in expelling the Mensuat. A decision favorable to the Chambri would also serve to confirm the strength of their position and their effectiveness as negotiators. However, the Chambri were not likely to regard as binding any decision by the commission that went against them. They would view such a decision as won through bribery, magic, invocation of kin ties or other forms of social connection, not by evidence that the Mensuat had a valid claim. Yet, the Chambri response to such a governmental decision favoring another group would reflect more than habitual Chambri-centrism or the view that politics (at least as exercised by others) should be kept in its place. The Chambri objection to such a decision would be, at least in part, that it was illegitimate for a body to claim the right to control them on the basis of authority superior to theirs.[11] Such a body, moreover, would be acting in an additionally illegitimate manner if it were to support the claims of others that were based on the "ways of white people." "Justice" was not the recognition of claims based on such abstractions as rights and obligations of citizens under a rule of law. Nor was it the recognition of claims pertaining to some transcendent public interest. Justice was in the Chambri view the full recognition of claims generated through social entailment and negotiated by and between the principals. (The Chambri, to be sure, regarded the claims generated by their own social relations as more valid and compelling than those generated by the social relations of others.)[12]

The importance of such claims based on social entailment was nicely illustrated when the conversation at Aron's about driving the usurping and slothful Mensuat off Peliagwi was interrupted by the arrival of a Mensuat woman. She was returning to Peliagwi with her ailing father from a visit to the Chambri aid post. Feverish and thirsty, the old man had instructed her to shore the canoe near Aron's house so that she could obtain water from the son of his trading partner, Kapiwon. She was greeted warmly and, amid expressions of what appeared entirely genuine concern for her father, given a plastic container of water, a watermelon, and extensive magical-herbal medical advice.

Contending with the state: the case of Remy's murder

While Chambri in Kilimbit were planning strategies so that they could re-engage the Mensuat on more satisfactory terms, those in Indingai were contemplating how best to negotiate an even more complex set of relationships with their neighbors and with the Papua New Guinea state itself. Remy Kembi, the maternal niece of Francis Imbang, had been beaten to death early one morning inside the Wewak police barracks by three policemen's wives.

The first news reaching Chambri Island of her death, described on the Mission radio as murder, without specifying the circumstances, plunged Chambri, especially those in her mother's natal village of Indingai, into mourning and anger. Francis lamented publicly that he had allowed his sister, Analise, to marry a non-Chambri; moreover, he said that he had continually warned her that Wewak was no place for her family of nine children. Continuing, Francis asserted that it was only because he had pressing business at Chambri that he had not left for Wewak immediately to investigate and avenge Remy's death. After all, he – not Remy's father – was still responsible for her, since no bride-price had ever been paid for her mother.

A few days later, we happened to be the ones to convey to Francis the latest news from Wewak describing the circumstances of the murder. We told him that Remy had been visiting an unmarried policeman, who had been having an affair not only with her but with one of his colleagues' wives. This woman became jealous of Remy and with the help of two of her friends, also policemen's wives, bludgeoned Remy to death with planks early in the morning inside the barracks. Subsequently, these women flagged down a passing truck and persuaded the driver to take the body to the hospital compound. He did so and dumped it just inside the gate. It was discovered a few hours later at dawn by a hungry Chambri youth searching for food. Looking down from a mango tree inside the hospital compound, he saw and then recognized the body. He immediately alerted those at the Chambri Camp of what he had seen and they collected the body. Once they discovered how she had died their mourning turned to anger. (Their informant was a young woman who had accompanied Remy to the barracks but left before her death.) Chambri youths from the Camp forthwith stoned a nearby police station and smashed windows of police vehicles. The women who had killed

Remy had fled, and although still at large, would soon be apprehended.

Francis listened to our report with great attention. When we concluded, he expressed relief that, since the killers were known and about to be apprehended, he would not have to discover their identity and whereabouts. Moreover, because it was obvious that it was the police who were responsible, there would be a very good possibility that he would be able to claim from the government the substantial compensation appropriate for the death of a young kinswoman. As we shall see, in his effort to be compensated for Remy's loss, he would seek to clarify and establish relations of entailment on several different levels. Indeed, he intended to negotiate with the state as if it were another kinship group.

First, he sought to clarify the entailments within his own (extended) kin group. He set to work in earnest to establish that in the absence of a bride-price for his sister (Remy's mother) he, not Remy's father, had the appropriate claim to the compensation for Remy's death. In large measure to affirm that Remy was still a member of his family, Francis held the ceremony that rid a house of the spirit of one of its deceased patrilineal members. Standing shirtless inside his house, before an audience of Indingai women, he rubbed an aromatic grass on his chest, groin and underarms. He then took three drafts from a coconut shell filled with sago soup and, with his right hand, passed the shell with the remaining soup and the grass under his left armpit to a classificatory sister (substituting for an actual sister) standing directly behind him. She then finished the soup and later secretly buried the grass.

The purpose of the ceremony, Francis explained to us, was to insure that Remy's spirit left the family lest he and others become sick. Moreover, the sweet-smelling leaves rubbed on his body would insure that animals he might wish to hunt would not smell the death on his person and run away.[13] Another man elaborated, repeating the motion of passing the right hand under the left armpit, that the ceremony made the spirit of the person who died pass *back through the groin* of his or her father and leave the living. This ceremony, thus, would seem to be a male reversal of birth, enacted in remarkably condensed form. With the assistance of his closest available female kin,[14] Francis was claiming Remy as his own by delivering her into the company of his dead clan ancestors.

After this ceremony, Francis left his house and joined the male guests, all non-clansmen, gathered outside. These included several men of his men's house and Suangin, whose son Francis hoped would marry his eldest daughter. Francis' wife and daughters served them soup, rice, canned mackerel, and flour pancakes. When they had finished eating, Francis discussed with them all that he planned to do when he went to Wewak concerning his "trouble." In so doing, he was not only seeking advice but was also establishing himself as socially competent. Much as Pekur had sought to demonstrate through pantomime how he proposed to deal with the magistrate, Francis sought to show he could assert and negotiate his rights and responsibilities. (Clearly, neither assumed that those rights and responsibilities would be enforced by the state.) Below (in translation) are the objectives and considerations Francis enumerated and the responses he received. We present this text to convey the perspectives of those committed to this system in which each group (and its constituent members) maintained responsibility for autonomy:

Number One. I must bring her body here – the body of my sister's daughter.

Number Two. I must find out who informed the leaders of the Education Department, the police and the Province of her death. What information was conveyed?

Number Three. I must learn what each leader has answered. What do they intend to do about this murder? When they tell me what they plan to do about it, I will ask: "When?" If there's time enough, I will come back home and then go back to Wewak again. They must hurry up, just as Somare [the former Prime Minister and leader of the opposition who described the murder over the radio as an outrage] advised them to, and finish this terrible grievance. If they do not hurry up, then they will be compounding the grievance.

Number Four. If Remy's father's people want the body, I know what I will say to stop them: "You never paid bride-price for her mother. If you had paid bride-price, then you would be welcome to the body." If the kin of her father try to shut me up, I will not let them. It was their fault. Many times I asked them to make something of this mother. But the father's side did not have the money. I am a little angry with them. Because of this, all of the nine children of this man really belong to me. I was the one who gave my kin at Mensuat some money to close their mouths when she married him. [Francis' sister (and Remy's mother), Analise, was nursed as an infant, when her Mensuat mother died, by her mother's clan sister. Francis eventually compensated members of this Mensuat family for their nurture when Analise married in order to terminate their claims for a portion of her bride-price. Francis in this speech was asserting that his

27   Francis Imbang enumerated his objectives concerning
Remy's death.

was the only remaining claim for Analise's yet unpaid bride-price and, thus, for Remy's death compensation.]

Number Five. I will ask a great deal of compensation from the government. If the government refuses to compensate me, I will cause real trouble. It is lucky I was not in Wewak when this came up. It is lucky also that this young man [pointing to Michael Kambon, one of the guests] who is not afraid to fight was not in Wewak. We would have gotten back at everyone responsible. It is real lucky. That is all I have to say. I was happy to hear Somare's talk. As soon as anything is decided, I will call you on the Mission radio.

Francis' speech met with clear approval, although several of the men had advice for him:

[Suangin:] You must get her body first; tell the government that you will come back for the court case. And tell them that the girl died straight inside the hands of the law.

[Michael:] The government must pay your transportation costs to bring the body home. It must pay for both the use of a car and motor canoe.

[Francis:] Yes, thank you, this is good advice. I wanted to hear what you had to say.

[Another guest:] You must make it clear to everyone that you are the boss; that all decisions must await you.

[Francis:] One member of the government [Provincial Parliament] from Boiken argued for a law which would allow murderers to be hanged. But the churches objected. They said that Papua New Guinea is a Christian country.

[Suangin:] This policeman was not married. He himself has said that he could not understand why these married women had killed this young girl. Francis, you must hurry up and go to Wewak. Peter Akaman [a member of Francis' extended family] is there, but he is too sick to represent you well. If another member of your family were there, then you could take your time.

[Francis:] Yes, Suangin, thank you.

[Suangin:] Tony Kembi [Remy's father] did not want to accept the teaching position the Mission had given to him. And if he had to go where it sent him, he wanted to take his family, but there was not a good enough house there for them to live in. He went alone, and then his family got into trouble. He wanted to tear his body apart when he heard the news. His headmaster did not tell him at first. He just said that a member of the family had become sick. If he had been told that his daughter was dead, he would have died on the highway while trying to reach Wewak. Remember, Francis, to say that it was something the government did. It was not an ordinary criminal who killed this girl, but a policeman's wife from [the Sepik River village of] Yamanambu. Her [the murderess'] father was initially from [the Sepik River village of] Japandai. Just she alone was angry. She was cross that this policeman had promised to marry Remy.

[Francis:] Remy was a good girl. She was like Tiameri [his eldest daughter]. She never talked back to her parents.

[Suangin:] Tell them right away that the law killed her, not a criminal. She was not sick, but she died. Do not be afraid; you have a large family who will come to support you if you need help.

[Francis:] Thank you for your good thoughts.

As we have seen, one of the attractions of town life was the freedom and excitement that came from encounters between relatively unentailed individuals. However, with an incident such as Remy's death, these individuals immediately acquired a density of social attributes, specifically those defined by kinship. Remy became socially embedded in the various kin groups with an interest in her, as did those implicated in her death. Indeed, the government itself was seen as enmeshed in the logic of (patrilineal) kinship: it had overall responsibility for the entire range of actions of its members and members' wives.

Francis and his advisors were concerned not only to specify which kin groups would become participants in the social field created by Remy's death but also to establish a strategy for dealing with them. There was agreement that, provided Francis acted forcefully, his position was strong. And Francis did stress his capacity for direct confrontation. Moreover, he could call on reinforcements from his own kin group if necessary.

Francis anticipated that, although the Mensuat who had nurtured Remy's mother might still assert an interest in Remy, he could remind them that their claims had already been satisfied. The claim to Remy by members of her father's group, which ordinarily in this patrilineal region would have been pre-eminent, could also be effectively contested because the bride-price necessary to make her a full member of their group had never been paid.

His most critical dealings, however, would be with the government. He should insist that the government transport the body at its own expense to Chambri for burial. Of most importance, the government should be compelled to pay heavy compensation. In addition, Suangin briefly considered whether the clan members of one of the killers in Japandai and Yamanambu should also pay compensation, but this possibility was dropped, presumably in recognition that the government was both easier of access and had a much "deeper pocket."[15] That the police, and the government more generally, must be held responsible for this killing was entirely evident to the Chambri: "it was something the government did"; "the girl died straight inside the hands of the law"; "the law killed her, not a criminal."

Such a view, though, that the act of policemen's wives was an act of the government, did not take into account certain critical distinctions on which the modern (bureaucratic) state was based. These distinctions focused on the nature of a citizen's legal individuality. Thus, in the eyes of the state, a person was defined as substantially different even from those in his or her family; of equal importance, his or her acts as a private individual (a private citizen) were different from those as an office holder who was exercising the (ceded) power of the state on behalf of the citizen and the public. Of special relevance to our discussion of the Chambri is this latter distinction: acting according to private interests and acting in the public interest created separate spheres of responsibility. The City of New York, for instance, would not be expected to pay compensation to the family of someone killed by one of its policemen who was off-duty, and clearly not pursuing official duties, much less to the family of someone killed by that policeman's wife. (Although there might be debates, based on the distinction between private and public responsibility, as to whether, for example, the City had reason to know that it was harboring a corrupt policeman, there would never be debates as to whether the City would be responsible for the action of the wife.)

Francis and his Chambri advisors had quite the opposite view. They considered Remy's death to be at the hands of the law, even though the policeman Remy had gone to visit was described as entirely uninvolved: "He himself," Suangin mentioned, "has said that he could not understand why these married women had killed this young girl." Moreover, no Chambri seemed to find our own concern in determining where the police were when the killing took place of much importance. The fact of police responsibility was already established to their satisfaction because it was known that the wives were the killers.

The Chambri were, in other words, viewing the police as a kin group, collectively responsible for the actions, in whatever capacity, of its members and their wives. In the context of expectations provided by kinship, responsibility for a death required payment of compensation from one kin group to another. And, as with the Chambri talk of using force with the Mensuat, one of the possible tactics of negotiation between groups was reprisal or threats of reprisal. In the Chambri dealings with the police, the attack on the police station was in part a warning that reprisals would surely follow for any continued refusal to accept responsibility for Remy's death. Thus, the Chambri in their grievance with the state, far from yielding to a superior authority, were asserting their efficacy and autonomy by forcefully negotiating their rights and responsibilities as they would with any other group.

On protecting your own from the state

A few days later, Francis, conspicuously adorned on wrists and ankles with mourning bands woven from shiny black plastic twine, accompanied us into Wewak. While he set off on his business with the government, we arranged to meet Martin Gawi for lunch at a local hotel. We wanted to get his version of the news. Martin told us that "everything at Chambri Camp went wrong at once." "First," he said, "the police killed the girl; then, seven young men robbed a local tradestore of K300; finally, Steven Manukin got stabbed because his son was one of the robbers." These latter two unfortunate occurrences formed part of a sequence of events during which the Papua New Guinea state claimed grievance against several Chambri; in response to these events, the Chambri community, for the first time that we were aware, seriously contemplated acknowledging to the state that in terms of offenses against outsiders some of its own members were criminals. As we shall see, to yield Chambri up to the police, who were acting in response to the complaints of non-Chambri citizens, would be to deprive Chambri of their autonomy as negotiators in a way they would find difficult to accept.

However, before we examine the Chambri response to these particular events, we should note that the Chambri themselves sometimes sent for the police to come into Chambri Camp to calm matters down between angry Chambri. Quarrels were most likely to arise in the context of drinking. For instance, a young man, who was drinking beer in the afternoon with some friends inside one of the Camp's rather makeshift men's houses, urinated in the corner. He was castigated by an older man for desecrating this ritual center. When he laughed derisively in response, the older man threw a multi-pronged hunting spear at him. The young man and his friends then began to tear the men's house apart, to the increasing fury of the older man. Bystanders, realizing their own efforts to bring order were proving inadequate, summoned the police. Their arrival was dramatic: three smartly uniformed men, two with batons and one with a tear-gas gun, moved with assurance to the site of the trouble. The antagonists were quickly separated and brought back by the police to the nearby station. The police then, as in the other three instances when they were summoned to Chambri Camp during the time we lived there,[16] sternly instructed the antagonists to return to the Camp and settle matters according to Chambri custom.

In these cases, a public meeting was subsequently convened, grievances were aired, compensation was set and paid and betel nut was exchanged by the antagonists. In the course of the meeting concerning the desecration of the men's house, the youths were lectured about the central importance of the men's house to Chambri cultural identity and political strength and about the traditional punishment through incineration of those who damaged a men's house. Agreement was reached for them to repair and refurbish the men's house under the supervision of knowledgeable seniors. Thus, summoning the police to the Camp inaugurated, rather than precluded, the process by which Chambri settled their affairs in their own way, so as to reaffirm Chambri custom.

But the events precipitated by the robbery of the tradestore were not so easily kept within Chambri jurisdiction. The robbery, Martin told us, took place in broad daylight near Chambri Camp. The seven young men, in their late teens and early twenties, held up the clerks in the store at knife-point and ran off with the money, which they subsequently claimed to have dropped in their flight. Unfortunately for the Chambri, the tradestore owner was a man reputed to defend his interests vigorously, even to the point of having his enemies killed. Thus, Chambri believed that the attack a few days later on Steven Manukin, whose son was known to have participated in the robbery, was arranged by this man. Steven was stabbed in the side, though not seriously, as he was walking home one night after selling artifacts at a local hotel.

According to Martin, several hours after the robbery police came to the Camp searching for the thieves, already identified as

Chambri youths.[17] One senior Chambri man, Anton Bascam, gave up two of the boys, Steven's son and Yarapat's son, to the police who took them to jail. Immediately afterward there was a meeting at the Camp, in which residents were joined by Chambri living elsewhere in Wewak, to discuss the crime and how to deal with the police.

One speaker, a man in charge of Catholic education in the province, was strongly in favor of turning the other youths in. (His special interest concerned student vandalism in community schools.) This, he felt, would at least partially restore the good name of the Chambri which had been impugned by the criminal, "copycat" (Western influenced) customs of some of its youths. Moreover, these youths were "big heads"[18] who would not listen to their elders; jail would teach them a much-needed lesson. Bascam and several others expressed their support of his position.

Martin told us that he had taken the opposite view and had been "a force to be reckoned with."[19] He had convinced the community that the only chance to reform the "big head" youths by teaching them proper Chambri ways would come if they were protected from arrest. So effectively did he speak that even Bascam changed his mind and, indeed, made (unsuccessful) efforts to secure the release of the two already in jail.

We asked Martin whether he felt that in harboring their criminals the Chambri might be creating further problems: emboldened by protection from punishment and given a secure base of operation, they might come to threaten those within their own community as well as others. Concerning the possibility of threat to Chambri, Martin admitted that Bascam had changed his position partially because Martin had warned him that he, Bascam, might well be stabbed in the future by one of the robbers for his failure to support them. Concerning the possibility of threat to others, to the public at large, Martin insisted that one could, with the correct magical knowledge, remain safe from criminal attack. We reminded him of a story he had once told us of an attack he had suffered in Port Moresby. Temporarily blinded by (what he said was) acid thrown in his face, Martin had been robbed of his money. (Ironically, his copy of *How to Win Friends and Influence People* was also stolen.) Martin, nonetheless, insisted that correct magical knowledge would have protected him even from such an assault.

He concluded his story by telling us that the stabbing of Steven had convinced most Chambri that, regardless of whether they protected their youths from the police (Steven's son was, after all, still in jail), they would have to compensate the tradestore owner. Because the youths continued to claim they were unable to return the money, having dropped it in their flight, Bascam raised about K350, somewhat more than had been stolen, in a community collection. This sum was presented to the tradestore owner who, after some negotiation, declared himself satisfied with this compensation and agreed to drop charges with the police.

As far as we could reconstruct, in no case did Chambri entertain, much less advocate, the proposition that they were obligated or that it was their public responsibility to turn the youths over to the police simply because they had broken the law. Even those who initially thought they should go to jail did so not because they regarded themselves as good citizens, controlled by and committed to the laws of the state and to the public interest, but as good Chambri, controlled by and committed to Chambri customs. As such, they considered it in the Chambri collective interest to show that they did not condone criminal activity. Chambri took pride in their capacity to resolve their own dilemmas, to govern themselves; and the presence of youthful criminals, that is, young men out of control, was a source of shame. Although the argument that a stint in jail might make these Chambri youths, the "big heads," more receptive to accepting Chambri customs had some plausibility to the Chambri, Martin convincingly argued that the most effective way to have them learn these customs was to keep them in the community.[20]

Thus, Chambri living in Wewak at this period in Papua New Guinea history could in substantial measure use the police as a resource: they could choose to enlist police help in quelling a disturbance yet be assured that the Chambri community (in cases other than capital crimes)[21] would retain responsibility for the resolution of the conflict; they could choose whether or not the police should be given custody of the young thieves. The use of such a resource by the Chambri and, as far as we know, their Sepik neighbors in Wewak, testified to certain underlying conditions: specifically, the existence of strong kin and ethnic groups operating within still viable systems of customary law in a context in which the police had real, but distinctly limited, power.

Commensurate differences within the public realm

That the Chambri, and we think most other Papua New Guineans, did not grant transcendent authority to the state meant that much of the interaction within the "public realm" followed the assumptions of the system of commensurate differences. Chambri, either as individuals or as members of a collectivity, encountered other Papua New Guineans as well as the government with the expectation that the entailments which defined the relationships between each must not only be negotiated but must be negotiated under circumstances in which the principals represented themselves and their particular interests.

For instance, in seeking access to the resources of the state, the Chambri sought to negotiate relations of entailment in very specific terms, again, somewhat on the model of a trading partnership.[22] Thus, one candidate, running for election to the Wewak seat in the provincial parliament, was informed during a campaign visit to the Chambri Camp that if he wished to represent them, he would have to convince them that he could further *their* development. One man demanded that the government must see to it that tourists bought at generous prices all the artifacts and baskets Chambri artisans produced. As it was, this candidate was told, many Chambri had little to show for their hard work and skill. Another insisted that the candidate would have his vote only if he promised to provide well-paying jobs for Chambri in the Wewak area. To be sure, an American electorate also expected its representatives to deliver benefits in the form of local projects; yet, these representatives were, at the same time, expected to be "statesmanlike" and balance local benefits against regional and national ones. The Chambri, however, would never accept an argument that their representatives should even consider the possibility that more general public interests outweighed their specific Chambri interests. The idea that national interests should legitimately subsume local interests was as antithetical to the Chambri system of commensurate differences as was the concept that the authority of the state should subsume the authority of particular groups.

Correspondingly, the form that Chambri criticism of the government, including elected representatives, took was not that there was an excessive concern with local interests but that there was insufficient reciprocity for Chambri support and/or there were others who had access to more compelling ties of entailment than did Chambri. It was in this latter regard that the term "wantok system" was likely to be employed. (The wantok system referred to a pattern of preferential treatment given kin and others of a primary social network.)[23] The Chambri (and we think other Papua New Guineans) objected to such patterns of preferential treatment primarily when they themselves were excluded from the networks of entailment which defined who the possible negotiators were. That is, the wantok system was troubling to the Chambri primarily when it precluded them as having insufficient relevance even to be players in the system of commensurate differences. Indeed, increasing numbers of Chambri and other Papua New Guineans were sensing that they were being ruled out of the game and that differences were becoming so great and so entrenched as to be incommensurate. (Whether these differences would become those of class, or those predicated on a relationship between persons who controlled the means of production and persons who sold their labor, was not clear.)

Stated another way, we suggest that a large number of Papua New Guineans had begun to suspect that despite their best efforts, including their most effective use of their networks, they would be barred by the wantok system from access to the most significant resources such as educational opportunities[24] and lucrative employment with the government or large businesses. They would be barred from those opportunities no longer controlled within the Chambri community and they would lose out, relative to others, on the advantages of development. These perceptions, we will argue, were partially responsible for what was being experienced as a serious problem with law and order. During our most recent research there was a distressing increase in crime in Papua New Guinea as individuals (including, as we have seen, Chambri youths) relied on their own kin or village networks for protection when they attacked those with better access to resources than they.

Chambri were very upset, for example, when their children at two provincial high schools were sent home in the middle of the semester as the result of criminal youth operating from the safety of their local villages and under the protection of their own wantok. In one case, the entire faculty composed of both indigenous and expatriate teachers left after a night of systematic robbery in which each of their houses was raided and their belongings stolen at knife point; in the other, all of the school equipment had been stolen. Rape and other forms of assault upon teachers, their families and students at such schools were commonly reported occurrences. As these cases suggest, it was especially when they were without the company of kin or others of their network that prosperous Papua New Guineans as well as Western residents and visitors were vulnerable to locally based banditry and assault.[25] (The previously mentioned assault on Michael Fox and the mining engineers suggests the same conclusion. Correspondingly, John Illumbui had told us that despite his extensive security precautions, he felt extremely insecure in his suburban Port Moresby house.)[26]

We conducted numerous discussions with Chambri about why criminal attack, especially by young men, took place. Perhaps the most thoughtful responses were that violent crime such as armed robbery, assault and rape took place in order to "pull others down." Anyone, we were told with a really good fortnightly salary, one of K200–K300, was an automatic target. Similarly, these youths would attack those who had good clothes, a car, a nice house, as they might attack women who dressed well and appeared disdainful. For many youths, precluded as they must have felt by wantok favoritism from becoming players in what was no longer entirely a system of commensurate differences, violent crime appeared as one way to establish themselves as potential equals.

Moreover, the Papua New Guinea state, based as it continued to be on kin and ethnic ties, was not only relatively partial but, as we have seen, relatively ineffectual, at least with respect to law enforcement. Under the circumstances we have described in which each group negotiated with the state on its own behalf, the police did not have sufficient power, certainly compared to that retained by kin groups and villages, to discourage such criminal attacks. Thus, the wantok system was providing a double impetus for the crime that Papua New Guineans found so distressing: when determining access to the public resources of the state, this system was fueling much of the anger that seemed to motivate many criminal activities; when determining relations of primary allegiance, it was precluding effective law enforcement.

During this period, Chambri and others were trying to negotiate with the state without accepting the assumptions and concomitants of the state. They did not accept the proposition that they had ceded authority to the state; they did not believe that within the state all citizens were formally equal; and they rejected the virtual inevitability of incommensurate differences based on control of the concentrated power and resources of the state. Because of their insistence on preserving a sovereign autonomy while negotiating entailments with each other and the state, relations in the public realm between unentailed individuals were frequently troubled. These relations were confrontational, evocative of envy, dangerous and resistant to adjudication.[27] Yet, to yield that autonomy – to cede authority – would be to give up the capacity to negotiate their identity as equals in efficacy and significance. It would be to accept representation and definition of interests by others and, thereby, risk the institutionalization of social inequalities.[28]

The Chambri, of course, never contemplated relinquishing their autonomy. Nor did they expect that the difficulties they were experiencing in negotiating with the state would abate if they did relinquish their autonomy. Indeed, in their view, to cede power would only exacerbate these difficulties. From the Chambri perspective, the best and the only way for them to deal with the future and the changes it would continue to bring was to hold firm to ancestral power, ensuring that it continued to work for their benefit. Simply put, this would mean that they must maintain full control over Chambri Island.

Such a strategy, it seems to us, would serve them reasonably well: at the very least, although they might never have sufficient power to dump cyanide into their neighbors' lakes, they might prevent it from being dumped into their own.

Will the center hold?

Virtually all Chambri realized that the future would not be any simple replication of the past. Although in most cases they were optimistic about what development held in store, they also recognized that it had brought continuing problems: Nick's death and then Remy's, were preoccupying indications that intergenerational conflict would increase as would also the hazards of negotiating in the public realm.

The most forceful exposition we were to hear of a solution to the problems associated with development came from Yarapat in response to Remy's death and his son's incarceration for robbery of the tradestore. He believed that the best and, indeed, the only context in which Chambri could safely incorporate the benefits of development would be at Chambri itself. Although his perspective was that of a Chambri big man and thus was not likely to please someone like Rex, we do think Yarapat was on the right track in trying to formulate a viable future for the Chambri at Chambri.

Yarapat had established an extensive and profitable garden and piggery on an island close to Chambri. However, at the time of our conversation with him, not only had his pigs become elusive but his wife sick. He had therefore decided to pledge to his ancestors that he would rebuild his (and their) men's house from its virtual ruins. His ancestors had, he believed, become angry since, with the men's house in essential disuse, they had no one to converse with or to eat with. At the feast Yarapat gave to provide formal notice both to his ancestors and to those living at Chambri of his (politically very ambitious) intentions, he explained to us that Chambri lives went wrong when connections with ancestral ways, the basis of both power and wisdom, were broken or attenuated.

He began the conversation with us by speaking about who would inherit his ancestral powers. He said that since Independence in 1975, it was possible for children to live according to their own inclinations: if they chose, they could just drift, going here and there and staying nowhere very long. It had also become possible for a father to bequeath his power to any of his sons, rather than as previously, to his eldest son.[29] Indeed, he continued, Independence provided both fathers and children with a variety of alternatives. Yet, Yarapat insisted, some were clearly more viable than others. He spoke with intensity to us and several of his very attentive young sons who were present about what would happen to the children who chose not to listen to the wisdom of their elders: these, he stated flatly, could expect to die. When people were lamenting Remy's death, he said he had told them it was her own fault because she should have come back home. Everyone who did not have a good job should come home to earn money by planting coconuts and gardens, fishing and raising pigs. One could, in fact, be a "businessman" at home.

(Yarapat described himself as such and referred to his pigs as his savings account. Of course, without feasible access to regional markets, the profitability of Yarapat's enterprises required that other Chambri who were his customers had sources of income. Thus, his particular solution to the problem of earning money at home would work only if money continued to come into Chambri, either through such usual means as remittances and tourism or, perhaps, through the creation of local industry. Martin Gawi had suggested in his campaign platform the possibility, for example, of a timber works or a furniture factory to be based at Chambri. In the Conclusion we will return to this topic of local employment when we discuss plans to develop an elaborate tourist hotel on a small island close to Chambri. Such an enterprise as this though, at some social and cultural cost, would probably guarantee regular income to at least a few of those who might be interested in buying Yarapat's pigs.)

Yarapat continued: those who rejected proper Chambri lives by drifting around aimlessly in town would surely encounter trouble, either by falling in with, or becoming victims of, criminals. Young people had been told this many times but were "big heads" who would not listen to this or any other counsel from their seniors. Nor did they show any interest in learning ancestral knowledge. Significantly, Yarapat then brought up the case of Nick Ambri who died because he did not listen to his father: because he was a know-it-all kid, he was killed (by sorcery). Although Nick, of course, was at Chambri when he fell ill, his case was, in Yarapat's view, comparable to Remy's in that death occurred when ancestral protection was lost through the rejection of Chambri truths.

(Given the force and clarity with which Yarapat expressed his position, it was with some trepidation that we asked him about the incarceration of his son as a criminal. He responded in typical Chambri style. He merged self-interest with Chambri-interest while at the same time denying legitimacy to the state. He had just heard on the Mission radio that his and Steven's sons were still in jail and that their cases were yet to be heard. This was all a great mistake for which Bascam was responsible. Even the store owner, content with the return of his money, did not wish them to be held. The store owner knew, Yarapat insisted, that the boys really had not done wrong because, if they were real criminals, they would have robbed one of the big stores in town. They had acted as they did, not because they were "big heads," but because they wished to provoke a confrontation with the police to repay them for what they had done to Remy.)[30]

Near the end of our fieldwork, we asked two of the older Chambri men, two on whom the action of the elements was still thought to depend, what they thought the Chambri future in this expanded and changing world would be like after they died. Although differing, each insisted that the only viable future would be one in which Chambri retained its sovereignty.

Maliwan, who was at the height of his physical and political power, believed that the future ultimately boded well for Chambri. True, there might be a break in inter-generational transmission of ancestral knowledge: nonetheless this knowledge would not be permanently lost. Because the ground of Chambri and its power remained, the ancestors themselves, perhaps communicating secrets through dreams, would ensure that "the shoots of understanding would sprout again."

Old and in failing health, our long-term friend Yorondu feared that after his death, and the death of other senior men, Chambri would be unable to regulate their lives. They would become as disconnected from the Chambri realm as were the white people who came as tourists. It would no longer be the Chambri but others who would determine when and if the various sorts of fish, birds, waters and winds were to come. Chambri, with its power dispersed, and dependent on others, would no longer be the center of order and signification. It would cease to exist.

Conclusion
Interlocking stories, intersecting lives

As we began working on this conclusion, the following letter arrived from Godfried. It was written from Wewak where he had once again returned to live. We print it here in translation, with his permission:

November 6, 1988

Dear Sister Deborah,

Here now I write to tell you about our father Andrew Tambwi Yorondu. Yes Deborah and Freddy, father died on October 5, 1988. I will write the story of his death soon but I wish to tell you that it was not a good death. All the elder men of Chambri ensorcelled him and he died. A death like his was not an ordinary death. He is gone.

In April I received the K20 you sent me along with the trousers. About the new cassette recorder, I received it and am using it. Yes, sister, and in-law, Freddy, everything that you have sent me I have gotten. So do not worry about them. I am using the recorder to collect stories to send you . . . I would like a camera so I can send you pictures of all the big ceremonies that will be held at Christmas. To commemorate father's death, there will be a ceremony of the fish that you two have not seen; also, two ancestral crocodiles, Ilasone and Pangasone, will also be invoked . . . It will cost me a lot of money, about K600. I must buy a pig and make all the presentations in father's name. So, you two, if you are concerned about helping me, now is the time to do it. You might also send some tourists to make a movie of these events.

We changed all of the thatch on the big [Walindimi] men's house at Wombun and then held a celebration. One hundred and seventy five tourists came to see this celebration. And another thing happened. We held a large party for the opening of the airstrip at Kilimbit village.

The next matter pertains to the island of Mungank [a small island only a few hundred yards from Kilimbit village]. Everyone knows that soon the tourist association board will build a men's house and hotel there.

196

This is the tourist board of Australia at Cairns . . . And, Deborah and Freddy, I want to give you a very large thanks from all the people at Chambri for your hard work in helping with the tourists. We are proud of you and wish you to come back soon to Chambri Lake; a big thanks also from the people of Wombun for writing the story of the [Walindimi] men's house there. Because of your help, many people in Wombun are now helping me by giving me stories. . . .One more thing, I want to ask you if you want carvings. Please let me know. I am ready to send them to you so that you can sell them in the U.S.A. So that is all now.
Your loving brother,
Godfried Kolly

Yorondu's death marked a conclusion for us. His life had begun in one context and had ended in another. He was born some 65 years before, during the exile that had followed the Chambri defeat at the hands of the Iatmul; he was initiated in a ceremony that included not only skin cutting but ritual homicide;[1] and he had been among the last of Walinakwan's contemporaries. (It may be recalled from the Introduction that it was Walinakwan who slept with his drums, Posump and Ponor.) Like Walinakwan, Yorondu was regarded as powerful, and, like Walinakwan, he was also regarded as anachronistic.

Because he was reputed to have extensive ritual knowledge, few doubted his claim – one among many – that it was he who annually brought a particular species of fish to Chambri Lake. Indeed, women returning from the lake sometimes presented him with small cash gifts to thank him for providing the fish they had just caught. Few disputed Yorondu's claim that by controlling the ancestral forces residing in the water hole in front of his house he held Chambri Island in place thus preventing it from drifting throughout the Sepik, as it once had.[2] Such claims for ritual efficacy were, as we have seen, typical and in fact, definitional of a big man. And, although others might contest his recent assertion that, in anchoring Chambri Island, he was as well, anchoring Papua New Guinea and America, no one would be surprised that a Chambri man of knowledge would make such a boast.

Nevertheless, what was worldly knowledge for those whose world was the regional system of the Chambri and their Sepik neighbors appeared as *somewhat* unsophisticated for those whose world had been shaped by a national and international system. Chambri, even those most committed to the idea of development, would still agree that Yorondu was correct to take his ritual concerns seriously. Yet, they would find in what was partly an aesthetic reaction that he often took them too seriously or, at least in a way that made him appear peculiar. Thus, while most if not all Chambri still believed that in times of illness, ancestral support must be mobilized, few would seek support in the way Yorondu did. As an example of Yorondu's peculiarity: when his youngest son fell ill with the painful headaches of malaria, Yorondu was not content with what had become the contemporary practice of placating offended ancestors with the *smell* of a singed and cooking chicken. He placated offended ancestors and evoked general astonishment by actually dropping pieces of cooked chicken into his water hole to facilitate his son's recovery.[3]

As might be expected, he was occasionally deprecated by Chambri children and youth. One morning as he was chatting with us at our house, he was brought into a conversation initiated by our neighbor, Scola. She was describing a government-sponsored class in nutrition she had attended with other Sepik women. In order for the women better to remember the "basic foods," each one was given the name of a food that began with the first letter of her name. Thus Scola was called "sago" for the duration of the course. Her three young sons who were running about found this story hilarious. Then, while she looked on somewhat apprehensively but without interfering, they began shouting that Tambwi Yorondu was really "Tambwi tomato." Yorondu was obviously annoyed that the boys were disrespectful and that Scola was doing nothing to stop them. (When one of the boys was stung by a wasp a few minutes later, Yorondu muttered that he, Yorondu, had made that happen.)

In fact, Chambri youth had, for some time, regarded his ritual preoccupations with indifference. During our research in 1983, while he constructed, virtually alone, a medium-sized men's house, the young men whose men's house it would also be, strummed their guitars and watched without offering any assistance.[4] In his turn, he took grim satisfaction in the extent of their ignorance. He would, for example, instruct us to play for the youth, lounging in the vicinity of our house, tape-recordings we had made of his chanting both exoteric and esoteric clan names. He would chortle and say privately to us that these youth were too stupid to recognize which the powerful names were.[5]

During our years of collaboration with Yorondu, we never discovered an area of traditional knowledge unfamiliar to him and about which he could not produce a full, though perhaps politically partisan, account. (We told him this on our last trip; he agreed and immediately challenged us to find something he did not know.) When we asked him how he had learned so much, he said that most of his knowledge had come from his father, Kwolikumbwi; the rest he had picked up as a young man by listening to the conversations of his elders in the men's house. Yorondu and other adult Chambri clearly recognized that present-day youth had neither the context nor the desire for such learning. Yorondu's death must, thus, have presaged for others, as it did for us, the end of an earlier way of being Chambri.

Yorondu's death, as well, marked for us another important transition in the anthropology of the Chambri. With his death, our connection was substantially diminished with the Chambri of Margaret Mead and Reo Fortune, whose writings had affected our own work. Yorondu, who had taught us so much, had learned from his father who had also taught Mead and Fortune.[6] And surviving Yorondu and that first generation of anthropologists was his son Godfried, who had decided to become an indigenous ethnographer, writing not only for us but for a Chambri audience.

In addition to the sense of finality and passage that Godfried's news of Yorondu's death evoked in us, his letter appeared a conclusion of another sort. Catching Chambri in process, Godfried alluded to and showed the persistence of many of the concerns and preoccupations we have written about in this book. His letter, moreover, provided the last Chambri words we can incorporate in our writing here about these continuing concerns and preoccupations.

By attributing Yorondu's death to ensorcellment at the hands of big men, Godfried voices the pervasive theme of Chambri male activity and identity: the virtually ceaseless efforts of mature men (such as Maliwan, Kapiwon, Aron, Pekur, Yarapat, and Nick Ambri's clansmen) to maintain equality within a system of commensurate differences by accumulating and displaying power in competition with one another. Any shift in the social field, particularly as manifested by the death of an elder man like Yorondu, would necessarily be interpreted by Chambri in terms of contention over power. If big men could combine to ensorcell someone as knowledgeable as Yorondu, those younger men like Rex must have continued to wonder how they would fare if they were to return to Chambri with their disruptive ideas.

Yet, however ambivalently individuals might feel about life at Chambri, clearly no other place would be adequate for the invocation and implantation of ancestral forces. It was to Chambri that Godfried would have to return in order to effect the final conversion of Yorondu into an ancestor. It would have to be there that the clan sisters would take the *mwai* mask with his spirit into his men's house. Nor would another location have an audience as socially complete. As even those youths close to Nick Ambri could attest, Chambri cosmological and social life was ineluctably grounded at Chambri. And, by planning that his father's last rites would take place during Christmas, Godfried sought to ensure the attendance (and, he hoped, the assistance) of those in Wewak and beyond. As we saw in the letter from the young migrant to his parents (Chapter 3), it was then, perhaps on Christmas break from schools or jobs, that migrants were most likely to visit Chambri. Christmas had in fact become the primary season for them to return to engage not only in Christian but in traditional rituals. (We might add that Maliwan's skin cutting and Nick's last rites had been scheduled to take place *before* Christmas so that participants would not be distracted by the rush of other ritual activities.)

The ceremony Godfried planned would be an involved and expensive display of the clan-based totemic powers Yorondu had exercised. Through staging, for instance, the elaborate ceremony of the fish, Godfried would commemorate Yorondu and, like Yarapat with his display to us of his totemic prerogatives (Chapter 5), exhibit his own enhanced identity as the heir to those important totemic powers. Moreover, to stage successfully such an expensive ceremony would provide both prestige and the proof that Godfried actually had those powers to which he was laying claim.

We also learned from Godfried's letter that he was continuing with his literary project and that it was − he claimed − still providing him with recognition. (Along with his letter he sent us three stories, comparable to those he had written earlier and none containing esoteric information. One, twenty-three pages long, provided Chambri with an infant Jesus.[7] Another concerned the deplorable fact that young men were dying, ensorcelled because they no longer obeyed the "good Christian custom" of respecting big men, elders, teachers, catechists, priests and bishops. The last, a well-known folk tale, related the seduction and murder of a Chambri ancestor by an autochthonous female spirit.) Godfried attributed the cooperation he had recently received from story tellers in Wombun to the success our story of the Walindimi men's house had in attracting tourists.

From Godfried's allusion to new thatch on the Walindimi men's house we concluded that Maliwan was prospering. Apparently his application to the national government for funds to refurbish Walindimi (Chapter 1) had been approved. If so, he had acquired prestige by pulling money from the government and by sponsoring a big work project (which had cost him nothing). In any case, he had profited by staging the men's house re-opening as a tourist event, for which admission was undoubtedly charged; and he had ensured that Walindimi, his men's house and tourist attraction, would continue to be a source of income.

Godfried, evidently wishing to duplicate Maliwan's success, asked us to send tourists to Yorondu's last rites. (It was believed that we had sent tourists to Chambri at other times.) Moreover, Godfried and other Chambri were excited by the increase in tourism that was to come with the opening of the airstrip at Kilimbit and the building of a men's house and hotel on Mungank Island. Kilimbit Chambri had long pressed to have an airstrip at their end of the island. Kapiwon had, at least by his own account (Chapter 5), donated the land, and the men, in response to Martin Gawi's promise of public funds (Chapter 3), had worked hard to level the ground. A men's house and hotel on nearby Mungank to attract and accommodate the tourists arriving by plane would provide a wonderful concentration of patrons for their artifacts and traditional ceremonies.

It should be noted that even Yorondu, despite the pessimism of his view that Chambri would themselves eventually become tourists in what had once been their domain (Chapter 6), would have been as enthusiastic as anyone about the proposed Mungank project. (Undoubtedly he would have asserted special ancestral connection to Mungank so as to claim payment for use of the land.) Although, as we have argued, important generational differences existed, all Chambri were, as far as we knew, enthusiastic about the development that they thought tourism would bring.

Finally, throughout his letter, Godfried reminded us, as others often had, that we were connected to him and other Chambri by a kinship constructed through a history of reciprocity, a history in which each had negotiated for resources from the other. Our special value to Chambri, and, we are sure, a source of periodic resentment, derived in large part from the fact that we were far more favorably situated within the world system than they. We could come and go as we pleased; we had trousers, tape recorders, money and cameras to send if we chose; we lived in the United States where many of the tourists who either bought or declined to buy their artifacts also lived. As they saw it – and we agreed – allowing and helping us to do anthropology among them had socially entailed us to them: they had extended a generosity to us, for which we should reciprocate. This book has been intended as an acknowledgement of our relationship.

Through presenting interlocking stories of intersecting lives we have sought to establish a density of connection within and among those lives. We have, as well, attempted to delineate the transformation of the contexts in which Chambri shaped their lives and gave them meaning. By evoking Chambri twisted histories and altered contexts we hope to have provided at least a partial rendering of Chambri actions and experiences during the twentieth century.

The aspects of their twentieth-century actions and experiences that have most engaged us were those focused on the "development" Angela referred to in her school notebook, the development most Chambri pursued with such interest, indeed with such excitement. In our effort to understand the significance of development to the Chambri we have focused on the choices they made in pursuit of the development they sought. (We are referring here to the quote found in Angela's school notebook, "When there is development there is always changes. We must choose the best way to cause development.")

In particular, we have tried to understand Chambri as agents of choice and of change, as negotiators of their political (and contested) interests under circumstances they were themselves in part intentionally and unintentionally altering. Thus, Maliwan (Chapter 2) had invited tourists to his initiation in order to fulfill traditional obligations in exemplary fashion. In so doing, he threatened the system in which those obligations took their meaning. Chambri youth (Chapters 3 and 4) had used Western representations to assert their freedom to choose their own social entailments. In so doing, they threatened the system in which entailments were of significance. And Godfried (Chapter 5) had tried to create the Chambri Bible to preserve the traditional knowledge and precedent on which individuals and clans had based and apportioned political efficacy. In so doing, he threatened the system in which efficacy was shared.

We must emphasize, however, that although these choices and changes did affect the context in which the Chambri operated, the reverse was true as well: the Chambri, as they full well knew, operated within a regional system of constraint, a system broader than that of their own society. They were also quite aware that this system had shifted within the twentieth century and were actively probing its parameters.

To characterize the nature of this shift: a regional system based on differences in ecologically given resources had become increasingly encompassed by a world system based on differences in development. In other words, a system based on commensurate differences had become incorporated into one based on incommensurate differences. Although both were systems of hegemony, the nature of hegemony, that which affected choice and change, differed correspondingly within each system. Simply put, the Chambri could become much more like the Iatmul than they could become like the Australians, Americans or Japanese: the Chambri could become "Iatmulized" in a way that they could not become "developed."

As we have said, the Iatmul did shape and maintain the regional system for their own benefit. For instance, their strategy of treating Chambri as allies and encouraging them to emulate Iatmul ritual and social forms existed only as long as it furthered Iatmul objectives of securing Chambri trade items. Yet, although the Chambri may have been somewhat misled by Iatmul flattery in the degree to which the Iatmul considered them valued allies,[8] both recognized a mutual advantage and, concurrently, a mutual dependency in the trade of stone tools and mosquito bags fabricated by Chambri for shell valuables procured by Iatmul. While the regional system remained intact, neither could readily dispense with the other. Indeed the trading partnerships through which these exchanges were conducted were long term, with the expectation that they be patrilineally inherited.

The hegemony exercised by the Westerners with their colonial and post-colonial influence and their concept of development was substantially different from that exercised by the Iatmul with their military strength and their ideas about proper ritual forms. The regional system had constrained the development of inequality in a way that the world system did not; consequently, the difference in power was far less between Iatmul and Chambri than between Westerners and Chambri.[9] For essentially the same reasons that Chambri rejected the structures of organization and authority of the Papua New Guinea state (Chapter 6), Iatmul villages in the pre-contact era acted largely autonomously and did not combine to form the higher level, encompassing organizations[10] that could administer Chambri or Sawos villages and extract Chambri commodities or Sawos sago.[11]

The promulgation by the first world of the idea of development carried far greater implications of inequality than had the promulgation by the Iatmul of their military and ritual superiority. Development, indeed, was pervasively hierarchical in its significance, based as it was on the differentiation between those more and those less developed and on the assumption that the more developed were those with hierarchical – more authoritative – organizational forms.

(In regard to the particular course that development might take among the Chambri, we worry about the possible effects that a nearby tourist hotel might have. [Because our greatest concern is that the Chambri would maintain their subsistence economy we are less troubled about this hotel than about the possibility of gold-mining operations near the lake.] We recently learned from a colleague that the airstrip at Kilimbit was in fact opened and was to accommodate this hotel, but that actual construction on Mungank was still to begin. The hotel was to be partially the enterprise of an Australian former colonial patrol officer who, demonstrating an authority greater than any the Papua New Guinea state would be likely to muster, had apparently obtained rights to the land from the many Chambri of different clans with ancestral claims to it. Indeed, Mungank was of considerable ritual significance to the Chambri. It was there, for instance, that senior men of the Kwalumembank clan annually performed the dry-season ritual that caused the fish to surge from the diminished Chambri Lake down the channel to the Sepik River. The opening of this hotel, it seems to us, would likely cause three interrelated changes which the Chambri, despite great initial enthusiasm for the project, might well come to regret.

Specifically: for the hotel to be built, land would need to have been purchased or leased from the Chambri, alienating it for the first time in their experience from their control and ritual use. For the hotel to be operated, Chambri would have to be induced to sell their labor as menials – as maids, janitors, and grounds keepers. Thus, for the first time class-relations would be created *at Chambri*. For the hotel to provide the kind of experiences tourists coming to Papua New Guinea required, the Chambri would have to be pressed into roles as self-conscious performers of Chambri culture, presenting themselves in a more intense and continuous way than before as the embodiment of the exotic. In all of these ways, though the hotel might bring relatively substantial income to those at Chambri itself, it would facilitate a further transformation of the system of commensurate differences into one of incommensurate differences.)

To return to inequality in the first world: the concept of development, holding out the promise of equality and a better life through increased consumption, served to conceal and thus perpetuate a system based both on enduring inequality and continuing change. Thus, Chambri were likely eventually to discover that despite their efforts, they had, at best, been only running in place, and that the equality they had sought would continue to elude them. If such were the case, they would remain as they had been for the tourists, peripheral and, as one "backward" people among many, essentially dispensable. Such an outcome to Chambri aspirations for development would be bitterly disappointing to them. They would greatly resent having their hopes raised and then dashed; and, as we have seen from Maliwan's response to the tourists from the Karawari Lodge who refused to pay to see his initiation (Chapter 2), they would greatly resent deprecation from those more "developed" than they.

Yet, despite the virtual inevitability of future disappointments, the course the Chambri had thus far negotiated for themselves during the twentieth century might continue to prove reasonably viable. The Chambri still defined their interests, even those focusing most directly on development, according to the quite explicit conviction that Chambri – both place and people – was the center and source of power and significance. The Chambri, hence, remained strongly committed to maintaining intact their Chambri center. In defense of their center they could, in our estimation, be expected to encounter the future with resilience, toughness and ingenuity.

One of the major concerns for older Chambri about the future was, we have seen, the realization that processes of sociocultural reproduction had become impaired through the course of development. True, no one, youth included, was contesting, or even finding implausible, the fundamental Chambri assumptions that ancestral power, controlled by secret knowledge, accounted for the condition of the natural and social world; no one, youth included, denied the capacity of big men (Nick Ambri's father, for instance) to make others, including their young clansmen, sick. The impairment was evident nevertheless: the expansion of the regional system by its incorporation into the world system, in addition to providing those such as Maliwan with new opportunities to expand their power, was providing youth with hitherto unavailable opportunities and justifications to evade the control of their seniors.

Strongly influenced by Western representations of the special status of youth and the importance of freedom and choice, young Chambri men and women often clashed with their elders about such issues as all-night parties and arranged marriages. However, what these Chambri "young lives" (Chapter 4) sought, and to some extent experienced as liberation, was seen by their Chambri seniors as "copycat" customs, adopted by "big heads," intent on evading clan responsibilities and ignorant of ancestral ways. That they were ignorant of ancestral ways would not only get them into serious trouble, as Yarapat righteously insisted, but might leave Chambri bereft of the knowledge necessary to activate ancestral power, as Yorondu darkly predicted. Yet, even as senior Chambri perceived the dangers of uncontrolled or ill-regulated development and even as the men, at least, recognized that the Chambri political system served their generational interests, *they too* wished to appear progressive, rather than anachronistic. (Yarapat, it may be remembered, defined himself as a businessman).[12]

Clearly no one – young or old, male or female – wanted to be left behind by development. Change – development – was therefore neither to be categorically rejected nor enthusiastically embraced. It was to be negotiated in particular cases and, as with most, if not all Chambri negotiations, the considerations were as much matters of particular political advantage as of public interest. (Godfried's project [Chapter 5] to write a Chambri Bible and the responses it engendered could be seen as typifying such negotiations.) In other words, what it meant to be a Chambri under conditions of development, would necessarily reflect Chambri political processes and the enterprise characteristic of these processes.

That cultural identity be politically established would strike the Chambri as both necessary and appropriate: indeed, from the Chambri perspective, the politically successful *was* the culturally, the cosmologically, correct. Most essentially, Chambri as a socio-cultural entity was the product of those who, through exercise of secret knowledge, were able to elicit and control ancestral power both to regulate the environment and to pursue their own political affairs. Simply put (and subject to some qualification), to be a Chambri was to be efficacious in the world: what was Chambri was what worked. Correspondingly, as the fears about cultural repro-duction indicated, cultural loss was feared primarily because it would result in the dissolution of power both individual and collective. (Suangin's concern over the sale of Posump and Ponor [Introduction] is an example.)

Yet, these same assumptions that were generating concerns about cultural loss also supported, in apparent compensation, an energetic self-validating and politically alert pragmatism: to effect a remedy for a collective dilemma or quandary would demonstrate control of ancestral powers that conferred both prestige on the author and legitimacy on the solution. As the Chambri came to comprehend better the nature of the world system and the ever-greater influence (either directly or through the Papua New Guinea state) it would have on their lives, they would fully expect that it, like their more familiar regional system, was based on political and economic interests. The fact that the Chambri had long been accustomed to engaging in political negotiations with those more powerful than they would also serve them well in a further transformed future.

However, as we have also suggested, it would be hard to visualize a viable future for the Chambri unless they could maintain their subsistence base. As long as Chambri Lake over-flowed with fish, even those who chose to remain in Wewak and beyond would not inevitably be at the mercy of a cash economy in a third-world country.[13] Moreover, for Chambri everywhere, but particularly for those at Chambri itself, as long as the home environment was in working order not only would food be provided in abundance but Chambri totemic efficacy would be confirmed. (Presumably, such a confirmation would eventually allay the most general fears of senior Chambri men concerning the loss of vital ancestral knowledge.)

Conversely, the Chambri were doubly vulnerable when the

home environment was not in working order. The ecological crisis lasting from the mid 1970s to the mid 1980s was profoundly alarming to the Chambri. At that time Chambri Lake and other Sepik waterways had been so choked by the exotic fern, *Salvinia molesta*, that fishing and travel were greatly curtailed. Although the fern had been eventually eradicated by the introduction of its biological enemy, the weevil, *Cyrtobagus singularis*, and although a Chambri big man had managed to take credit for mobilizing his and others' ancestral powers to bring the research scientist who introduced the weevil, the Chambri were shaken by the experience.[14] To judge by their reaction to the possibility that gold extraction in the area might pollute Chambri Lake (Chapter 6), they would do whatever they could to protect their particular environment in the future.[15]

Our book has been about interconnections, about the twisted histories that have linked Chambri to one another, to their neighbors within Papua New Guinea, to tourists, to us as friends and ethnographers, and to the first world system from which we, the tourists and others have come. We chose to write an ethnography of a particular kind – a collective biography – because this form allowed us to present as fully as possible Chambri lives in altered contexts. Convinced by the social theories that show action, experience, and social change as linked, we sought to convey the particularities of Chambri lives in transition. We sought to convey how Chambri have practiced, elaborated and transformed their culture in circumstances they were attempting to understand, exploit, and shape. However in such circumstances power was not only negotiated; it was also imposed.

As we have argued throughout this book, the Chambri whose lives we have invoked and inscribed were maneuvering within drastically changing circumstances: the regional system of commensurate differences had become increasingly and undeniably encompassed in a world system of incommensurate differences and the linkages between regional and world systems had developed to such an extent that the world system has had power to change the regional system.[16] It is because the Chambri were negotiating their futures within a system imposed upon them by those of the first world that we, their Western ethnographers, have found it important to write about their lives.

We earlier suggested that ethnographic representation of a

third world society such as the Chambri was politically justified if it impelled us as members of the first world to understand, and thereby take responsibility for, the effects of first-world actions. Having examined the consequences, both intended and unintended, of the Chambri encounter with many of the processes of the world system, we reaffirm this position. At this period in history, ethnography, although an endeavor compromised by the politics of representation, can be justified so long as it sustains an anthropology that focuses on the encounter between systems: on infiltration, negotiation, clash, transformation, and resistance.[17] As ethnographers, we may be part of the problem of hegemony, but not to write ethnography is not part of the solution.[18] It is because ethnography is inherently political that it continues to have potential value.

Appendix A
Godfried Kolly's life story

This life story is about the time I spoiled my Christian life and as well about what I saw in a dream. I said "yes" in 1974 when I was married and in 1957 when I was baptized. I promised to become a follower of Christ.

I took my first Holy Communion in 1965 but, brothers and sisters, I wasn't a man to follow Christ's customs too well. I was in the habit of thinking too much about the customs of the ground and was a man of sin. In 1975, I was given a sign by Father God above.

I had a present God had given me but I didn't watch over this present well.

The present God had given me was a child, a daughter named Martwina Kolly.

Father God above took back this daughter with his own hand. But in 1977 he gave me back this present. He gave it to me back with his own hand. He gave me back another daughter who looked just like the one he had taken from me. In 1975, I was in the habit of fooling and fighting around. It was during this year, during 1975, that I ruined my Christian life and my Holy Communion.

And I took a second wife and I stayed with her. And I lived with both her and my first wife. My second wife was pregnant in August of 1976 through April; on Tuesday night, April 13, I dreamed that Jesus came down to me as a white light, I was asleep and dreaming and I looked above at a cloud and there was a hole in the cloud. From this hole a white light streamed down and by the time it reached me, it was very big. By the time it became big, I looked and it had changed. A man was standing on my right side and he stared at me for five minutes. I began to see more clearly and I saw brother Jesus. He was angry with me and he showed me a cross that had a picture of Jesus on it. He berated me and asked me why I had broken my promise, become a sinful man and ceased to think about him: "You don't think about the promise you made when you were baptized. You must lose your customs of fornication and follow me. Here take this cross. If you take it then you will not forget about me. Take the cross and don't lose it. Now I am going to tell you something. The present you lost in 1975 will be given back to you tomorrow, April 15, 1977, Thursday night at 2 o'clock in the morning by Father God above."

And what Jesus said to me in the dream happened. This account is completely true. I held the cross and the daughter lives with me now. Yes, brothers and sisters, I can tell you because I twice have dreamed. And everything I dreamed about came true.

The second time I dreamed of the prophets coming down on a ladder. This ladder was on top of a cloud and it came down and it stood on the ground by my right hand side. You know about the story of Jacob. He dreamed as I did. At this time I dreamed of the ladder and the prophets came down from the ladder. This was the time I married my third wife. It is because of this that I am telling you that you must beware of bad customs and sins or else you will dream and then you will know that you have made a big transgression toward God the Father. Well, people of God, I can tell you. At the time you were baptized you should know the promise that you made to God and you must follow the promise. Whatever customs you make in the eyes of God are not very good. I spoiled my life in the eyes of God above. But I can tell you that my life with all my wives and children was no good. I found a great deal of sickness, of pain, of trouble.

All of these things I found, why did I find them? Because I didn't try to think about Father God and abandon my ways of fornication. And I didn't try to change my habits and become a follower of Christ again. Beginning in 1975 until 1985 my life and my circumstances were not good and in 1986 on New Year's night I changed my thoughts and my life and I promised that I would try to turn my attention and go back to Father God and stand strong and remain a follower of Christ. I promised to Father God that I would be strong in following Christ. And then I turned my thoughts and went inside and stood up as one of Christ's followers. I became completely straight, I didn't have quarrels or fights or trouble. I met again the good life.

Now, at this time, my life has changed and it has been good. And I have become a man of belief and turned my back on all sinful customs of the ground. So this is the life story of a true Christian. God bless you all. This story, I myself, Godfried Kolly, wrote.

Notes

Introduction: On writing the Chambri

1   Angela had received minimal instruction in English, Mathematics, Social Studies, Health and Science in a nationally prescribed curriculum designed for both those who remained in their villages and those who were allowed to continue their schooling. For those who remained in their villages, it was to provide sufficient knowledge so that they might be competent and healthy citizens. For those few others who continued their schooling it was to provide a basis for more advanced instruction. (In 1987, only four of the forty children completing the sixth grade at the Chambri Community School were able to pass the examination for entrance into the seventh grade at one of the provincial high schools.) There had been great controversy among government and academic officials as to whether this – or any single – curriculum could be successful both in meeting the basic educational needs of villagers and in preparing those who would become the educated elite. For an analysis of some of the issues debated during the creation of this educational system see Howie-Willis, 1980.

2   The "Twelfth Independence Anniversary Survey," conducted and published by *The Times of Papua New Guinea*, provides evidence that Papua New Guineans generally accepted the importance of development. One 16-year-old girl from Popondetta, for example, is quoted as saying: "The government should think about more agricultural development in the villages so that the people can have something to do and stay at home" (1987:21). To the same end a 32-year-old man from Tapini said: "In order for everyone to be happy, the government must help improve the situation in the rural areas by providing electricity and a water supply" ('Anniversary Survey':22). As these statements indicate and as we shall see, for instance, in Chapter 3 where we analyze literature for a political campaign, a major role of the government was defined as facilitating development.

These statements reveal also that many Papua New Guineans wanted their government to foster development that would significantly increase the viability of village life relative to that in the towns. They were aware that many had already left the villages for the towns and they considered this state of affairs unsatisfactory, not only because they thought life in the villages had lost vitality but also because they thought life in the towns was corrupting. Indeed many Papua New Guineans saw that it was not in their interests to adopt without discrimination the products and preoccupations of the urbanized industrialized nations. As a 34-year-old man from the Eastern Highlands put it in *The Times* "Survey": "The encouragement of disco clubs and alcoholism are two other factors that I have seen spoil a lot of marriages as well as encourage prostitution" (op. cit.). Thus, at least the essential difference between modernization and development seemed to be generally recognized. (See Frank, 1969, and Wallerstein, 1974, for thorough analyses of the significance of this distinction.)

For some of the recent literature about modernization and development in Papua New Guinea see: Gerriston, et al., 1981; Gregory, 1982; Marshall, 1982; May, 1982; Morauta and Ryan, 1982; Grossman, 1984; Strathern, 1984; Boyd, 1985a, 1985b; and Lederman, 1986.

3   For a detailed analysis of these processes of regional interaction and integration see Gewertz, 1983. For the linguistic evidence of patterns of prehistoric contact in the Sepik see Foley, 1986; for archaeological evidence, see Swadling, 1986. Comparable processes of regional integration have been described elsewhere in the area by Tuzin, 1976; Harrison, 1987; and McDowell, n.d.

4   For historical and sociocultural descriptions of the Iatmul see, for instance, Bateson, 1933, 1958; Metraux, 1978; Schuster, 1965, 1969; Hauser-Schaublin, 1977a, 1977b; Weiss, 1981; Wassman, 1982; and Stanek, 1986.

5   For an analysis of the Sawos see Schindlbeck, 1980.

6   The complexity of this strategy in practice, described in detail in Gewertz, 1983, stemmed from the fact that the regular supply of fish the Iatmul provided to the Sawos enabled the Sawos to develop villages of sufficient size to challenge periodically Iatmul control of the river. Although it was true that each became dependent on the other, it was necessary for the Iatmul to perpetuate this dependency by military and cultural means.

7   Bateson was, of course, the first to describe Iatmul organizational problems and attempt to delineate the Iatmul solution to them. (See also Rubel and Rosman, 1978: 36–50.) However, in our view, Bateson's argument that village cohesion depended on patterns of

self-correcting behavior needs to be augmented by an analysis recognizing the importance of both regional and internal patterns of exchange.

8 We regard hegemony as domination by military, political, economic, and, significantly, ideological means. We therefore adopt the position of Gramsci, 1977, that a central aspect of hegemony is the projection by a dominant group of its view of the world on another so that this view comes to be accepted as common sense.

9 Scott, 1985, presents evidence that Gramsci's concept of hegemony does not necessarily apply to circumstances in which interests are class-based: particular interests, he shows, are not always reformulated and presented as general interests. Yet, within the Middle Sepik, Chambri did admire, strive to emulate and accept as generally valid the Iatmul view of reality. The Middle Sepik, however, was never a Iatmul empire nor were the Iatmul a dominant class.

10 We argue in Errington and Gewertz, 1987a, that, largely because they were protected from Iatmul attack, the Chambri never developed a male-oriented military organization comparable to that of the Iatmul; relations between Chambri men and women were, therefore, much more egalitarian than between Iatmul men and women. (For a description of gender relations among the Iatmul see Bateson, 1958, and Hauser-Schaublin, 1977b.)

Moreover, Chambri relations of trade also discouraged development of male dominance. Specifically, because Chambri access to shell valuables was substantially dependent on the availability of these to their trading partners among the Iatmul, Chambri men could not appreciably increase the flow of shells to themselves by increasing their production of items of trade. Thus, the control of women and their products – mosquito bags in particular – was irrelevant to either the military or political viability of Chambri men. (See Weiner, 1976, and Etienne, 1980, for discussions of comparable circumstances in which the surplus production of women was not subject to male appropriation.)

11 In this Middle Sepik context, in which headhunting was ritually significant, the peace that Chambri enjoyed was not absolute. They themselves both periodically took and lost heads. Indeed, the wars that led to the Chambri exile were begun by a Chambri who, humiliated by recent successes of Chambri rivals in taking heads from Sepik Hills groups, killed a Iatmul from the village of Parambei in order to have a head for display in his own men's house. In this later case, however, because the Iatmul were no longer concerned with the eventual restoration of amicable trading relationships, they could escalate the war and, indeed, strive to annihilate the Chambri.

12 We argue in Errington and Gewertz, 1987a, that Mead is wrong in

this regard: Chambri women did not dominate over Chambri men. Nor, because the political strategies and spheres of Chambri men and women were largely distinct, did Chambri men dominate over Chambri women.

13 On the devastation caused by *Salvinia molesta* see Mitchell, 1979; Gewertz, 1983; and Errington and Gewertz, 1987a.

14 See Mead, 1935; 253.

15 We have argued that in the *context of marriage transactions* money had been acting for some time as the functional equivalent of the shell valuables it displaced. (The process of displacement, completed by the early 1960s, began in the 1930s when the axes and money brought by returning labor migrants became incorporated into marriage presentations.) For instance, in marriage presentations money became used as shell valuables had been, to construct the effigies that were symbolic women; these effigies were presented by wife-takers to wife-givers, as one presentation in a life-long series in return for the actual women received. Whereas shell valuables could be used only in restricted ways (shells of one variety were, in fact, explicitly regarded as wombs), money could be used to buy almost anything. It did not, however, generate further relationships (see Errington and Gewertz, 1987a: 111–28). Thus, the meaning of money had come to depend on its context: in the context of marriage transactions it was the functional equivalent of symbolic wombs – it was part of a gift economy; in the context of most other transactions, as for instance at a tradestore, it was a generalized media of exchange – it was part of a commodity economy.

We therefore agree with Gregory (1982) that Papua New Guinea had developed both a gift and commodity economy. However, at least in the Chambri case, it was unclear whether this separation of context and meaning would persist. Certainly there were some indications that the meaning money had in the commodity economy might displace the meaning it had in the gift economy such that presentation of bride-price might come to be regarded as the purchase of a woman rather than as a marriage presentation (Errington and Gewertz, 1987a: 117).

Nor do we dispute Lederman's argument (1986) that, prior to European intrusion, there were (at least) instances in which both types of economies existed together. In fact, such would not be surprising if one accepts Appadurai's point that the basis of exchange, whether of gifts or commodities, is political (1986b: 56–58). Certainly Papua New Guineans, *always* alert for opportunities to increase power, could define their political advantage on some occasions in terms of transactions that produced highly entailed social relations and, on others, in terms of transactions that incurred no future obligations.

16 In 1987, K1.00 was equivalent to $US1.15.

17 We thank Seroi Eoe and Pamela Swadling of the National Museum for permission to photograph Posump and Ponor.

18 Not only do non-indigenous anthropologists shape the data they collect by asking questions designed to address their own, culturally determined problems (see, for interesting elaborations of this point, the essays in Clifford and Marcus, 1986), they also may affect the data they collect by becoming involved in the lives of those with whom they work. Long-term fieldwork, hence, is in part the study of a social field which has come to incorporate the presence of the anthropologist. See in regard to this last point the essays in Colson, et al., 1979.

19 That Posump and Ponor were made at a time when men would sleep with their power-objects might have contributed to what a Western sensibility perceived as their aesthetic power: that they were constructed with the utmost seriousness might have resulted in an intensity of execution which made them museum quality. Certainly Forge (1967) reports that the objects the Abelam regarded as most powerful were those he himself found most aesthetically pleasing.

20 For important general works which clarify the nature of a world system, see Frank, 1969; Wallerstein, 1974, Stavenhagen, 1975; Taussig, 1980; Wolf, 1982; Hobsbawm and Ranger, 1983; Worsley, 1984; and Scott, 1985.

21 The Chambri at the time of our study produced nothing which gave them a significant role in the world market. In 1972 a report to the Commonwealth Scientific and Industrial Research Organization described the Chambri land system as having "no agricultural land use capability" (Haantjens, et al., 1972: 182). The report also stated that "land reclamation does not appear feasible, or would not produce good land" (op. cit.). Moreover, an economic planner for the Papua New Guinea government described the Sepik area as "out of the mainstream of [economic] development" (Philpott, 1972: 37). To date, the Chambri have derived some measure of protection from the fact that they had no resources that could be appropriated. (Such an appropriation could derive from both external and internal sources. For a Melanesian study which meticulously argues that the suitability of land for cash cropping has resulted in the development of a local land-owning class, see Rodman, 1987.) However, as we will discuss later, there had recently been talk of gold in the nearby Sepik Hills. Any exploitation of this gold would be likely to have considerable impact on the area.

22 Both Meillassoux (1981), with respect to Africa, and Fitzpatrick (1980), with respect to Papua New Guinea, contend that village life may have a persistently non-capitalist configuration within a larger capitalist system. However, as the Carriers (1989) lucidly show, not

only do villages subsidize the larger system by absorbing labor costs and providing migrants as Meillassoux and Fitzpatrick argue, but migrants subsidize the village by providing remittances. Indeed, the Carriers demonstrate (as do our own data), that money acquired in the capitalist national economy frequently generated a vigorous village-based gift economy. Chambri village life would hence be significantly and, in the views of most Chambri, adversely affected if the Chambri were cut off from the cash economy. Nevertheless, the preservation of their subsistence economy would provide Chambri with an essential security if life away from the home villages were to become oppressively harsh or otherwise untenable.

23 Elsewhere we argue that a person in the West acquires validity through developing an identity that has at its core a distinctive subjectivity – a unique cluster of dispositions, capacities and perspectives. (See Errington and Gewertz, 1987; for other discussions of individualism in America, see Varenne, 1977 and Bellah, et al., 1986.) Field research in a remote culture is likely to be understood as contributing to the development of such an identity by providing the unusual experiences which would help form a distinctive subjectivity.

24 This view that cultures should be assumed to be discrete entities, historically unrelated to one another, unless clear evidence could be found to the contrary, was promulgated by Boas and others early in the twentieth century as a refutation of the conjectural history of the unilinear evolutionists (Boas, 1948). According to the evolutionists, human cultures had a common history and progressed (at different rates) through the same stages of savagery, barbarism, and civilization: they would regard all the cultures in Papua New Guinea as very similar since all were in the same historical stage of "savagery."

25 For various aspects of this argument, see Dumont, 1977; Mintz, 1977; van den Berghe, 1980; Boon, 1982; Hamilton, 1982; and Crick, 1985.

26 Organizations such as the National Geographic Society persist in presenting Papua New Guineans as entirely "primitive" – as still unaffected by outside influences. Recently, for example, Deborah was asked to review the sound script for a film that the Society was producing about music in Papua New Guinea. She commented that it portrayed Papua New Guineans as if they were living in the "Stone Age" when in fact many of the musical events depicted were staged, at least partially, to earn money from tourists. In response, she was told explicitly that nothing could be done about this aspect of National Geographic policy because its subscribers "buy" (the term used) this image of the still untouched primitive. Comparably, Clifford (1988b) demonstrates that the American Museum of

Natural History does not acknowledge in its displays that tribal peoples now inhabit a world system such that, for example, they are likely to wear wrist watches.

27 On writing ethnographies as dialogues see, in particular, Clifford, 1986 and the first two chapters of Clifford, 1988a.

28 In our focus on the experience of social change in a world system, we adopt an approach similar to that advocated by Marcus 1986, and embodied by Taussig, 1987.

29 We hence distinguish our effort to convey Chambri lives not only with immediacy but as caught up in world historical processes of the twentieth century from two recent, important studies of social action in Melanesia: Munn's (1986) stimulating analysis of the relationship between local and wider worlds in the Massim, and Strathern's (1988) challenging theory of agency in Papua New Guinea and Vanuatu.

30 Several anthropologists have been struggling of late, with the difficulty of creating politically compelling texts about terror and genocide. One problem they face is to find a prose which neither reduces the horror nor repels the reader. For one successful attempt see Taussig, 1987.

31 Much of *Writing Culture* (Clifford and Marcus, 1986) calls for experiments and innovations in ethnographic presentation. Indeed, Marcus and Clifford edit a new series from the University of Wisconsin Press called "New Directions in Anthropological Writing".

32 It has been argued that anthropologists as products and agents of capitalist systems objectify those they observe (Fabian, 1983; Pratt, 1986), regarding the "other" as available for their acquisition and use. In this process, the other stripped of power and volition, becomes defined to meet Western standards of conceptual utility. See, Asad, 1973; Appadurai, 1986a; Haraway, 1985; and Spooner, 1986.

33 We are not contending, however, that the kind of self-knowledge gained through a contrast between ourselves and others is not useful. Nor, despite the critique presented on the idea of the remote, do we deny that contrast between Chambri culture and society, for instance, and our own way may be relatively great and informative. For a discussion of the importance of ethnography in generating an American cultural critique see Marcus and Fischer, 1986.

1 The new traditionalism: tourism and its transformations

1 See Gewertz, 1982a, for description of these earlier initiations.

2 The literature on initiation in Papua New Guinea has become extensive. See, among others, Barth, 1975; Tuzin, 1980; Herdt, 1982; Godelier, 1982; Modjeska, 1982; Bowden, 1983; Whitehead, 1986; Hays, 1988; and Strathern, 1988.

3   For analysis of similar circumstances in which *the concept* of tradition has achieved political and economic importance, see Said, 1978; Hobsbawm and Ranger, 1983; Clifford, 1988; Fienup-Riordan, 1988; and Lass, 1988.

4   The relationship between tourists and anthropologists has become a matter of some recent concern. Several anthropologists have argued that, despite an ideology to the contrary, anthropologists are, in fact, little different from tourists. See Dumont, 1977; Mintz, 1977; van den Berghe, 1980; Boon, 1982; and Hamilton, 1982. The most forceful formulation of this view comes in a recent article by Crick, 1985, who suggests that anthropologists have lost their authority because, like tourists, they do not reach an objective understanding of the other. We provide a detailed discussion of this comparison between anthropologists and tourists in Errington and Gewertz, 1989, arguing that extensive and politically important differences exist.

5   Ordinarily, several patriclans would have their sons initiated at the same time. Although each clan would be responsible, for example, in compensating its own in-laws, many other expenses, such as providing food for those of the opposite initiatory moiety, would be shared. Chapter 2 presents a relatively complete account of the initiation procedure and attendant expenses.

6   In *Cannibal Tours*, a recent film about the interaction between tourists travelling on the Melanesian Explorer and Sepik peoples, Dennis O'Rourke (1987) depicts the tourists as less well disposed. We suspect, however, that he was somewhat selective in choosing footage.

7   Tourism was promoted not only by the Chambri and other Papua New Guineans but by the government as an important source of income. For instance, in 1987 the East Sepik Minister of Culture published a newsletter, to be distributed to the Wewak hotels. In it "traditional cultural events" were announced so that tourists could attend programs such as the opening of a men's house or the staging of ritual songs and dances.

8   We discuss the migration to the towns in detail in Chapter Three.

9   For a description of recent changes in and variations among men's houses and domestic houses at Chambri see Errington and Gewertz, 1987a: 117–23.

10   Our debt to Lévi-Strauss is obvious here. See, for instance, Lévi-Strauss, 1969.

11   For Walindimi to have seduced Yambukay's wife meant that he had enough power to pull her away – more power than Yambukay had to hold her. Moreover, at least in accounts of the past, big men would on occasion show their superior power by remaining unmoved in the face of attack. In both instances, power was shown as focused into a

concentrated, almost magnetic, center *around* which activity took place.

12 The most powerful Chambri were often regarded as those who had refused to share their power: they were frequently depicted as socially disengaged, either as living apart from their families or, in some cases, as having killed them.

13 The importance of particularistic ties made it difficult for Chambri to cooperate both with other Chambri belonging to different clans or villages and with those from other Papua New Guinea societies. Probably the relative tranquility of Papua New Guinea during the post-World War 2 Australian administration stemmed in part from the position of the Australians as outsiders. This position enabled them to act in a way no Papua New Guinea group could – that is, without provoking complementary opposition. We discuss the persistence and significance of particularistic ties in post-independent Papua New Guinea in Chapter 6. See also Evans-Pritchard, 1947, for a brilliant analysis of the comparable role of the outsider in a very different ethnographic context.

14 See Errington and Gewertz, 1985, 1987a and 1988, for more complete discussion of Chambri ideas about the relationship of power and social life and the virtual inevitability of entropy. Harrison, 1985; McDowell, 1986; and Barth, 1988, also discuss the concept of entropy in Papua New Guinea groups.

15 See Errington and Gewertz, 1986, for a more extended discussion of Chambri views of their social origins. For comparative Papua New Guinea data on the constitution of society on the basis of immigration see Battaglia, 1990.

16 In fact, the owners of the Melanesian Explorer planned to replace their present ship with a far more luxurious one, equipped, for instance, with phones in each cabin that would allow direct dialing worldwide.

17 See MacCannell, 1976: 91–107, for a discussion of how important the appearance of authenticity is in tourist settings.

18 Indeed, considerable sums of money, sufficient to buy large trucks, could be raised in this way. See Gregory, 1982: 203–9, for a discussion of just how successful gift exchange could be in capital accumulation.

19 Perhaps basing their view of "primitives" on their stereotypes of Native Americans, many tourists, even when we attempted to explain the achieved leadership of big men, refused to change their views that Papua New Guinea social organization focused on chiefs.

20 Although not used on this scaffolding, triangular bracing was common and was, for instance, used on a small bridge we had crossed that morning.

21 We discuss the distinction between travelers and tourists in Errington and Gewertz, 1989. For other recent analyses of those we call travelers see Teas, 1988 and Cohen, 1989.

22 This is quoted from a notebook, kept in a Wewak guest house, in which travelers entered their comments to make their experiences available to others.

23 For comparative discussions of the relationship between forms of initiation and types of adult status see Modjeska, 1982; Whitehead, 1986; Hays, 1988; and Weiner, 1988.

24 For a discussion of the Western view that persons are unique subjectivities which summarizes some of the extensive literature on this subject, see Errington and Gewertz, 1987a:129–41. A recent historical survey of this subject of the Western constitution of the self is provided by Johnson, 1985.

25 These plans would be checked by listening to the daily radio broadcast of shipping news to determine the location of the Melanesian Explorer in its journey between the coastal port of Madang and the upper Sepik town of Ambunti.

26 Chambri men were aficionados of outboard motors and by listening to the sound of a distant engine could identify its make and model. In contrast to the 40 horsepower of the largest Chambri engines those on the speedboats of the Melanesian Explorer were a most impressive 125 horsepower.

27 Children in Papua New Guinea could attend school only if school fees were paid for them, usually by their parents. In 1987, the annual fee at the Chambri Community School was K5.50; at Saint Mary's Elementary School in Wewak, K26; at one of the provincial high schools, K150.

28 The following may provide some indication of the cash expenditures of Chambri families. According to figures collected by an adult male member of a family consisting of seven adults and six children, K37.50 was spent between December 9–25, 1987, for betel nuts, betel pepper catkins, kerosene, biscuits, beer, flour pancakes, sugar, canned mackerel, tobacco, cigarettes, cigarette newspaper, batteries, rice, sago, and for a contribution (of K13) to a ceremonial exchange to settle a kinsman's domestic disagreement. According to figures collected by an adult male member of another family consisting of 8 adults and 2 children, K70.80 was spent between December 6–27, 1987, for these same items (minus the cigarettes and including used clothing) and for a contribution (of K35) to the payment of a man who had built a house for the widow of a clansman.

29 Unlike the circumstance described by the Carriers (1989) for Ponam, most of the money those living on Chambri Island spent on goods and exchanges was earned locally and did not come from remit-

tances. According to data collected by Seby Asawi, Deborah Gewertz and Cony Tangi, the Chambri earned approximately K9,900 by selling artifacts to tourists in the Walindimi men's house between October 7, 1987 and October 6, 1988. This figure is an extrapolation based on detailed accounts kept between October 7, 1987 and December 23, 1988. During the time that these accounts were kept, 68 men sold 219 artifacts, earning K2082.60. (Many more men attempted unsuccessfully to sell artifacts; the total number is unknown.) The average price of the artifacts sold was K9.50, with prices ranging from K1 to K80. The 68 sellers earned an average of K30.63 each, with their revenues ranging from K1 to K144. In addition to the artifacts sold at Walindimi, 73 additional ones were purchased for K600 by an artifact dealer on November 13, 1987. Chambri also earned money through such means as selling fish and crocodile skins. According to our figures, between January 1, 1987 and December 30, 1987, 103 Chambri – 89 women and 14 men – journeyed to towns in the West and East Sepik to sell fish. They stayed away from Chambri for an average of three weeks and brought home, after subsistence and transportation expenses which consumed an average of two-thirds of their earnings, K6,504.60, or approximately K63.15 apiece. Between November 30, 1986 and December 1, 1987, eighteen Chambri men killed crocodiles. They sold the skins for between K10–K115, and earned a total of K605.30, or an average of K33.60 each.

30 See Graburn, 1976: 14–21, for a discussion of the stylistic modifications that are made in the development of tourist arts.

31 This nicely illustrates Sahlins' point that "the symbolic object represents a differential interest to various subjects according to its place in their life schemes" (1985: 150).

32 That Sepik peoples were encouraged in this manner to represent themselves to Westerners in ways Westerners defined as traditional suggests the operation of the same processes of modernization and control that Ranger, 1983, describes as resulting in the invention of tradition in Africa.

33 Graburn, 1976: 26–27, describes this process by which tourist art comes to represent a country to outsiders.

34 Maliwan regarded his arrangement with Peter Barter not only of mutual benefit but based on mutual help. In exchange for the help he gave Barter by arranging performances for the tourists, he often requested help from Barter in the form of specialized commodities such as cases of canned fish, to feed those giving the performances that the tourists would observe, and nails and carpentry tools to repair the Walindimi men's house.

35 In Errington and Gewertz, 1985, we discuss an instance in which, by

virtue of his success in directing outside resources to Chambri, a local politician declared himself, virtually without opposition, as the "chief" of the Chambri. He was at the height of power in 1983, but was voted from provincial office in 1987, in part because his eminence, and the arrogance it seemed to foster, aroused greater resentment than he could offset through his diminishing command of resources. Although, as Harrison, 1985, argues, the control of important outside networks was an incipient form of hierarchy in the Sepik, at least in the Chambri case, that hierarchy was likely to be short-lived. See also, Chapter Six, note three, and Conclusion, note 14, for more information on this "chief".

36 As has been mentioned, to the extent that Chambri were successful in earning money from tourists, they might change in ways that would make them appear less "primitive," and thus less appealing to tourists. However, regardless of how the Chambri might change – whether they would spend their earnings on traditional ceremonies or Western goods – any recognition that they were valued by tourists because they seemed "primitive" would be resented.

37 Basso, 1979, analyzes similar jokes concerning the status differentials existing between Apache and Whitemen. See also Apte, 1985: 108–148.

2 *The initiation: making men in 1987*

1 Cords around wrists and ankles were worn at times of transition – birth, initiation and death – and, accompanied by a variety of taboos, these cords indicated a constriction in normal relationships with the world. Woven by women, they were usually attached to men by their sisters who as clan members of the same generation were their closest female relatives. See Errington and Gewertz, 1987a: 83–98 and discussion later in this chapter for further consideration of the tie between Chambri brothers and sisters. For comparative Pacific data on this relationship see, for example, Strathern, 1972; Gailey, 1980; Shore, 1981; and Feil, 1984.

2 Formerly, first menstruation was also celebrated in a ceremony considered the female equivalent of male initiation, in which members of a woman's clan made large payments to their in-laws. For the last twenty years, however, wealthy mothers' brothers and fathers have instead displayed their resources by scarifying young women, although not secluding them in the men's house. In 1987, 10 per cent of Chambri women over 17 had been scarified.

3 Strathern, 1988, describing assumptions about social life held by Melanesians who do not form named groups, argues that society *per se* does not exist and that, therefore, initiation should not be viewed as a process by which society puts its imprint on unformed youths.

Instead, she argues, initiation is a process whereby basically androgynous youths are deconstructed so as to become gendered. We find her reanalysis of Melanesian initiation extremely provocative. Yet we must add the Chambri did name themselves – they were, after all, a small, linguistically distinctive group, surrounded by those speaking completely unrelated languages. As well, they regarded themselves both as distinguished from others by their customs and as constituted by various social categories, including the initiatory moieties. Furthermore, their social networks of gift exchange, although extensive, were understood as cosmologically centered on Chambri. (We have seen the importance of this centering in our discussion of Maliwan's account of his ancestor, Yerenowi.) It also seems to us that the processes in which they have been caught up since colonization were such as to increase their consciousness of themselves as an entity.

4   For a detailed analysis of the relationship between the timing of male initiation and marriage and the availability of clan resources, see Gewertz, 1982a.

5   In addition to the initiation moieties of Yambuntimeri and Pombiantimeri, there were the only partially exogamous marriage moieties of Nyauinimba and Nyeminimba. These two sets of patrilineal moieties were partially cross-cutting – Yambuntimeri men for example, might belong to either marriage moiety. Moreover, approximately one-eighth of all Chambri men claimed membership in both initiation moieties or in both marriage moieties. Indeed, there were some individuals who belonged to all four groups.

6   The smoke from the burning feathers and the smell of cooking meat served both to block and distract the attention of spirits.

7   Such taboos during initiation, marking liminality, are common throughout the world. For the classic analysis of liminality see Turner, 1969.

8   For discussion of the range of possible effects of making culture a commodity in the context of tourism see, for example, Finney and Watson, 1974; MacCannell, 1976; Smith, 1977; Goldberg, 1983; and Cohen, 1988.

9   See Bateson, 1958 and 1972, for a discussion of the way that feedback operates to maintain systems within existing parameters.

10 Frequently on festive occasions a Chambri woman would stop her dancing to crawl through the legs of another woman, calling the woman who had just "given birth" to her "mother" and being called "daughter" in return. This behavior served to collapse generational and kinship differences between women, since it took place between women of any generation, related in any sort of way. As such, it reflected the strategy employed by a Chambri woman to achieve worth through reproducing those who had produced her: that is to

say, by having her descendants replace certain of her own ascendants. In particular, she wished thereby to reproduce her own mother who, in this patrilineal system, belonged to a different kinship group than she. See Errington and Gewertz, 1987a and 1987b, as well as Introduction, note ten, and Chapter Three for a more complete discussion of male and female strategies for achieving worth.

11 Forge, 1972, argues persuasively, using Sepik data, that competition can only take place among relative equals.

12 However, while the first instance could be appropriately characterized as precluding what Bateson termed symmetrical schizmogenesis, the second instance could not be regarded as precluding complementary schizmogenesis, the other pattern of cumulative interaction that Bateson had described as important among the Iatmul, particularly in the context of male–female relationships. In cases of complementary schizmogenesis between Iatmul men and women, increased differentiation resulted as the display of aggressive behavior on the part of men was matched and evoked by a display of its opposite, submissive behavior on the part of women (Bateson, 1958: 176). In fact, neither the process of complementary nor of symmetrical schizmogenesis, as Bateson described them, would seem to affect the relationship between Chambri men and women.

13 See Errington and Gewertz, 1987a and 1988, for an extensive discussion of the relatively egalitarian nature of Chambri gender relationships. See also Introduction, note ten.

14 The kind of schizmogenesis that relations between Chambri men and women would, therefore, be subject to would be symmetrical rather than complementary, but symmetrical based on difference, rather than on similarity. Indeed, schizmogenesis of either sort ran a more extensive course for the Iatmul than for the Chambri who would try to resolve and neutralize internal oppositions at an earlier point. Moreover, unlike the Iatmul, Chambri men did not dress as women in order to ridicule them. See Bateson, 1958: 130–41.

15 The man who presented Maliwan with food was his *tsambunwuro*, the man upon whom Maliwan had lain when he was scarified. For an analysis of the role of the *tsambunwuro* within Chambri society, see Gewertz, 1982a.

16 All four of them had joint membership in both Yambuntimeri and Pombiantimeri. See note 5.

17 For a discussion of how important the appearance of authenticity is during cultural contact see, for example, MacCannell, 1976; Handler, 1986; and Spooner, 1986.

18 In this analysis, the emergence of the ludic was something of an accident: it had not been the Chambri intention to allow the initiates

respite from their double binds. It is, moreover, difficult to compare this occurrence of the ludic among the Chambri to that which Handelman, 1979, describes among the nearby Iatmul. In his view, the Iatmul employed the ludic in their *naven* ceremonies to escape sociocultural contradictions. Unfortunately, for purposes of comparison, his analysis is based on what we consider to be a misreading of the relationship of mother's brother and sister's son. He argues that there was a contradiction in Iatmul life between maleness and nurture which appeared in the relationship between mother's brother – a male mother – and sister's son. Because of this contradiction, their relationship was regarded as factitious. The evidence for this facticity was that the mother's brother referred to his sister's son by a name, the suffix of which meant "mask." Handelman argues from this that their relationship was "masklike" and, hence, one of paradox and play.

This interpretation of the ludic in Iatmul culture is, it seems to us, flawed in two ways. The category of mother's brother need not be regarded or experienced as constituted from other elements such as maleness and nurture: as Strathern, 1986, points out, a mother's brother can be regarded as a thing in itself, rather than as a composite. Moreover, and more directly relevant to a discussion of the ludic, was the meaning of masks and masking in the Sepik. In cultures such as the Iatmul and the Chambri, masks were the repositories of ancestral power and identity. In these cultures, all power was ancestral power, and men strove to embody their ancestors and their power: indeed, men would be most fully themselves as they became the ancestor whose mask they controlled (see Bateson, 1946). Thus, when a mother's brother referred to his sister's son by the name of a particular mask, he was giving him access to that ancestral power which would comprise a significant portion of his identity. Masks in this region did not, hence, hide real identity; they revealed it. Rather than marking the playful or paradoxical, they comprised the most serious and direct statements that could be made about power and identity.

19 It may be that the bifurcation Harrison describes whereby the hierarchy of the ritual domain coexists with the relative egalitarianism of the political and social domain is a product of the same historical process that has transformed Ponam. Thus, Manambu hierarchy may be more residual than incipient. We might mention, as well, that in our comparison between Chambri and tourists we are not intending to present an exhaustive social typology. We recognize, for instance, that unentailed relationships could in some cases (such as the Manambu) be hierarchical, entailed relationships could exist in the absence of commodities, and commoditized relationships could be egalitarian.

20 Even though, as mentioned in the Introduction, Suangin had complained about the sound of these new Posump and Ponor drums, we heard no criticism of their sound on this occasion. Perhaps it was only in the context of interpreting why his life had gone awry that it occurred to Suangin that the drums did not sound right.

21 These were the modern version of symbolic women that we describe in note 15 of the Introduction.

22 Maliwan would contribute to these donors when they collected money for comparable presentations.

23 Such a payment to the wife's maternal kin was expected in this context in which all who had contributed to the creation of the newly initiated young men were compensated. This particular payment reflected the importance of maternity. It reflected the recognition that the initiates had been produced by a line of mothers.

24 Maliwan had been, in fact, pleased that the tourists had taken so many photographs of him posed with his sons and of other aspects of his initiation. These, he told us, would extend his reputation throughout the world.

25 This phase of the initiation should not be regarded primarily as an instructive delineation of social structural components: rather than edify, it enthralled. Schieffelin, 1986, makes a similar point about the impact of ritual performances among another Papua New Guinea group.

26 We describe the possible effects of this transformation in Errington and Gewertz, 1987a: 111–28.

3 The town
1   The diocese which included the Sepik had its administrative center in Wewak. For a history of Catholic mission activities in this region see Huber, 1988.

2   Hospital services in Papua New Guinea were minimal. A patient's kin would frequently provide the food, company, and care needed by the patient, including protection from the sorcery that might be encountered among strangers.

3   Huber, 1979, describes the traditional land owners around Wewak as often eager to rent land as business ventures to these settlers.

4   For a history of Wewak, see Fleetwood, 1984.

5   Unlike Chambri Mountain which served to anchor both Chambri Island and Chambri ancestral spirits, the coastal range had no particular significance for the Chambri. Consequently, replication in Wewak of the spatial arrangements of their home was probably for aesthetic rather than cosmological reasons.

6   According to data collected by Seby Asawi, Deborah Gewertz, Michael Kamban, Cosimos Kompar, and Theo Pekur in 1987, 117

adults (those 18 years or older) and 78 children lived in 39 houses at Chambri Camp; 141 adults and 135 children lived in 44 houses at Kilimbit; 105 adults and 76 children lived in 39 houses at Indingai; and 196 adults and 137 children lived in 56 houses at Wombun.

7 The average adult (those 18 years or older) living at, and defining him/herself as a permanent resident of, Chambri Camp had spent 11 years there and had visited Chambri Island slightly more than twice during these years, with each visit lasting about 27 days.

8 No Chambri worked regularly in such an industrial context. For an analysis of the solidarity sometimes existing among workers in the roughly comparable coastal town of Madang, see Stevenson, 1986.

9 Our data agree with those of Strathern, 1975; Oram, 1976; Levine and Levine, 1979; and Battaglia, 1986, that the primary basis for relationships in urban settings was shared ethnicity. (According to the 1987 Catholic Church census there were twenty-nine of these ethnically-based settlements in Wewak.) For instance, during our three-month period of research in Wewak, we never saw a child from another camp visiting a schoolmate at the Chambri Camp. On only two occasions did we observe non-Chambri adults do more than pass through the Chambri Camp on their way to the main road or to a nearby market. Once, after prior arrangement, a political candidate and his entourage arrived to campaign; once, the relatives of a young Chambri woman brought the putative non-Chambri father of her yet unborn child along with three of his friends to the camp in order to demand that he pay child support. For more of the important and growing literature about the maintenance of ethnic identity in the towns of the Pacific, see: Burton-Bradley, 1968; Brown, 1972; Rew, 1974; Strathern, 1975; Levine and Levine, 1979; Morauta, 1979; Larcom, 1982; Keesing and Tonkinson, 1983; Premdas, 1986; and Nash and Ogan, 1987.

10 Occasionally organizations within these ethnic enclaves – like the Chambri Youth Group – would stage an all-night, fund-raising dance (with highly amplified, popular music) open to anyone who paid admission.

11 See Levine and Levine, 1979, for a comparable discussion of the ambivalence townsmen felt about their lives away from the village.

12 A higher proportion of the Chambri who had salaries lived elsewhere in Wewak; this was because they were provided with housing by their employers. According to data collected during 1987, 31 per cent of those Chambri living elsewhere in Wewak held regular jobs. Of the total number of Chambri living in Wewak who had regular jobs, nine men and seven women lived at Chambri Camp and thirteen men and three women lived elsewhere. Among these men, four worked as tradestore clerks, three as teachers, three as government clerks, two

as carpenters, two as construction workers, two as policemen, one as a hospital manager, one as a hospital orderly, one as an electrician, one as a secretary, one as a musician and one as director of Catholic education. Among these women, four worked as secretaries, two as teachers, two as nurses' aides, one as a nurse, and one as a tradestore clerk.

13 According to data collected by Deborah Gewertz and Cosimos Kompar, the Chambri living in Wewak earned K1,784.81 by selling artifacts to tourists and dealers visiting there between July 27, 1987 and September 27, 1987. During this time 52 men and women sold 209 artifacts. An additional 39 attempted without success to make a sale. The average price of the artifact sold was K8.50, with prices ranging from K1.40 to K110. The 52 sellers earned an average of K34, with revenues ranging from K2 to K340.

14 The total of K1,316 was based on the following calculations: K40 for rent, K26 for school fees, K36 (3K/month) for water, K1,095 (3K/day) for food, 52K (1K/week) for betel nut, K40 (10K/person) for clothing, 11K (K.20/week) for kerosene, 6K (K.50/month) for flash-light batteries.

If we had included data from all of Wewak and not just from Chambri Camp, and assumed that all of the money earned there was redistributed among the full total of 280 men, women and children (including the 195 at Chambri Camp), then the average family of four would have K1,824 available to it. However, we did not include these data in the text: we reasoned that unlikely as it was that there be full redistribution within the Camp where there were daily face-to-face relationships, it would be even less likely for there to be full redistribution between those in the Camp and those living apart from it.

15 The Chambri themselves noted that they had become very quick to charge each other in the community court, demanding substantial compensation for minor offenses. Thus, a youth who had staggered around the Camp one night, uttering drunken and random curses, was later taken to court by a householder, claiming K10 compensation, for the abuse he and his family had suffered. Although most thought the claimant more interested in acquiring money than in defending family honor, the K10 was paid by the youth's family to put an end to the matter.

16 Battaglia, 1986, describes a contrasting case in which Trobriand Islanders living in Port Moresby engaged in redistributive feasts of considerable scale and complexity.

17 One anthropologist characterized the situation in this way: "Public opinion . . . is that crime has been increasing and that particular types of offenses, crimes of violence and rape, have been increasing faster

than others. All over the country, people in different walks of life feel
that there is a law and order problem that has worsened during the
years of independence. Rural and urban people alike see towns as the
worst places for crime and see crime spreading into the countryside
along the roads and under the influence of urban models" (Morauta,
1986: 7). See also O'Collins, 1986, for an analysis of the law-and-
order problem in Papua New Guinea as it concerned youth.

18 Certainly the richness of Sepik ritual life and material culture
    testified to the relative ease with which subsistence needs were
    satisfied.

19 Rex was quite well-educated: this citation and those following from
    him are not translations but are in the English he used.

20 Gabriella Apak is a pseudonym.

21 See Errington and Gewertz, 1987a, for a detailed discussion of the
    strategies of Chambri men and women and for an argument that
    these strategies were sufficiently separate that neither men nor
    women sought to dominate each other. In this regard our position
    differs from Mead, 1935, who thought Chambri women dominated
    Chambri men.

22 See also Errington and Gewertz, 1988b, for a more complete
    discussion of the fact that in Chambri political theory the concentra-
    tion of power necessarily entailed its use in sorcery.

23 Not only did bad feelings provide the motivation for sorcery but
    these feelings could themselves, through the direct power of thought,
    cause illness.

24 This strong conviction that the older sister should precede the
    younger into a joint marriage was probably related to the ideal that
    older – and stronger – siblings should marry before the younger –
    and weaker – ones. Although no one could explicate this conviction
    for us, it seemed to rest on a sense of appropriate order that perhaps,
    in turn, reflected the cultural recognition of entropy – in this case,
    the stronger was to precede the weaker. See Chapter One, note 14,
    and Errington and Gewertz, 1987a: 28–30, for a discussion of the
    Chambri view that power becomes diluted and lost over time.

25 The twisted history in which Ambun and Yorondu played significant
    roles was even more complex: Yorondu was Ambun's father's sister's
    son; Yorondu's wife was Ambun's father's brother's daughter.
    Yorondu's line, thus, had been engaged in what was the preferred
    form of marriage among Chambri, mother's brother's daughter's
    marriage, with Ambun's line. Consequently, Yorondu's payment of
    Ambun's fine could be seen as a marriage payment, owed to the
    group from whom Yorondu had taken his wife, as well as an expense
    necessary to elicit Yandi's bride-price.

26 Mariana explained to us that the reason she had not been previously

inclined to marry was that her mother's father had ensorcelled her so that she would not find any one man sufficiently pleasing to settle down with. Why he had thus acted she did not know.

27 Both Strathern, 1975, and Battaglia, 1986, emphasize that ethnicity was an essential component in personal identity.

28 See Bourdieu, 1977, for an excellent discussion of the processes of cultural learning in the course of everyday life.

29 Martin Gawi is a pseudonym.

30 From a more general perspective, both sorts of music could be considered as self-expression, but they expressed different sorts of selves: Martin's music expressed a self defined in terms of unique sensibility; Chambri traditional music expressed a self defined in terms of clan-based powers and relationships with the living and dead.

31 Dale Carnegie wrote this work in 1936, primarily to help Americans develop attitudes necessary for success.

4 Western representations at home

1 For a more complete discussion of the social composition of self among the Chambri see Errington and Gewertz, 1987a. For a comparative discussion see the articles in White and Kirkpatrick, 1985.

2 According to our Chambri sources, only two Chambri had been away so long from the village or from other Chambri as to forget Chambri language and customs. Even those few who had broken contact with other Chambri were still regarded as Chambri and considerable efforts were made by their kin to regain contact with them. Anyone traveling where they were thought to be would be asked to seek them out. The police might even be asked to persuade such a person to go home.

3 The Chambri Camp in Wewak had become sufficiently permanent so that burial in the cemetery of the Catholic Church in Wewak was acceptable but far from ideal. Sufficient numbers of Chambri lived at Wewak to provide a social context for the dead buried there; yet, separated as these dead were from the seat of power at Chambri, they could never provide much ancestral support for their living descendants.

4 Disturbed social relations, especially with primary kin, signaled, as would any kind of misfortune, either misuse or loss of ancestral power. This in turn suggested vulnerability, either from sorcery exercised from within the clan or from some enemy outside the clan. Moreover, disruptions of the social relations constitutive of the self were likely to be experienced as not only leading to sorcery but as inherently depleting.

5 The nature of intergenerational conflict may have changed since

pacification in that youth formerly had a productive social role as warriors.

6   This is a translation of the full Pidgin English text of the eulogy:

Nick was born on February 2, 1961 and he entered Grade One of the Chambri Community School in 1969. In 1974 he finished Grade Six.

In 1979 he went to school again, to Talidic Vocational Center in Madang. He finished training in 1979 and returned to his [Wombun] village. When he returned home he thought about clearing land for a dance ground. All his mates worked with him on this project and finished it. This dance ground remains and we have parties on it now. It was Nick who started this project.

Nick was the head guitarist of our string band and also composed music for it. He composed songs for the band. When we started a Youth Group, he was Vice-Chairman.

Nick worked hard to help our community. He cut grass and cleaned the village and also worked hard to clear the Kumalio channel. [This was the project that Martin had contracted but never paid for.] Moreover, he helped many men with house building and other work. Furthermore, he led others at working for the church, at working in various ways for the church. He also worked at the school.

Nick was a man who liked his friends. He was a man who fought for the rights of all young men and women. Mainly he helped his mates through all kinds of trouble. He was a man who was not afraid to face the problems that met him.

After he finished all this good work, he got engaged, married and fathered two daughters. Nick Ambri left his brothers and sisters on this earth to go to the place of our father in order to rest for all time. The date he left us: May 9, 1987.

Significantly, even in this account of the young man whose life embodied the trials and aspirations of contemporary Chambri youth, we see Nick defined primarily in terms of his projects and his social relations. His friends did not apparently see his life as the expression of a subjective self. They did not see him as an individually distinctive set of dispositions, sensibilities, capacities, and perspectives that might give rise to and thus explain his activities.

7   These devil-men, called *simandankin* in Chambri, were short, black, red-eyed, nasty, and autochthonous. They acted both on their own initiative and as agents of sorcery.

8   For discussion of the degree to which big men attempted to control their sons see Gewertz, 1982b, and Errington and Gewertz, 1987a: 93–96; 1988b. Such big men were known to have seduced the wives of their sons; frequently they were believed to have effected their sons' deaths through sorcery.

9   Whereas a Chambri man's relationships with the other men of his clan were competitive and those with his in-laws, tense, his matrilateral relationships were supportive. Martin, it may be recalled, in

referring to the trouble he was having with his family, described his mother, not members of his clan, as a reliable source of unqualified support. In addition, as we have already seen, for instance, in the initiation ceremony, sisters and brothers were expected to sustain each other.

10   Through bearing children Chambri women were able to achieve worth by replacing those who provided themselves with life. This strategy of reproductive closure is described at length in Errington and Gewertz, 1987a. See also Introduction, note 10; Chapter 2, note 10; and Chapter 3.

11   In this view, the primary role of ritual is not didactic. Ritual is important to the degree that it is enacted rather than consulted. For an elaboration of this perspective, see Schieffelin, 1985.

12   *Mwai* were long-nosed masks, studded with cowry shells, believed by Chambri to embody ancestral powers.

13   For interesting comparative data about the deconstruction of persons during mourning rituals among the closely related Iatmul, see Bateson, 1958; 152–59; for such data about matrilineal Papua New Guinea societies, see Weiner, 1976, and Battaglia, 1989.

14   As we have said, the Waykumbunmank flute complex consisted of seven transverse flutes and a hand drum, each of which was owned by a different clan. Four of the flutes comprised Waykumbunmank; two, her children; one, her brother; and the drum, her husband. The four Waykumbunmank flutes were considered the most important. They were named Anumank, the line along which the initiates walked as they were struck with switches by the men of the opposite moiety; Oronanump, the stone of Chambri Island; Mandoi, the rat totem of the ancestor from Wombun who first made the flutes; and Kewan, the sago tree when laden with seeds. Thus, the Waykumbunmank flutes exemplified and substantiated – in their very names and through their use – major aspects of Chambri life: initiation, Chambri Island, totemism, and the staple food, sago. Furthermore the complex also represented the entire community of Wombun and, when fully activated, elicited the participation of virtually all in Wombun as well as most in the other two villages. They were, in their significance and efficacy, the essence of Chambri tradition.

15   See Gewertz, 1982a, for a complete discussion of the complex role of *tsambunwuro* in Chambri life.

16   We should note that Chambri had a variety of beliefs concerning the whereabouts of a dead person's spirit. Even though we were told that with the uprooting of the *sirilkam*, Nick's spirit would fly away, his spirit was also thought to be residing in the *mwai* mask. Moreover, one of our best informants admitted being confused about where Nick's spirit would go after the final ceremony since he had been told

of two quite different destinies – in addition to the Christian heaven. His fathers and ancestors had told him that when a man dies he stayed in his ancestral ground. This, as we have seen, was consistent with bringing the *mwai* mask containing Nick's spirit back into the men's house. He had also been told about a journey the dead took. It was because of this journey, he explained, that the women baked for the final day of the ceremony six-foot long, leaf-wrapped, loaves of a bread made of sago and coconut. Although eaten by the living, these loaves were used by the dead as bridges as they left the land of the living: the first time the spirit laid one of them down, it extended to the Sepik River; the second time, it extended to the ocean; the third time, to a place no living being had visited. Regardless of this latter view, Chambri also insisted that the dead were never very distant: they believed that the living and dead readily engaged in each other's affairs.

These alternative views of death, we suspect, became politically significant as men sought to demonstrate in debates that they had distinctive knowledge. Wagner, 1983, describes a comparable political use of differences in conception theory among the Barok of New Ireland.

5 *The written word*

1   Although by no means believing everything they read, Chambri (and, we think, many other Papua New Guineans) were inclined to give relatively careful consideration to claims that appeared in print. This may have partially accounted for the Chambri fascination with pamphlets describing get-rich schemes. It might be remembered, as well, that Martin pinned much of his campaign strategy on his hope that his printed platform would be efficacious. However, as Martin's case also showed, the power of the written word was not complete.

2   For discussions concerning the eventual effects of literacy on "traditional" societies see Goody, 1968, 1977, 1986, 1987; Ong, 1977, 1982; and Street, 1984.

3   Ogan, 1985, provides an especially moving analysis of his own relationship to a Papua New Guinea political leader.

4   While in Chambri Camp, we met Kore Ami of the Maprik area, an indigenous curer hired by a Chambri man to diagnose his illness. He showed us what he and others described as a "license." This was a typed certification in English that this man was a "good sorcerer" and a "native healer." It was signed by three local officials – two policemen and a patrol officer.

5   Through their capacity to document, anthropologists in these circumstances necessarily have a political role. See Errington and Gewertz, 1987c, for an elaboration of the problems inherent in this role.

6   We have earlier mentioned that the Chambri regarded their island as settled largely by a succession of immigrants from throughout the surrounding area. As we will see in this chapter, there was much political disagreement over whose ancestors arrived first and what of importance they brought with them. For an analysis of the basis of Chambri ethnic identity, given the belief that their ancestors were virtually all immigrants, see Errington and Gewertz, 1986.

7   For more about the history of this family including the activities of Kindui Yukindimi as the first *luluai*, see Gewertz, 1982b.

8   Michael Somare was from a Sepik village in the Murik Lakes where a language the Chambri recognized as related to their own was spoken. In the context of national politics, Chambri gave their overwhelming support to Somare as a fellow Sepik.

9   A few weeks before, several of Yarapat's clansmen had played their flutes to prolong the season of low water so that the gardens planted on the exposed lake bottom would have time to mature.

10   During the season of low water, the lake began to shrink as it drained back into the depleted Sepik River. At a certain point, the increasingly crowded fish surged in a thrashing flow from the diminished lake down the channel toward the Sepik. Various men took credit for bringing about this time of plenty when the fish could simply be scooped into canoes. Some claimed totemic control over the fish themselves; others, over the currents and winds; still others – Yarapat, in particular – over the water level.

11   Thus, although Fabian, 1983, may well be correct about the significance for members of our own culture of the anthropological objectification of the other, we should not assume that this particular form of objectification necessarily has universal significance. Strathern, 1988, makes a similar point in her discussion of the different meaning objects take in gift cultures such as those of Melanesia and in commodity cultures such as our own.

12   Chambri ordinarily wrote in Pidgin, not in Chambri. Godfried also chose to write in Pidgin so that other Sepiks would be able to read his stories.

13   Below is an example of one of Godfried's discussions of the "good" and "bad" customs which now exist at Chambri:

To Proclaim and Story

The past, the time of our fathers and ancestors, was a time at Chambri for the telling of the ancestral stories. The older men would build an enclosure, summon the young men and put them inside the enclosure. They would proclaim and recite stories to them all. When it was the time to debate, it wasn't the big men who started the story – no indeed – it was the young men who did. And if a young man went wrong in telling a story, all the big men would correct him.

This practice of holding meetings still remains among people of the Sepik River. But we have lost it which is why all the young people no longer know the ancestral stories or any of the good laws of Chambri.

All the good Christian laws of our fathers and ancestors at Chambri are lost, and now we only have bad customs belonging to other people. We are filled up with these at Chambri. Many young Chambri do not know the stories of the fathers and the ancestors. In particular, they do not know:

1. How to sing the songs.
2. That the ancestral stories are true.
3. The ways of helping other men and women.
4. The ways of playing all kinds of flutes.
5. The ways of working businesses.
6. The ways of cooperative work and service.
7. The ways of respecting the big men.
8. The ways of respecting the men's houses and churches.
9. The ways of making gardens and houses and canoes.
10. The ways of making all ancestral carvings.
11. That you cannot steal things belonging to other men.
12. The custom of marrying a good woman and having domestic peace.

And there were plenty of other good customs that all the fathers and ancestors of Chambri had, but that nowadays we have lost.

In this discussion of the present as inferior to the past, Godfried was thus equating ancestral and Christian knowledge and precept. His solution to the problems Chambri faced was a program of (re)education – through a simultaneous relearning of the Chambri–Christian truths, and a shedding of imported and deleterious practices. As might be expected, Godfried's depiction of Chambri's Edenic past, the past that must be revived, was not entirely realistic. He discounted the fact that in Chambri culture knowledge was power. He seemed to forget that it was a culture in which male competition was so intense that senior men never shared the details of their knowledge freely (even to other clansmen) or responded with other than delighted derision to the mistakes that others might make in mythological allusion. And, of course, in his comparison of the corrupt ways of the present with the virtuous practices of the past, Godfried ignored the fact that a major component of a big man's reputation for knowledge, and hence for power, was his capacity to protect that knowledge from those who wished to learn it, by working sorcery and causing illness. Godfried's picture of the past as a time in which knowledge was freely shared may have been colored, as well, by his own particular need for big men to contribute to his collection of Chambri stories.

14   The recent spread of evangelical Protestant sects in the Sepik often resulted in at least a temporary discrediting of previous forms of

Christian knowledge. This was not the case among the Chambri, who were politically – indeed, architecturally – invested in their role as staunch Catholics. For comparative data about the sociocultural effects of missionary effort elsewhere in the Sepik, see Smith, 1980, and Tuzin, 1989; for elsewhere in Oceania, see Barker, 1989.

15 As Huber, 1988, documents, the Catholics dominated the missionary field in the Sepik for many years. However, as we relate in note 14, within the decade of the 80s, evangelical Protestant sects became increasingly active. The charismatic movement in Catholicism was a response to the popularity of these sects in the Sepik and elsewhere.

16 Lawrence, 1964, provides what may still be the most extensive analysis of religious syncretism in Papua New Guinea.

17 Huber, 1988, describes the influences of Vatican II in the Sepik as stimulating a concern with economic development and indigenization of religious forms. Several priests we spoke to, while endorsing such changes as the performance of traditional music during services, were very uneasy about what they believed was the concomitant process of syncretism in the area of doctrine. It was clear that they were not inclined to exchange their own processes for the production of truth for those indigenous to Papua New Guinea. For a more comprehensive discussion of what was at stake, see, for example, Foucault, 1980.

18 The titles introducing Godfried's texts are his own.

19 For a more extensive analysis of this process of ancestral embodiment see Errington and Gewertz, 1987a.

20 Since the Chambri generally employed a rather stylized Christian rhetoric to discuss Christianity, it is difficult to know with precision what Christianity in fact meant to them. In this regard, Godfried's comparisons of Christian and Chambri stories are useful since our relatively extensive knowledge of the latter can be used to interpret the former.

21 It may be recalled that in Chapter 1, while analyzing the story concerning Walindimi's seduction of Yambukay's wife, we indicated that for the Chambri, seduction of another's wife was a manifestation of superior power.

22 In Chapter 3, we discussed the Chambri expectation that big men necessarily came into conflict with others. To accumulate power, a big man had to deprive others of it; it was therefore expected that he would have many enemies and that he would vigorously defend his interests by sorcery and other means. See, for further elaboration of the "amorality" of Chambri leaders, Errington and Gewertz, 1988b.

23 As discussed in Chapter 1 (including note 11) with reference to Walindimi allowing Yambukay to beat him without retaliation, to act

as an unmoved center in the face of attack was a demonstration (however ultimately futile) of power.

24 It was these circumstances that led the Chambri to regard the continued importation of power in the form of ritual complexes and paraphernalia as so desirable. See Errington and Gewertz, 1986, for further explication of what Mead, 1970, described as the remarkable proclivity in Sepik societies for such importing from their neighbors.

25 Although not relatives, Kosemp and Godfried belonged to the same men's house and therefore were accustomed to sharing the knowledge necessary for cooperation in ritual matters.

26 In constructing the Chambri Bible, Godfried was elaborating – indeed, constructing – a cosmology. This cosmology, moreover, was explicitly designed to provide truth not only for the Chambri but for other Sepiks as well. In analyzing this process of "cosmologies in the making" we concur with Barth that "[W]e must always struggle to get our ontological assumptions right: to ascribe to our object of study only those properties and capabilities that we have reasonable ground to believe it to possess" (1987:8). However, we must stress that in the Sepik, getting the ontology right necessarily means understanding the political interests of the cosmologist as well as those of his group. Gardner, 1988, makes a similar point about the Mountain Ok cosmologists on whom Barth focuses. See also Sahlins, 1985, for a theoretical treatment of the necessity of considering interests in processes of cultural replication and elaboration.

27 The Chambri, thus, like the Maori described by Sahlins, justified and determined action according to mythological precedent, according to a "mytho-praxis" (Sahlins, 1985: 54–72).

28 Kosemp's portrayal of Kwimembi's activities also included a careful description of those that took place at the area where Kosemp lived. He mentioned, for instance, the name of the stone in front of his house where Kwimembi had moored his canoe. In his exposition, Kosemp was not only seeking to establish his account of Kwimembi's activities as authoritative but also was confirming his claim, by virtue of his residence, to be Kwimembi's descendant. In this context in which the invocation and elaboration of ancestral deeds formed the basis of political efficacy, Bourdieu's observation, concerning *habitus*, that "[T]he schemes of thought and expression [an agent] has acquired are the basis for the intentionless invention of regulated improvisation" (1977:79), seems particularly apt. It might also be noted that, although there was controversy over which ancestors had which powers and priorities, all Chambri accepted as self-evident – as *doxa* (op. cit.:164) – that ancestral powers and priorities determined the state of the natural and social world.

29 See Bateson, 1958, and Harrison, 1982, for corroborative discussion of debating in the Sepik.

30 Godfried had not, in other words, developed a concept of culture as a system of only relative truth.

31 Goody suggests that the advent of literacy has had profound historical effects on social, psychological, cognitive and, even, physiological processes (1968, 1977, 1986, 1987). Our concentration here is primarily on the political changes writing has been bringing to Chambri. We do not, therefore, mean our discussion of literacy's implications to be taken as exhaustive.

6 Negotiating with the state

1 For recent analyses of the rhetoric of politics elsewhere in Oceania see the collection of essays edited by Brenneis and Myers, 1984.

2 Although Chambri society was based on kinship units of the sort regarded by Durkheim, 1984, as providing a mechanical solidarity, these units in their interaction as components of a totemic division of labor more nearly conformed to Durkheim's description of organic solidarity.

3 Godfried's effort to become the repository of collected Chambri wisdom was comparable to that of a politician several years before who proclaimed himself "chief" of the Chambri. In both instances, Chambri supported such individuals only while their own particularistic interests were served. The chief lost credibility when he was unable to deliver benefits from the outside world. See Chapter 1, note 35, and Conclusion, note 14, for additional information on this man.

4 For a comprehensive analysis of the relationship between written authority and centralized control see Goody, 1986: 87–126.

5 Among the many analyses of the relationship between the democratic Western state and the idea of the citizen are Gellner, 1983, and Anderson, 1983. For an exploration of how the models developed by Gellner and Anderson fit the Papua New Guinea context, see Ploeg, 1989.

6 Obviously there may be cultural differences in the definition of appropriate tolerance and forbearance.

7 Anderson, 1983, argues that an important characteristic of the state is the capacity for citizens to be conscious not only of the existence of particular others as citizens but of a citizenry.

8 The universalistic ethic often promulgated to Chambri in church was immediately discounted under circumstances of actual conflict in favor of attack or retribution in support of kin or fellow Chambri.

9 It might be noted that, in Pekur's scenario, no one actually had read the book. Pekur himself did not read English. Nor was the magistrate

depicted as studying the book, weighing the evidence of its particular accounts, before reaching his conclusion. Pekur envisioned that the book would be effective, not so much because the accounts it contained of the settlement of Chambri Lake would document the Chambri claim to Peliagwi, but because it was a powerful object, an object that would by its very nature have immediate efficacy. Pekur, in his anticipated encounter with the magistrate, was a big man. He was one who could convince through forceful assertion that he had secret and powerful knowledge.

10 For a discussion of the relationships which prevailed over time between the Chambri and the peoples of the Sepik Hills see Gewertz, 1983.

11 For an excellent, ethnographically rich analysis of law and order in the New Guinea Highlands that provides comparable case material see Gordon and Meggitt, 1985.

12 In Chapter 3 we discuss in detail a case in which Sisilia charged her sister Mariana in a Chambri village court. As was usual, the primary concern of the village court and the large number of interested bystanders was to air all grievances and to effect a mutually satisfactory reconciliation. However, as Mariana's refusal to shake hands with her sister and her subsequent departure from the scene indicated, decisions of even local – far from transcendent – courts were not regarded as binding. Yet, because all Chambri were entailed to each other in numerous ways and therefore found serious and long-term conflicts difficult to manage, the local court's suggestion for the resolution of the conflict was usually accepted. For an analysis of the operation of local courts within the Sepik, see Scaglion, 1983; for a discussion of national legal priorities, see Scaglion, 1981.

13 For classic discussions of the sensitivity of animals to human pollution see Douglas, 1966.

14 See Chapter 2 for examples and discussion of the special link between brothers and sisters.

15 Only one of the women responsible for Remy's death was from the Sepik River area. The home villages of the other two – an East Sepik village near Maprik and someplace (no one was sure where) in the Highlands – were too distant to be socially useful.

16 These are the other three instances. A married daughter with three children whose non-Chambri husband had just abandoned her called the police when her drunken father, angry that he had received no bride-price, struck her. The police took them both to the station and reprimanded the father for hitting his daughter who was no longer a child.

A young drunken man wanted to borrow a radio late one night from his kinswoman; when she refused, saying she wanted to sleep, he tore the siding off her house. She called the police the next morning. They told the young man to repair the damage.

Another young man, while drunk, severely beat a boy of about fourteen, whom he suspected of spying on, and intending to rape, several teenaged girls who were bathing. The boy's father called the police. They took everyone concerned – witnesses to the beating, kin of the boy, the girls, and the young man, camp leaders – to the police station where they were told to discover what the boy's intent toward the girls had been before deciding what compensation should be paid by the drunken man to the boy's family.

17 As we mentioned in Chapter 3, residents of Wewak were known to each other, if not by name, then by ethnic group.

18 This Pidgin term has essentially the same meaning as in English, namely stubborn, conceited and a general pain.

19 Martin and Bascam clashed periodically during the time we were living in Chambri Camp. On a previous occasion, Martin had been intimidated by Bascam's mastery of traditional rhetorical forms: in particular, Bascam had shown himself to be Martin's vanquisher by wearing the flowers that marked him as an initiator. Martin was undoubtedly delighted to find a context allowing him to retaliate, a context in which he, not Bascam, was upholding traditional perspectives.

20 Most Chambri hoped that these "big heads" would simply outgrow their more reprehensible behaviors.

21 In response to our inquiry, Chambri told us that a Chambri committing a capital crime such as murder would be given up to the police. However, it is not clear to us how they would in fact respond if such actually were to happen. We suspect that close kin would attempt to protect such a person. For those living at Chambri, the relative unavailability of the police meant that they were largely in control of their own affairs. (The nearest policeman was stationed at Pagwi, three to four hours distant.)

22 Hence, Maliwan justified his request for funds to renovate the Walindimi men's house by explaining that since the Chambri had built the house to celebrate Papua New Guinea's independence, the government should reciprocate by helping to reconstruct it.

23 The Pidgin English components of the term "wantok" mean, literally, "one language." The term referred, originally, to those from the same language group who worked together on European-owned plantations.

24 In our view, however, the educational system, although highly restrictive past the primary level, was based not on a wantok but on a merit system. Exams for entry into secondary and tertiary levels were generally fairly administered.

25 Assaults on Europeans in Papua New Guinea were discussed at length in the foreign – especially the Australian – press. Dinnen, 1986, presents the interesting argument that such accounts concerning the difficulties of maintaining law and order in Papua New Guinea were often exaggerated to provide a rationale for the diversion of investment away from socially useful, local-level projects in favor of capital intensive and extractive projects such as large mines.

26 John and Sisilia Illumbui read the Papua New Guinea newspapers regularly, where they learned of attacks on middle-class families. Articles like the following greatly increased their anxiety about their vulnerability:

Mother of five raped and slain

A family dinner in Popondetta turned to horror on Wednesday – and five children have been left without a mother.

The 28-year-old mum was seized in front of their eyes by a gang of men as a knife was held to the father.

The men had stormed in and when they had found no money, grabbed the helpless Sepik woman and took her away.

Then she was repeatedly raped – and after exhausting themselves, the gang members stabbed her to death.

Late yesterday, about 50 relatives took her body to Popondetta police station demanding the police be responsible for airfreighting the body to her home province.

After peaceful negotiations, the relatives are collecting money to send the body home and the police club in Popondetta has donated K200.

Popondetta police have arrested three suspects (Post Courier, 1987:3).

27 To be sure, Americans (for example) as well as Papua New Guineans found relations in the public realm frequently confrontational, evocative of envy, dangerous, and resistant to adjudication. However, the understanding of these relations was likely to be different in each case. Americans were likely to regard them as indicating a breakdown in the system, as an erosion of civic virtue especially concerning respect for the rights of others. Papua New Guineans, we think, were likely to regard such relations, not as aberrations, but as normal, as what could be expected from those not entailed.

28 Unlike the political situation in some third world countries such as Nigeria, New Guinea has no one ethnic group sufficiently large to dominate over all or most others.

29 It should be noted, however, that because of inter-generational competition, a father was, in fact, likely to transfer his power to the *youngest*, and therefore the least formidable rival, among his sons. This had been the case for Yarapat himself. Certainly, fathers had been able in the past to exercise a substantial degree of choice concerning such matters.

30   Few not of Yarapat's clan so exonerated his boy from the charge of
     "big head"; Yarapat's rivals were pleased at evidence that his power
     had been insufficient to control his own children.

Conclusion: interlocking stories, intersecting lives

1   Prior to effective Australian control of the Sepik, a Chambri male,
     during a phase of his initiation, earned the right to wear the black
     paint of a homicide by spearing a child purchased for him from a
     neighboring group by his mother's brother.

2   See Gewertz, 1980, for a more complete discussion of this water hole
     which the Chambri regarded as a microcosm of the world.

3   Yorondu believed that his son had fallen ill because his ancestors
     were angry that Yorondu had revealed their secret names to us. In
     offering them the chicken – provided by us, at his insistence, as our
     responsibility – he assured them of our reliability.

4   For a description of these events and a photograph of Yorondu
     laboring on this men's house see Errington and Gewertz, 1987a:
     120–23.

5   Not surprisingly, Yorondu appeared most anachronistic on the
     relatively few occasions he was in Wewak. Although competent in
     pressing his claim for a share of the money to clear Mariana's name
     (see Chapter 3), he was generally ill at ease and querulous; indeed, we
     were told directly by a young man in Chambri camp that, although
     Yorondu might be a big man at Chambri, he was a rubbish man at the
     Camp.

6   See Errington and Gewertz, 1987a: 1–4, for a discussion of the
     relationship of Mead and Fortune to Yorondu and his father,
     Kwolikumbwi.

7   This infant Jesus was the child of the sun in a myth that had been, we
     have argued, about responsibility to in-laws. For a rendition that
     preceded Godfried's, see Errington and Gewertz, 1987a: 21–26.

8   In fact, the Iatmul referred privately to the Chambri as *numanki*,
     (ritually) inadequate ones.

9   As Gewertz, 1983: 17–36, suggests, the Sawos, for example, did on
     occasion *become* Iatmul.

10   Bateson, 1958, regarded the endemic competition of Iatmul life as
     limiting the Iatmul capacity for collective action. Not only would they
     be unable to form an empire; it was remarkable, in Bateson's view,
     that they could organize into large villages.

11   Gewertz, 1983, discusses some of these limiting mechanisms in detail.

12   Pekur once related to us with enormous indignation that he had
     overheard Chambri youth in Wewak referring to him dismissively (in
     a combined English and Pidgin) as a "fucking lapun [old man]."

13   Gregory argues that Papua New Guinea was unique among third-

world countries in that there were "many legal and social forces working against the emergence of land as a commodity . . . [but that these] forces have created a contradictory situation, whereby cash crops are being produced on clan land" (1982: 165). Among the non-agricultural Chambri, however, primary resources remained both communally owned and in subsistence production.

14 Once the Chambri realized that they were no longer cosmologically self-sufficient, even in their own territory, they faced the urgent problem of trying to use Western power for Chambri ends. To achieve this objective, they believed they would have to accumulate sufficient power of their own to attract to them those Westerners who had power. They were looking for someone who could embody and concentrate the hitherto dispersed Chambri power. To this end, they created a new social role, a "chief." This role was a significant departure from the existing clan-based pattern of political organization. Although the chief was not granted the right to command, he was acknowledged as the representative of the Chambri to the world of the Westerners and as the leader who would enable the Chambri to acquire the power and influence that would enhance their efficacy, not only so that they could meet their crisis at home but could, as well, enhance their influence in the larger political and economic context of Papua New Guinea. (See Errington and Gewertz, 1985, for a discussion of this case.) Interestingly, we discovered during our most recent field trip that, with the control of *Salvinia* by the introduction of its natural enemy, life in Chambri resumed as if there had been no ecological disruption. Moreover, with the passing of the crisis, the "chief" had lost his support. See, also, Chapter 1, note 35, and Chapter 6, note 3.

15 It is our strong impression from reading national newspapers and from conferring with colleagues commissioned to perform environmental impact assessments in areas where mining operations were proposed, that the Papua New Guinea government was concerned to protect the environment. The government was, however, much in need of foreign capital.

16 It seems to us that any ethnography concerned with tourism should note that although tourists and tourists' "attractions" alike were linked by a world system in mutual process of cultural creation and re-creation, they might as agents within that system have very different political positions and very different effects on each other.

17 Ethnographies must not be based on a vision of simplified humanity, protected by its isolation from processes of change. This view, for example, has characterized the Bushmen in such representations as the popular film, *The Gods Must Be Crazy* (Uys, 1980). Comparably, the Tasaday have been depicted as "gentle" and alleged to have no

word for "war" (see Nance, 1988). Rather, ethnographies must be based on a respectful recognition that our informants are our equals in their full engagement with the complexity of history.

18 Although we agree with Sahlins that the "heretofore obscure histories of remote islands deserve a place alongside the self-contemplation of the European past ... for their own remarkable contributions to an historical understanding" (1985: 72), we insist that more than our own intellectual interests are at stake.

References

Anderson, Benedict 1983 *Imagined Communities* (London, Verso).

Appadurai, Arjun 1986a "Theory in Anthropology: Center and Periphery," *Comparative Studies in Society and History* (28: 356–61).

1985b "Introduction: Commodities and the Politics of Value," In *The Social Life of Things*, Arjun Appadurai, ed.(Cambridge, Cambridge University Press) pp. 3–63.

Apte, Mahadev 1985 *Humor and Laughter* (Ithaca, Cornell University Press).

Asad, Talal, ed. 1973 *Anthropology and the Colonial Encounter* (London, Ithaca Press).

Barker, John, ed. 1989 *Christianity in Oceania* (Lanham, Maryland, University Press of America).

Barth, Fredrik 1975 *Ritual and Knowledge among the Baktaman of Papua New Guinea* (New Haven, Yale University Press).

1987 *Cosmologies in the Making* (Cambridge, Cambridge University Press).

Basso, Keith 1979 *Portraits of the Whiteman* (Cambridge, Cambridge University Press).

Bateson, Gregory 1933 "Social Structure of the Iatmul People," *Oceania* (1: 245–91, 401–53).

1946 "Arts of the South Seas," *The Arts Bulletin* (2: 119–23).

1958 *Naven* (Stanford, Stanford University Press).

1972 *Steps to an Ecology of Mind* (New York, Ballantine).

Battaglia, Debbora 1986 *Bringing Home to Moresby* (Port Moresby, Institute of Applied Social and Economic Research).

1990 *On the Bones of the Serpent* (Chicago, University of Chicago Press).

Bellah, Robert, et al. 1986 *Habits of the Heart* (New York, Harper and Row).

Boas, Franz 1948 *Race, Language and Culture* (New York, Macmillan).

Boon, James 1982 *Other Tribes, Other Scribes* (Cambridge, Cambridge University Press).

Bourdieu, Pierre 1977 *Outline of a Theory of Practice* (Cambridge, Cambridge University Press).

Bowden, Ross 1983 *Yena* (Oxford, Pitt Rivers Museum).

Boyd, David 1985a "We Must Follow the Fore: Pig Husbandry, Intensification and Ritual Diffusion among the Irakia Awa, Papua New Guinea," *American Ethnologist* (12: 119–36).

1985b "The Commercialization of Ritual in the Eastern Highlands of Papua New Guinea," *Man* (20: 325–40).

Brenneis, Donald and Fred Myers, eds. 1984 *Dangerous Words* (New York, New York University Press).

Brown, Paula 1972 *The Chimbu* (Cambridge, Schenkman Publishing Company).

Burton-Bradley, B.G. 1968 *Mixed-Race Society in Port Moresby* (Canberra, Australian National University).

Carnegie, Dale 1936 *How to Win Friends and Influence People* (New York, Simon and Schuster).

Carrier, James and Achsah Carrier 1989 *Wage, Trade and Exchange in Melanesia* (Berkeley, University of California Press).

Clifford, James 1986 "Introduction," *In Writing Culture*, James Clifford and George Marcus, eds. (Berkeley, University of California Press) pp. 1–26.

1988a *The Predicament of Culture* (Cambridge, Harvard University Press).

1988b "Histories of the Tribal and the Modern," In *The Predicament of Culture* (Cambridge, Harvard University Press) pp. 189–214.

Clifford, James, and George Marcus, eds. 1986 *Writing Culture* (Berkeley, University of California Press).

Cohen, Erik 1988 "Authenticity and Commoditization in Tourism," *Annals of Tourism Research* (15: 371–86).

1989 "Primitive and Remote," *Annals of Tourism Research* (16: 30–61).

Colson, Elizabeth, et al., eds. 1979 *Long-Term Field Research in Social Anthropology* (New York, Academic Press).

Crick, Malcolm 1985 "Tracing the Anthropological Self," *Social Analysis* (17: 71–92).

di Leonardo, Micaela 1989 "Malinowski's Nephews," *Nation*, March 13, pp. 350–52.

Dinnen, Sinclair 1986 "Perspectives on Law and Order," In *Law and Order in a Changing Society*, Louise Morauta, ed. (Canberra, Australian National University) pp. 76–89.

Dorst, John 1989 *The Written Suburb* (Philadelphia, University of Pennsylvania Press).

Douglas, Mary 1966 *Purity and Danger* (London, Routledge and Kegan Paul).

Dumont, Jean-Paul 1977 "Review of MacCannell," *Annals of Tourism Research* (4: 223–25).

Durkheim, Emile 1984 *The Division of Labor In Society* (New York, Free Press).

Errington, Frederick and Deborah Gewertz 1985 "The Chief of the Chambri: Social Change and Cultural Permeability among a New Guinea People," *American Ethnologist* (12: 442–54).

1986 "The Confluence of Powers: Entropy and Importation among the Chambri," *Oceania* (57: 99–113).

1987a *Cultural Alternatives and a Feminist Anthropology* (Cambridge, Cambridge University Press).

1987b "The Remarriage of Yebiwali: A Study of Dominance and False Consciousness in a Non-Western Society," In *Dealing with Inequality*, Marilyn Strathern ed. (Cambridge, Cambridge University Press) pp. 63–88.

1987c "On Unfinished Dialogues and Paper Pigs," *American Ethnologist* (14: 367–76).

1988a "Myths of Matriarchy Re-examined: The Ideological Components of Social Order," In *Myths of Matriarchy Reconsidered*, Deborah Gewertz, ed. (Sydney, Oceania Publications) pp. 195–212.

1988b "Exemplars and the Reproduction of Everyday Life," *Dialectical Anthropology* (13: 31–43).

1989 "Tourism and Anthropology in a Post-Modern World," *Oceania* (60: 37–54).

Etienne, Mona 1980 "Women and Men, Cloth and Colonization: The Transformation of Production-Distribution Relations among the Baule," In *Women and Colonization*, Mona Etienne and Eleanor Leacock, eds. (New York, Praeger) pp. 214–38.

Evans-Pritchard, E.E. 1947 *The Sanusi of Cyrenaica* (New York, Oxford University Press).

Fabian, Johannes 1983 *Time and the Other* (New York, Columbia University Press).

Feil, Daryl 1984 *Ways of Exchange* (St Lucia, University of Queensland Press).

1987 *The Evolution of Highland Papua New Guinea Societies* (Cambridge, Cambridge University Press).

Feld, Steven 1982 *Sound and Sentiment* (Philadelphia, University of Pennsylvania Press).

Fienump-Riordan, Ann 1988 "Robert Redford, Apanuugpak, and the Invention of Tradition," *American Ethnologist* (15: 442–55).

Finney, Ben and Karen Watson 1974 *A New Kind of Sugar: Tourism in the Pacific* (Honolulu, East-West Center).

Fitzpatrick, Peter 1980 *Law and State in Papua New Guinea* (London, Academic Press).

Fleetwood, Lorna 1984 *A Short History of Wewak* (Wewak, The East Sepik Provincial Government).

Foley, William 1986 *The Papuan Languages of New Guinea* (Cambridge, Cambridge University Press).

Forge, Anthony 1967 "The Abelam Artist," In *Social Organization: Essays Presented to Raymond Firth*, Maurice Freedman, ed. (London: Oxford University Press) pp. 65–84.

1972 "The Golden Fleece," *Man* (7: 527–40).

1973 "Style and Meaning in Sepik Art," In *Primitive Art and Society*, Anthony Forge, ed. (London, Oxford University Press), pp. 169–82.

Fortune, Reo 1933a "Field Notes," Unpublished manuscript, University of Auckland.

Foucault, Michel 1980 *Power/Knowledge* (New York, Pantheon).

Frank, Andre Gunder 1969 *Capitalism and Underdevelopment in Latin America* (London, Monthly Reader Press).

Gailey, Christine 1980 "Putting Down Sisters and Wives," In *Women and Colonization*, Mona Etienne and Eleanor Leacock, eds. (New York, Praeger) pp. 294–322.

Gardner, Don 1988 "Review of *Cosmologies in the Making* by Fredrik Barth," *American Ethnologist* (15: 795–96).

Gellner, Ernest 1983 *Nations and Nationalism* (Ithaca, Cornell University Press).

Gerriston, R. et al. 1981 *Road Belong Development* (Canberra, Australian National University).

Gewertz, Deborah 1977 "The Politics of Affinal Exchange: Chambri as a Client Market," *Ethnology* (16: 285–98).

1980 "Of Symbolic Anchors and Sago Soup," *Journal of Polynesian Society* (89: 309–28).

1982a "The Father Who Bore Me: The Role of the Tsambunwuro During Chambri Initiation Ceremonies," In *Rituals of Manhood*, Gilbert Herdt, ed. (Berkeley, University of California Press) pp. 286–320.

1982b "Deviance Unplaced," *Social Analysis* (12: 29–35).

1983 *Sepik River Societies*: A Historical Ethnography of the Chambri and their Neighbors (New Haven, Yale University Press).

1984 "The Chambri View of Persons: A Critique of Individualism in the Works of Mead and Chodorow," *American Anthropologist* (86: 615–29).

1985 "The Golden Age Revisited: A History of the Chambri between 1905 and 1927," In *History and Ethnohistory in Papua New Guinea*, Edward Schieffelin and Deborah Gewertz, eds. (Sydney, Oceania Publications) pp. 58–76.

Godelier, Maurice 1982 *The Making of Great Men* (Cambridge, Cambridge University Press).

Goldberg, A. 1983 "Identity and Experience in Haitian Voodoo Shows," *Annals of Tourism Research* (10: 479–95).

Goody, Jack 1968 *Literacy in Traditional Societies* (Cambridge, Cambridge University Press).

1977 *The Domestication of the Savage Mind* (Cambridge, Cambridge University Press).

1986 *The Logic of Writing and the Organization of Society* (Cambridge, Cambridge University Press).

1987 *The Interface Between the Written and the Oral* (Cambridge, Cambridge University Press).

Gordon, Robert and Mervyn Meggitt 1985 *Law and Order in the New Guinea Highlands* (Hanover, University of Vermont).

Graburn, Nelson 1976 "Introduction: Arts of the Fourth World," In *Ethnic and Tourist Arts*, Nelson Graburn, ed. (Berkeley, University of California Press) pp. 1–32.

1983 "The Anthropology of Tourism," *Annals of Tourism Research* (10:9–33).

Gramsci, Antonio 1977 *Selections from the Prison Notebooks* (London, Lawrence and Wishart).

Gregory, Christopher 1982 *Gifts and Commodities* (New York, Academic Press).

Grossman, Lawrence 1984 *Peasants, Subsistence Ecology and Development in the Highlands of Papua New Guinea* (Princeton, Princeton University Press).

Haantjens, H. A., et al. 1972 *Lands of the Aitape-Ambunti Area* (Canberra, C.S.I.R.O.).

Hamilton, Annette 1982 "Anthropology in Australia," In *Anthropology in Australia: Essays to Honour 50 Years of Mankind*, Grant McCall, ed. (Sydney, Anthropology Society of New South Wales) pp. 91–106.

Handelman, Don 1979 "Is Naven Ludic?" *Social Analysis* (1: 177–91).

Handler, Richard 1986 "Authenticity," *Anthropology Today* (2: 2–4).

Haraway, Dona 1985 "Teddy Bear Patriarchy," *Social Text* (4: 20–64).

Harrison, Simon 1982 *Stealing People's Names: Social Structure, Cosmology and Politics in a Sepik River Village*, unpublished PhD Thesis, Australian National University.

1985 "Ritual Hierarchy and Secular Equality in a Sepik River Village," *American Ethnologist* (12: 413–26).

1987 "Cultural Efflorescence and Political Evolution on the Sepik River," *American Ethnologist* (14: 491–507).

Hauser-Schaublin, Brigitta 1977a *Mai-Maken der Iatmul, Papua New Guinea: Stil, Schnitzvorgang, Auftritt und Funktion* (Basel, Naturforschende Gesellschaft im Basel).

1977b *Frauen in Kararau* (Basel, Ethnologisches Seminar der Universität und Museum für Völkerkunde).

Hays, Terence 1988 "Myths of Matriarchy and the Sacred Flute Complex of the Papua New Guinea Highlands," In *Myths of Matriarchy*

Reconsidered, Deborah Gewertz, ed. (Sydney, Oceania Publications) pp. 98–120.

Herdt, Gilbert 1982 "Fetish and Fantasy in Sambia Initiation," In *Rituals of Manhood*, Gilbert Herdt ed. (Berkeley, University of California Press) pp. 44–98.

Herzfeld, Michael 1983 "Signs in the Field," *Semiotica* (46: 99–106).

Hobsbawm, Eric and Terence Ranger, eds. 1983 *The Invention of Tradition* (Cambridge, Cambridge University Press).

Howie-Willis, Ian 1980 *A Thousand Graduates* (Canberra, Australian National University).

Huber, Mary 1979 "Big Men and Partners: The Development of Urban Migrant Communities at Kreer Beach," *Yagl-Ambu* (6: 39–49).

1984 "War and Bisnis in the History of Settlement in Wewak," unpublished manuscript, presented at the 1984 meetings of the American Anthropological Association, Chicago.

1988 *The Bishop's Progress* (Washington, Smithsonian Institution Press).

Johnson, Frank 1985 "The Western Concept of Self," In *Culture and Self* Anthony Marsella, et al. eds. (New York, Tavistock) pp. 91–138.

Keesing, Roger and Robert Tonkinson, eds. 1982 "Reinventing Traditional Culture," *Mankind*, Special Issue No. 3.

Larcom, Joan 1982 "The Invention of Convention," *Mankind* (3: 330–37).

Lass, Andrew 1988 "Romantic Documents and Political Monuments," *American Ethnologist* (15: 456–71).

Lawrence, Peter 1964 *Road Belong Cargo* (Manchester, Manchester University Press).

Lederman, Rena 1986 *What Gifts Engender* (Cambridge, Cambridge University Press).

Levine, Harold and Marilyn Levine 1979 *Urbanisation in Papua New Guinea* (Cambridge, Cambridge University Press).

Lévi-Strauss, Claude 1969 *The Raw and the Cooked* (New York, Harper and Row).

Lightbody, Mark and Tony Wheeler 1985 *Papua New Guinea: A Travel Survival Kit* (Victoria, Lonely Planet Books).

MacCannell, Dean 1976 *The Tourist* (New York, Schocken Books).

MacCormack, Carol and Marilyn Strathern, eds. 1980 *Nature, Culture and Gender* (Cambridge, Cambridge University Press).

Marcus, George 1986 "Ethnography in the Modern World System," In James Clifford and George Marcus, eds. *Writing Culture* (Berkeley, University of California Press) pp. 165–93.

Marcus, George and Michael Fischer 1986 *Anthropology as Cultural Critique: An Experimental Moment in the Human Sciences* (Chicago, University of Chicago Press).

Marshall, Mac, ed. 1982 *Through a Glass Darkly* (Port Moresby, Institute of Applied Social and Economic Research).

Mathie, Alison and Elizabeth Cox 1987 *New Directions for Women in*

Non-Formal Education (Office of Women's Affairs, Waigani, Papua New Guinea).

May, R. J., ed. 1982 *Micronationalist Movements in Papua New Guinea* (Canberra, Australian National University Press).

McCarthy, J.K. 1963 *Patrol into Yesterday* (Sydney, Robert Brown and Associates).

McDowell, Nancy 1986 "Exchange and Entropy: The Mundugumor Case," unpublished manuscript presented at the Wenner-Gren Symposium, *Sepik Culture History*, Mijas, Spain.

n.d. *The Mundugumor: From the Field Notes of Margaret Mead and Reo Fortune*, unpublished manuscript.

Mead, Margaret 1933 "Field Notes," unpublished manuscript, Library of Congress, Washington, D.C.

1935 *Sex and Temperament in Three Primitive Societies* (New York, William Morrow and Company).

1970 *The Mountain Arapesh: Arts and Supernaturalism* (Garden City, New York, Natural History Press).

Meillassoux, Claude 1981 *Maidens, Meal and Money* (Cambridge, Cambridge University Press).

Metraux, Rhoda 1978 "Aristocracy and Meritocracy: Leadership among the Eastern Iatmul," *Anthropological Quarterly* (51: 47–58).

Mintz, Sydney 1977 "Infant, Victim and Tourist: The Anthropologist in the Field," *Johns Hopkins Magazine* (27: 54–60).

Mitchell, D.S. 1979 *The Incidence and Management of Salvinia Molesta in Papua New Guinea* (Port Moresby, Office of Environment and Conservation).

Modjeska, Nicholas 1982 "Production and Inequality," In *Inequality in New Guinea Highlands Societies*, Andrew Strathern, ed. (Cambridge, Cambridge University Press) pp. 50–108.

Morauta, Louise, ed. 1986 *Law and Order in a Changing Society* (Canberra, Australian National University).

Morauta, Louise and Dawn Ryan 1982 "From Temporary to Permanent Townsmen," *Oceania* (53: 39–55).

Munn, Nancy 1986 *The Fame of Gawa* (Cambridge, Cambridge University Press).

Nance, John 1988 *The Gentle Tasaday* (Boston, David R. Godine).

Nash, Jill and Eugene Ogan 1987 "The Red and the Black," unpublished paper presented at the 1987 meetings of the Association for Social Anthropology in Oceania, Monterey, California.

O'Collins, Maev, ed. 1986 *Youth and Society: Perspectives from Papua New Guinea* (Canberra, Australian National University Press).

Ogan, Eugene 1985 "Participant Observation and Participant History," In *History and Ethnohistory in New Guinea*, Deborah Gewertz and Edward Schieffelin, eds. (Sydney, Oceania Publications) pp. 127–44.

Ong, Walter 1977 *Interfaces of the Word* (Ithaca, Cornell University Press).
 1982 *Orality and Literacy: The Technologizing of the Word* (London, Methuen).
Oram, Nigel 1976 *Colonial Town to Melanesian City* (Canberra, Australian National University Press).
O'Rourke, Dennis 1987 *Cannibal Tours* (Los Angeles, Direct Cinema Limited).
Ortner, Sherry 1984 "Theory in Anthropology since the Sixties," *Comparative Studies in Society and History* (26: 126–66).
Pfaffenberger, B. 1983 "Serious Pilgrims and Frivolous Tourists," *Annals of Tourism Research* (10: 57–74).
Philpott, Malcolm 1972 *Economic Development in the Sepik River Basin* (Port Moresby, Department of Transport).
Ploeg, Anton 1989 "Citizenship in Papua New Guinea," In *Man and a Half: Essays in Honour of Ralph Bulmer*, Andrew Pawley, ed. (Auckland, University of Auckland Press) in press.
Post Courier 1987 "Mother of Five Raped and Slain" (Port Moresby, September 4, p. 3).
Pratt, Mary Louise 1986 "Fieldwork in Common Places," In *Writing Culture*, James Clifford and George Marcus, eds. (Berkeley, University of California Press) pp. 27–50.
Premdas, Ralph 1986 "Ethnicity and Nation-Building in Papua New Guinea," unpublished manuscript, presented at the United Nations symposium, *Ethnic Diversity and Nation Building in the Pacific*, Suva, Fiji.
Ranger, Terence 1983 "The Invention of Tradition in Colonial Africa," In *The Invention of Tradition*, Eric Hobsbawm and Terence Ranger, eds. (Cambridge, Cambridge University Press) pp. 211–62.
Rebel, Henry 1989 "Cultural Hegemony and Class Experience," *American Ethnologist* (16: 117–36).
Rew, Alan 1974 *Social Images and Process in Urban Papua New Guinea* (New York, West Publishing).
Rodman, Margaret 1987 *Masters of Tradition* (Vancouver, University of British Columbia Press).
Rubel, Paula and Abraham Rosman 1978 *Your Own Pigs You May Not Eat* (Chicago, University of Chicago Press).
Sahlins, Marshall 1985 *Islands of History* (Chicago, University of Chicago Press).
Said, Edward 1978 *Orientalism* (New York, Vintage).
Salzman, Philip 1989 "The Lone Stranger and the Solitary Quest," *Anthropology Newsletter* (30: 44 and 16).
Scaglion, Richard 1981 "Samukundi Abelam Conflict Management," *Oceania* (52: 28–38).
 1983 "The Effects of Mediation Styles on Successful Dispute Resolution," *Windsor Yearbook of Access to Justice* (3: 256–69).

Schieffelin, Edward 1985 "Performance and the Cultural Construction of Reality," *American Ethnologist* (12: 707–24).

Schindlbeck, Markus 1980 *Sago Bei Den Sawos* (Basel, Ethnologisches Seminar der Universität und Museum für Völkerkunde).

Schuster, Meinhard 1965 "Mythen aus dem Sepik-Gebeit," In *Festschrift Alfred Buhler*, Carl Schmitz and Robert Wildkaber, eds. (Basel, Pharos-Verlag Hansrudolph Schwabe) pp. 369–84.

1969 "Die Topfergottgeit Von Aibom," *Paideuma* (15: 140–59).

Scott, James 1985 *Weapons of the Weak* (New Haven, Yale University Press).

Shore, Bradd 1981 "Sexuality and Gender in Samoa," In *Sexual Meanings*, Sherry Ortner and Harriet Whitehead, eds. (Cambridge, Cambridge University Press) pp. 192–215.

Smith, Michael French 1980 "From Heathen to Atheist," *Oceania* (51: 40–52).

Smith, V.L. 1977 *Hosts and Guests* (Philadelphia, University of Pennsylvania Press).

Souter, Gavin 1963 *New Guinea: The Last Unknown* (Sydney, Angus and Robertson).

S.P.A.T.F. n.d. *The Artifacts and Crafts of Papua New Guinea* (Hong Kong, South China Printing Company).

Spooner, Brian 1986 "Weavers and Dealers," In *The Social Life of Things*, Arjun Appadurai, ed. (Cambridge, Cambridge University Press) pp. 195–235.

Stanek, Milan 1986 "An Analytical Model as a Basis for Cultural Comparison of the Societies on the Middle and Lower Sepik River," unpublished manuscript presented at the Wenner-Gren Symposium, *Sepik Culture History*, Mijas, Spain.

Stavenhagen, Rudolph 1975 *Social Classes in Agrarian Societies* (Garden City, N.Y., Anchor Press).

Stevenson, Michael 1986 *Wokmani: Work, Money and Discontent in Melanesia* (Sydney, Oceania Publications).

Strathern, Andrew 1982 *Inequality in New Guinea Highlands Societies* (Cambridge, Cambridge University Press).

1984 *A Line of Power* (London, Tavistock).

Strathern, Marilyn 1972 *Women in Between* (London, Seminar Press).

1975 *No Money on Our Skins*, New Guinea Research Bulletin No. 61 (Canberra, Australian National University Press).

1986 "Increment and Androgyny," unpublished manuscript.

1987 "Out of Context: The Persuasive Fictions of Anthropology," *Current Anthropology* (28: 251–81).

1988 *The Gender of the Gift* (Berkeley, University of California Press).

Street, Brian 1984 *Literacy in Theory and Practice* (Cambridge, Cambridge University Press).

Swadling, Pamela 1986 "Glimpses of Prehistoric Contacts Within and Beyond the Sepik-Ramu," unpublished manuscript presented at the Wenner-Gren Symposium, *Sepik Culture History*, Mijas, Spain.

Taussig, Michael 1980 *The Devil and Commodity Fetishism in South America* (Chapel Hill, University of North Carolina Press).

  1987 *Shamanism, Colonialism and the Wild Man* (Chicago, University of Chicago Press).

Teas, Jane, 1988 "I'm Studying Monkeys; What Do You Do?" *Kroeber Anthropological Society Papers* (67/68: 35–41).

The Times of Papua New Guinea 1987 Number 403, September 17–23, Port Moresby.

Travcoa n.d. Tourist brochure, Travel Corporation of America.

Turner, Victor 1967 *The Forest of Symbols* (Ithaca, Cornell University Press).

  1969 *The Ritual Process* (Chicago, Aldine).

Tuzin, Donald 1976 *The Ilahita Arapesh* (Berkeley, University of California Press).

  1980 *The Voice of the Tambaran* (Berkeley, University of California Press).

  1989 "Visions, Prophesies and the Rise of Christian Consciousness," In *Religious Imagination in Melanesia*, Gilbert Herdt and Michele Stephen, eds. (New Brunswick, Rutgers University Press) pp. 187–208.

Uys, Jamie 1980 *The Gods Must Be Crazy* (Botswana, C.A.T. Films).

van den Berghe, Pierre L. 1980 "Tourism as Ethnic Relations," *Ethnic and Racial Studies* (3: 375–92).

Varenne, Herve 1977 *Americans Together* (New York, Teachers College Press).

Wagner, Roy 1983 "The Ends of Innocence: Conception and Seduction among the Daribi of Karimui and the Barok of New Ireland," *Mankind* (14: 75–83).

Wallerstein, Immanuel 1974 *The Modern World-System* (New York, Academic Press).

Wassman, Jurgen 1982 *Der Gesang an den Fliegenden Hund* (Basel, Ethnologisches Seminar der Universität und Museum für Völkerkunde).

Weiner, Annette 1976 *Women of Value, Men of Renown* (Austin, University of Texas Press).

Weiner, James 1988 "Durkheim and the Papuan Male Cult," *American Ethnologist* (15: 567–73).

Weiss, Florence 1981 *Kinder Schildern Ihren Alltag* (Basel, Ethnologisches Seminar der Universität und Museum für Völkerkunde).

White, Geoffrey and John Kirkpatrick 1985 *Person, Self and Experience* (Berkeley, University of California Press).

Whitehead, Harriet 1986 "The Varieties of Fertility Cultism in New Guinea," *American Ethnologist* (13: 80–99; 271–89).

Wolf, Eric 1982 *Europe and the People Without History* (Berkeley, University of California Press).

Worsley, Peter 1984 *The Three Worlds* (Chicago, Universty of Chicago Press).

Index